Dec. 3rd. 1949.

Mrs Reuben Hoffstetter

Moments With God

A Bible Selection
A Short Bible Text
A Prayer

for Each Day in the Year

BY
WALTER E. SCHUETTE

COLUMBUS, OHIO
THE BOOK CONCERN
1927

Made in U. S. A.

To My Fellow Pilgrims:

ONE of the pilgrims on life's way not long since wrote these words: "The Church is the only institution which definitely undertakes to help me in my struggle between the streets and the skies." His words went straight to my heart. You and I know what he meant when he spoke of the struggle, for we are traveling streets every day which make our lives a continuous experience of arduous exertion. The streets of daily toil, the weary days of grief and bereavement, the enticing roads of pleasure, the dark paths of lonely vigil — on which of them can we relax from our bearing as soldiers constantly under arms?

We of the Church have not been helpful enough to each other in this struggle. We have not aided one another as we should in heeding our Master's admonition, "Watch and pray."

These pages have been written to help you put into words feelings and thoughts which you have perhaps wished to utter, but somehow did not; and to help you entice thoughts and feelings into utterance, the presence of which in your own soul was not clearly known to you; and to enable you to learn how easily possible it is, even in the busiest and most harassed life, to take time for daily expressed communion with God.

This little helper asks you to let it become your confidential friend. Its maker has tried to arrange its pages so that not only all your soul's needs and moods will be considered, but also that the year's festival changes will be observed — an exercise which is now almost universally acknowledged to be salutary.

By a unique arrangement of the following pages, those who allow this little helper to become their daily companion will always enter Lent and arrive at Eastertide with the calendar (See notes under date lines on pages 42, 45, 46, 48, 49, 52, 53, 54, 57, 58, 60, 61, 65, 66, 69, 70). A prayer for Ascension Day will be found on page 166, and a prayer for Pentecost, or Whitsunday, on page 172. The fixed festivals, for both Church and Nation, have all been accorded consideration.

WALTER E. SCHUETTE.

Sewickley, Pennsylvania, 1924.

JANUARY 1

Read Genesis 1:1-16

VERSE 3 — *And God said, "Let there be light," and there was light.*

LORD JESUS CHRIST, Thou art the same yesterday, to-day, and forever: it is by Thy mercy and long-suffering that we are permitted to enter this new year. We have not deserved to have our lives lengthened unto this time. If Thou, who art the righteous Judge of all, wouldst deal with us according to our sins, Thou wouldst long since have cut us off and called us to our last account. But with Thee there is plenteous mercy, and Thou hast given us another year of grace. We thank Thee; and now, Lord, since Thou hast given us this new year, help us to make it a time of rejoicing in Thy salvation. Be Thou our Light, our Sun, our Shield. Without Thee we can do nothing. This year will not be a blessing to us if Thou art not with us day by day and hour by hour. We need Thee always, everywhere. Thy blood and Thy righteousness are our only hope. Draw us day by day closer to Thyself as this year goes on its course. Enfold us in Thy redeeming love. Let us be joyful in the happiness which cometh because Thou didst put Thyself under the law of God in our stead, because Thou didst fulfil all righteousness for us. And, as Thou dost continue to apply Thy saving blood to us, do Thou likewise make us more like Thee. Grant us Thy spirit of unselfishness. Make us better servants in Thy kingdom. When all our years have been told, take us to that life in which days and years are unknown — for Thy mercy's sake. *Amen.*

JANUARY 2

Read Romans 1: 8-17

VERSE 16 — *"I am not ashamed of the gospel of Christ, for it is the power of God unto salvation."*

LORD, our God, we have begun this year with Thee, trusting in the redeeming and cleansing blood of Jesus, relying on Thy constant care and companionship. We know it pleaseth Thee to come to us in Thy blessed Word. What marvelous love Thou hast revealed to us in the precious story of the coming of Jesus into our flesh, the story of His life, His labors, His suffering, His death, His resurrection. Truly, Thou didst bring the world good news when Thou didst send Him, as Thou hadst long foretold. We thank Thee not only for giving us the gospel, but for entering our hearts with Thy Holy Spirit and drawing us by this gospel to faith and trust in its promises. We thank Thee for making us childlike followers of the Christ. Do Thou not now forsake us. Make Thy grace mighty in our hearts and minds to preserve us from growing weary of the gospel's sweetness. Make Thy Word so powerful in our lives that we can never admit one thought of proving faithless. Teach us to see the blessedness of sending Thy Word to those who have despised it or who have not yet heard its message. Make us unashamed to speak of our Christ among those who do not yet belong to Him. Keep before our eyes the words which He once spoke, saying that He will not be ashamed to confess those before Thee who have not been ashamed to confess Him in this life. Hear us, Lord, our God, for His sake. *Amen.*

JANUARY 3

Read Genesis 1:20-31

VERSE 27 — *So God created man in His own image: in the image of God created He him.*

O GOD, who hast created us and given us our bodies and souls, our eyes and ears and all our members, our reason and all our senses, and who dost still preserve them to us: we rejoice in this, that Thou art our Maker. We bless Thy glorious name because Thou didst raise us up from the dust and didst give us Thine image. Thy Word doth teach us that we are Thine offspring, and that Thou didst fashion us, giving us spirits which were like Thee in righteousness and true holiness. Alas, that we sinned against Thee, and chose the vanity of wanting to be equal with Thee instead of the true joy of being in Thine image and resting as children in Thy bosom. How good Thou art, promising that Thou wilt restore us to Thy likeness. How merciful Thou hast been, sending Thine only-begotten Son, Jesus, to bring back Thine image to us. Such love, such tender mercy, is too wonderful for us. We cry out with Thy servant, "What is man, that Thou art mindful of him, and the son of man, that Thou visitest him?" But, unspeakably wonderful as Thy mercy is, we know it is real and true. Thy Son did become the Second Adam; and, as by one man sin entered into the world, and death by sin, so new life hath come by one Man, the Man Christ Jesus. Eternal praise be to Thee. And now, O God, make Thy restored image plaine in us every day, until we see our Savior face to face, awaking in His likeness. *Amen.*

JANUARY 4

Read Matthew 3: 11-17

VERSE 17 — *And lo, a voice from heaven, saying, "This is my beloved Son, in whom I am well pleased."*

HEAVENLY FATHER, Thou who art in truth the Father of our Lord Jesus Christ, we love to bear in mind that, although He took upon Himself the form of man, humbling Himself and making Himself of no reputation, lowering Himself to the rank of a servant, submitting even to the shameful death of the cross, Thou didst at all times acknowledge Him as Thy Son, Thy well beloved Son, in whom Thou wast well pleased. Well might Thy heavens open when He, unflinchingly minded to fulfil all righteousness for us, entered upon His sacred mission of saving the souls of all sinners. Thou wast well pleased with Him because He came not to be served but to serve, to do Thy will, even to the dread day when He could not but cry out, asking Thee why Thou hadst forsaken Him. Father, we stand amazed at this mystery, Thy Son, our God, made manifest in our own poor flesh, taking on Himself our sad burdens, preparing Himself for the ordeal of meeting the eternal punishment which we had merited. Yes, well might the heavens open when He accepted Baptism, proclaiming that He had come to do Thy will in order to bring about our redemption. Can we ever sufficiently thank Thee? What shall we offer Thee, mindful of Thy wisdom and grace? We can but bring our repentant hearts. We know that in Jesus we, too, are now Thy beloved — well pleasing to Thee. Take us, Father, into Thy keeping, under Thy guidance, and in Thy good time let the heavens open to receive us, for His sake. *Amen.*

JANUARY 5

Read Genesis 4: 3-15

VERSES 4, 5 — *The Lord had respect unto Abel and to his offering, but unto Cain and to his offering He had not respect.*

LORD GOD, how often our hearts tempt us to believe Thou art not just and righteous. How often the world doth ask us to think Thou art not worthy to be followed. Happy are we in possessing Thy holy Word; for it showeth us how, through generation after generation, Thou hast always dealt fairly with men. It is only when we are not willing to do Thy pleasure that Thou turnest from us. If we will but listen to Thy voice we will find Thee always true and faithful. How plain Thou hast made the way of life to us. We need but yield to the wooing of Thy Holy Spirit, we need but accept, in the strength which He giveth us, Thy way of salvation, and all will be well with us. Lord, deal with us according to our several needs. If we grow proud and self-willed, send us Thy rebukes. If we come to Thee with gifts which are not holy, with hearts which are perverse, with thoughts which are of our own unhallowed reason, do Thou deal with us according to Thy wisdom, not according to the will of our own flesh. Keep us ever mindful of our unworthiness. Make us understand that no service can please Thee unless it is the true service of a heart purified by the blood of Jesus Christ. And oh, lead us away from our inborn selfishness into a self-sacrificing spirit which is willing to lay all upon Thine altar, asking only that Thou wouldst in mercy accept what it bringeth to Thee. We ask it in His name who offered up Himself for us. *Amen.*

JANUARY 6 (Epiphany)

Read Matthew 2: 1-12

VERSE 2 — *"We have seen His star in the East and are come to worship Him."*

LORD CHRIST, this is the day which doth commemorate Thine Epiphany, Thine appearing to the heathen, Thy revelation that Thou didst come into the world to save not only the souls of God's people, Israel, but the souls of all the Gentile world, even to the ends of the earth. We treasure the story of the star which led wisemen from the distant East to Thy cradle, when Thou didst lie a babe in Bethlehem. It hath been dear to us from our own babyhood, this sweet story of God's goodness to men who in far-off lands were groping for Thy light. It hath touched our hearts, this story of their generous gifts, the gold, the frankincense, and the myrrh. We know not who they were, whether kings, or priests, or philosophers, or astrologers. But this we know, Thy Father made Himself and Thee known to them, and they heeded the leadings of God, despite whatever knowledge of earthly things they had stored in their minds. Truly, they were led by Thy Spirit, and they were Spirit-filled. So peace and joy came to them, and courage to disregard the will of an earthly monarch, obeying God rather than men. Lord Christ, guide us by the star of Thy presence through the days of our lives, through the temptations which assail us, through the imaginations of our own minds. In days when men's wisdom vaunteth itself, preserve to us the disposition to look to Thee alone for guidance. Make Thyself dear to our hearts, and move us to lay all we have at Thy feet, for Thy sweet love's sake. *Amen.*

JANUARY 7

Read Matthew 5: 13-20

VERSE 17 — *Think not that I am come to destroy the Law or the Prophets. I am not come to destroy but to fulfil.*

LORD JESUS, what strange perversity of human hearts is this, that they refuse to understand Thee and to receive Thee as Thou art? Thou hast plainly proclaimed Thyself the Redeemer and the Savior. Thou dost call Thyself the Lamb of God, that taketh away the sins of the world. We read that Thou art the End of the law to them that believe. All this, because Thou wouldst have us know we no longer need to fear the wrath of God on account of our transgression of the law, a law which we are unable to keep because we are born in sin. What comfort Thou hast brought to us, Lord Jesus. Yet, again and again the natural man, not yet drowned out of our hearts, doth rise and put into our minds the thought that Thou art a destroyer of the law, and that, since Thou hast put it away, we may live according to the flesh, that we may disregard the righteousness and holiness which befit Thy followers. Preserve us, Lord Jesus, from the foolish and hurtful thoughts of minds which do not bow down to Thee. Make clear and firm in our souls the truth of Thine atonement. Thou, who gavest the law, didst obey the law. Thou didst take its yoke from our shoulders upon Thine own, freeing us from the curse of our disobedience, but freeing us into a liberty in which Thou dost give us strength to do the Father's will. Preserve us in this faith and life unto our end, in Thy great mercy. *Amen.*

JANUARY 8

Read Isaiah 60: 1-11

VERSE 1 — *Arise. Shine. For thy Light is come, and the glory of the Lord is risen upon thee.*

DEAR HEAVENLY FATHER, what glory Thou dost shed abroad in this world and into our hearts. Daily Thou dost send marvelous light to us, for Thou dost preserve unto us Thy Word, Thy holy sacraments, Thy Church. Daily we dare to come to the throne of unchangeable light, for we have the privilege to come to Thee in prayer. Thou hast lighted the darkness of the world's ignorance, the night of the world's sorrows, the shadows of the world's doubts, the blackness of the world's ungodliness. If we do not see the light, it is because we have closed our own eyes to the streams of brightness which come from Thee. Do Thou continue to send the sun-rays of Thy love upon us and all other men. Do not let the light which cometh from the cross of our Savior be dimmed by the darkness of unbelief and human wilfulness. Let Thy Church remain a tower from which beams of brightness reach to the uttermost parts of the world. Kindle anew each day the fires of faith and devotion in our own breasts. And, while we delight in the beauty of Thy light, make us torch-bearers to our fellow men. No matter what the cost, fill us with zeal to bear Thy truth to the ends of the earth. Make us light-bearers to those of our own households and communities. Send us to the distressed and the afflicted with brightness for their relief. And at last take us where endless light doth stream throughout the city above. Accept our prayer, for the sake of Him who is the Light of the World. *Amen.*

JANUARY 9

Read Romans 3: 20-28

VERSE 24 — *Being justified freely by His grace through the redemption that is in Christ Jesus.*

JESUS, Redeemer of our souls, our only Savior from sin and eternal death, what peace doth dwell in our hearts because we know our salvation resteth upon Thy life and suffering and death, and not upon our own poor efforts. What confidence doth dwell in our hearts because we know we are indeed fully justified, even in the sight of Holy God, who can not permit one single sin to go unpunished. We know that Thou hast made our salvation complete. Nothing is wanting of all that God in His infinite righteousness must demand of us. Thou hast rendered all He must require, Thou hast paid all He must demand. Freely and fully Thou hast secured our justification. There is no condemnation for us. Thou hast so fully accomplished our justification that we need have no thought of trying, by work or merit of our own, to add to that which Thou hast done for us. O our Redeemer, grant us freedom from hours of doubt and darkness, when we might perhaps feel that our sins are not fully forgiven. Preserve us from those temptations of the devil in which he doth suggest that our sin can still condemn us in God's sight. Help us to beware of those who teach that our own works are the way to justification in the eyes of God. But, as Thou dost keep us safe from these errors, grant that we may not become ensnared in the false belief that we can have true faith in Thee and still remain in the works of the flesh. We ask it for Thy name's sake. Amen.

JANUARY 10

Read Luke 6: 17-26

VERSE 19 — *The whole multitude sought to touch Him, for there went virtue out of Him and healed them all.*

JESUS, Thou wondrous Healer of all humanity's diseases, we look back to the days of Thy sojourn on earth in the visible flesh; and the thought of Thee, as Thou didst move about among the suffering people of those days, bringeth comfort to our souls. Only a touch of Thy divine hand, and sickness and deformity and evil spirits vanished, and the afflicted praised God for their deliverance. Thou art mightier than all the woes which can burden us, in body or in soul. Thou art stronger than any evil spirit who might come to vex us. With Thee nothing is impossible. Oh, make this truth vivid to our minds. Teach us to believe Thou art as truly with us as Thou wast with the people of olden times. Convince our hearts that, when our earthly ills are not taken away, it is not because Thou art not near, or because Thou hast lost Thy helping healing power, but because sometimes in Thy wisdom Thou canst use us better beneath our afflictions than Thou couldst if we were free from their restraint. Above all else, lead us to bear in mind that the ills of our souls, from which Thou dost daily deliver us, are the real ills which should concern us; and keep alive in us the faith that it is only through Thy divine touch the evils which afflict our souls can be banished. We know, dear Lord, that at the last Thy touch will free us from every ill. We look forward to that happy day, and are content. We rest and trust in Thee alone. *Amen.*

JANUARY 11

Read Deuteronomy 8: 2-9

VERSE 3 — *Man doth not live by bread only, but by every word that proceedeth out of the mouth of the Lord doth man live.*

O GOD, who hast given us our life, Thou wouldst have us know the secret of true life; namely, that the life of the soul is far higher than the life of the body. Thou wouldst have us comprehend that, just as these poor wasting bodies of ours need daily supplies of food and drink, so our immortal souls must be fed to keep them from perishing. Thou hast taught us that earthly food and substance can not sustain our souls. Thou hast provided for our souls the plenteous feast of Thy holy Word, which is milk for those who are infants in faith, yet at the same time strong meat for those who have grown to manhood in Thy household. Make us ever mindful of these things. Busy with the affairs of our earthly existence, we are inclined to overlook the needs of our souls. Ofttimes Thou must send us trial and tribulation to bring us back again to the remembrance that bread of this earth can not satisfy us, and that, in order truly to live, we must nourish ourselves with the words which proceed from Thy mouth. Lord God, when Thou dost find us forgetful, spare not; but send us whatever chastening we need to drive worldly delusions from our foolish minds. When Thou hast cleared our minds of folly, show us our duty to be the heralds of Thy truth to other starving souls. Attend to this our prayer, for Thy Son's sake. *Amen.*

JANUARY 12

Read First Corinthians 1: 1-13

VERSE 9 — *God is faithful, by whom ye were called into the fellowship of His Son, Jesus Christ, our Lord.*

O GOD, Thou faithful, changeless heavenly Friend, why do we ever doubt Thy wisdom, or Thy might, or Thy love, or Thy constancy? Among all Thy promises given to the children of men there is not one Thou hast ever failed to keep, even though it had been given to the least of Thy children. Among all Thy prophecies, there is not one which, when its time came, was not fulfilled, even to the very letter. Thou art true, but we are often false. Thou art a constant Friend, but we are often inconstant. Thou dost not change, but we are variable as the vagrant winds. Blessed be Thy great name, that Thou, although no other abideth firm, art forever faithful. To Thee we commit ourselves wholly, unreservedly, in earthly and in heavenly things. In Thy tender bosom we repose all our cares. Under Thy firm shepherding we go in and out, secure from dangers, supplied in all our wants. When Thou didst call us into the fellowship of Jesus, Thou didst not deceive us. In Him we have found whatever our deepest longings desired. The wealth of His grace is boundless, the resources of His power to bless us can never be exhausted. O God of Truth, so fill us with Thy Spirit that we may never waver in our allegiance to Him who died for us. Strengthen our wills, that we may prove constant in every time of storm or stress. We pray this in His name alone. *Amen.*

JANUARY 13

Read Genesis 18:1-10

VERSE 1 — *The Lord appeared unto him in the plains of Mamre, and he sat in the tent door.*

LORD GOD, Thou dost say, in Thy holy Word, that Thou art not a god who is far away. Thou wouldst have us know Thou art near us; that, no matter where we may roam, Thou art still with us; no matter where we dwell, Thou hast not forsaken us. Oh, the blessedness of the thought of Thy nearness. How dear to our hearts is the knowledge that, even if we are but weak mortals, even if we are not worthy that Thou shouldst come under our roof, Thou dost deign to visit us and dost delight in granting us Thy companionship. There is no land where Thou art not. There is no far journey on which Thou dost not accompany Thy children. There is no fireside at which Thou art not willing to sit within the family circle. With Thy presence Thou dost make our homes sacred. How different our homes would be if Thou wert not there. How different wedded life would be if Thy companionship were absent. How different fatherhood and motherhood would be if Thou didst depart. Thanks be to Thee because Thou art the God of our households. Grant that we may realize Thy presence with us, and always live as before Thee. Keep from our homes the blight of discord, the gloom of sorrow, the wolf of poverty, the pain of distress. Help us keep erect the family altar, about which we gather daily to worship Thee. Make Thy Son, Jesus Christ, the Head of our household, and let us enjoy His visitations day by day. We ask this, confiding in His love. *Amen.*

Read John 5: 26-35

Verse 30 — *I seek not mine own will, but the will of the Father, which hath sent me.*

O CHRIST, Thou wondrous Son of God and Son of Man; Thou who art called the Lily of the Valley, and the Bright and Morning Star, because of Thy glorious beauty: wherever Thou dost meet us in the gospel story Thou dost make us pause and marvel at Thy person and Thy work. Thou art the eternal Son of the Father, equal with Him in majesty, in power, in wisdom, one with Him in the Godhead — yet Thou dost subject Thyself to Him, dost make His will Thy law, dost permit Him to send Thee forth upon the errand of our salvation. The mystery of Thy two natures joined in one person is far above our understanding — yet we know that in this mystery our eternal hope is bound up. Accept our praise, our reverence, our worship, for Thy Saviorhood. There is none like Thee, there can be none to displace Thee in our faith and in our love. O Master, do Thou so employ our thoughts with the sublime vision of Thyself as Thou art, that we may never heed the voices of those who will not bow the knee of their proud reason before Thee as the Mediator and Redeemer. Defend us from the temptation to place Thee lower than the exalted station which is Thine and Thine alone. Make us valiant champions of Thy gospel truth. Bend our wills to Thine; and, when Thy great day hath come, let us be among those who worship before Thine eternal throne. *Amen.*

JANUARY 15

Read Matthew 8:5-15

VERSE 13 — *Go thy way; and, as thou hast believed, so be it done unto thee.*

JESUS, beloved Helper in need and distress, how light our burdens grow when Thou dost come to brighten our lot with Thy loving-kindness and gentle compassion. How dare we permit the thought to arise in our minds that we are ever bearing sorrows unremembered by Thee? Thou wast always ready to hasten to the side of those who, when Thou wast upon earth in our visible flesh, cried to Thee in their troubles. It was not their persons, or their merits, or their deeds, for which Thou didst have respect. It was their need, their dependence upon Thee, which moved Thee to impart Thine aid to them. Nor did the bodily blessings Thou didst bestow form the whole abundance of Thy favor; for Thou didst bring health and strength for the soul whenever Thou didst bring healing to the body. What wonder that men could trust Thee? What wonder that they could have faith in Thee? We ask Thee now to fill our hearts with faith, with faith so strong that we may have consolation in every new grief which may visit us. We can not by our own reason or strength come to faith in Thee; nor will our faith endure if Thou dost not watch over it. Blot out the remembrance of all our transgressions, and favor us with the gift of unafraid faith, unafraid beneath the crosses which we must bear, unafraid in the hour of death, unafraid before the judgment seat of God; and let our faith always be so pure that it will glorify Thy holy name among men. *Amen.*

JANUARY 16

Read Psalm 19

VERSE 1 — *The heavens declare the glory of God, and the firmament showeth His handiwork.*

MIGHTY GOD, in whose hands are all things in heaven and on earth and under the earth, Thou who rulest the wind and the wave, Thou who ridest upon the storm, Thou who sendest the sun and the rain, Thou who numberest the stars and fixest the constellations of the skies; with all Thy greatness and Thine infinite majesty Thou art yet our Father, our Friend, our Lover. Give us eyes to see what Thou hast written in the limitless book of the universe. May Thy heavens and their hosts, the days and nights of the years Thou dost send, the working of Thy power in the tireless processes of nature, preach to us of the might and the wisdom and the love and the providence which Thou dost unceasingly exercise. Protect us from the folly of viewing this vast universe with unseeing eyes and unimpressed minds. Deliver us from the foolishness of men's puny guess-work science. But let us hear, even dearer and clearer than Thy voice in nature, Thy revelations in the Word, which is more to be desired than much fine gold, sweeter also than the richest droppings of the honey comb. Grant us the insight to behold that Thou art the same when Thou speakest in this Word and when Thou dost write the story of creation in Thy handiwork. We will keep silence before Thee and let Thee lead us, knowing Thou wilt not rest until Thou hast taken us to the cross of Christ, where the darkened heavens and the hidden sun proclaim Thy greatest glory, the love that saveth to the uttermost. *Amen.*

JANUARY 17

Read Genesis 18: 20-32

VERSE 25 — *"Shall not the Judge of all the earth do right?"*

MERCIFUL HEAVENLY FATHER, it is with fear and trembling we come before Thee when we remember Thy greatness and our own sinfulness and unworthiness; yet it is always with confidence and perfect trust Thou wouldst have us appear in Thy presence. Thou hast shown us in Holy Writ how easy Thou art of approach. Not once hast thou turned a deaf ear to one of Thy children who came to Thee in worship and godly fear. But how hard it is for us to keep misgivings from our minds. Sometimes we are so filled with fears, sometimes we have so little faith, that we entirely hush our voice of prayer and remain away from Thy presence. We thank Thee that Thou hast given us the examples of those holy men who dared to come to Thee unabashed, even when they had great things to plead, knowing that Thou, the Judge of all the earth, must always be right and do right. Let us profit by their examples. Make us bolder in our asking. Prevent the foolish fears of our old nature from coming between us and Thy loving heart. Fill us with a sense of our filial right to come to Thee with all that is in our hearts. Make us understand that when we doubt or grow timid we are showing distrust of our Savior's blood rather than humility of our own minds. Teach us to expect great things of Thee, in reliance upon His merits. *Amen.*

JANUARY 18

Read First Corinthians 1: 18-29

VERSES 23, 24 — *We preach Christ crucified . . . Christ, the Power of God and the Wisdom of God.*

LORD JESUS, despised and rejected Son of Man, what shame and mockery were poured upon Thee by Thy chosen people and by the mighty ones of the Gentiles. The story of Thine innocent sufferings, the picture of Thy terrible cross, will never fade from human memory. Never was sufferer more innocent, never was judgment more depraved. Yet, what wisdom of the Father in heaven, when Thou didst bleed and die on that cursed cross, on that black day when Hell seemed to win its highest victory. For Thou, even in Thy disgrace and death, art the Power of God. Thou art His Power to overwhelm the forces of the prince of darkness. Thou art His Power to lift up our deep-fallen race. Thou art His Power to satisfy the requirements of His own unbending justice. So Thou art preached to the utmost parts of the earth, throughout all generations; and with the preaching of Thy Cross there goeth forth a power the like of which is not known even in the highest seats of the mighty of this world — a power to bless, to comfort, to cleanse, to strengthen, to preserve. We feel Thy power within us, a power as of One who is our loving Lord and God, a power as of One whom we must love because He first loved us. Hold Thy cross before us as we journey onward. We know streams of power will come to us if we but look up to it with unwavering faith in Thy redemption. *Amen.*

JANUARY 19

Read Matthew 5: 38-48

VERSE 45 — *He maketh His sun to rise on the evil and on the good, and sendeth rain on the just and on the unjust.*

GOD OF LOVE, tender, compassionate, and forgiving, how canst Thou be so good to those who have disobeyed Thy commandments, who have rebelled against Thee, who have trampled Thine honor in the dust? What mercy is Thine, that Thou hast not destroyed this world and all our human race! Daily we see the proofs that Thy fatherly goodness doth encompass us all, whether we be Thy children through Jesus Christ, or whether we be estranged from Thee in unbelief and worldliness. The lands of this earth abound in proofs that Thou hast not withheld Thy bounties from the sons of men; that, while Thou dost hate sin with a hatred which can not yield, yet Thou dost yearn for the soul of the sinner, vile though he may be. It was when the world still lay in unbelief and rebellion that Thou didst exercise the love which sent Thy best Gift, Thy Son, to offer Himself a Ransom for the guilt of the sinners who would not own Thy sovereignty. We know Thou dost desire that we, as we have redemption through Thy mercy, shall deal mercifully with those of our fellow men who have done us wrong. Speak to these wicked vengeful hearts of ours, and make them forgiving and considerate. Remove the evil hatred from our natures. Grant us patience and gentleness even though we be provoked by a brother's most hateful wrong-doings. Make us true followers of Jesus' perfect example. *Amen.*

JANUARY 20

Read Genesis 19: 15-26

VERSE 16 — *The men laid hold upon his hand and upon the hand of his wife and upon the hand of his two daughters, the Lord being merciful unto him.*

O GOD, our Defender and Protector in all the evils which befall us: how many endangered ones Thou hast rescued from their peril, even though they had been heedless of Thy timely warnings. How dull our senses are to Thy repeated admonitions. Yes, how we often chide with Thee because, caring for us, Thou dost point the way of safety, when we prefer to choose our own ways and abiding-places. How we love to tamper with the evil, to risk our safety to the limit, for a little earthly gain, a little worldly pleasure, a little more companionship with the giddy world and its gayeties. If Thou shouldst deal with us according to our deserts Thou wouldst abandon us to our well deserved fate. But Thou art so desirous of our welfare that Thou dost save us even against our own choices, sending Thine angels to lay their hands upon us and withdraw us from the path of destruction. It is all Thy mercy to which we owe our safety. A hundred perils surround us, of which we know nothing. But Thou dost see and know, and in Thy kind providence dost make our paths safe. Thou hast kept us to this hour, hast led us to this day. Tarry with us longer, O our God, and let Thy guardian care surround us in soul and in body. Choose our paths for us, in spite of our wilfulness; and by and by lead us to a better understanding of those providences which too often bring only murmuring to our lips. We ask it for Christ's sake. *Amen.*

JANUARY 21

Read Matthew 8: 18-27

VERSE 26 — *He arose and rebuked the winds and the sea, and there was a great calm.*

JESUS, Thou mighty Prince and Deliverer, we can not be afraid when we know Thou art near. Hast Thou not revealed to us that Thou art always with us, even to the end of the world? Our lives are filled with storm and tempest. In infancy our little hearts are tossed and driven by childhood's passions and disappointments. In our youth there are the foamings and dashings of our turbulent natures. All through our maturer years our ship of life must ride the storms and outlive the gales of temptations and ambitions, of discouragements and failures. Even in our old age the poor beaten ship of our life must encounter the blasts of this cheerless world. All these unrests come because we are sinners. How blessed are we, because Thou art with us in the boat. In the midst of tempests which try the stoutest hearts among us Thou art calm and majestic. Nothing can disturb the perfect control which Thou dost at all times possess. Thou canst command, and there will be a great calm. We worship Thine omnipotent power, and we cling to Thee in storm and in calm. What manner of man Thou art we know; for Thou art the eternal Son of the everlasting God. Even the storm of eternity's judgment must bow at Thy word; for Thou hast satisfied the righteous wrath of the Judge of heaven and earth. Jesus, we give ourselves to Thee, wholly, in repentance and faith. Grant us repose, here in our daily life, and one day in the hour of death. *Amen.*

JANUARY 22

Read First Corinthians 2: 1-9

VERSE 9 — *Eye hath not seen, nor ear heard, neither have entered into the heart of man, the things which God hath prepared for them that love Him.*

SAVIOR of our souls, Thou incomparable Christ, Thou Peerless One among all the lords and kings: we need not look beyond the years into the lands of the new heavens and the new earth in order to behold what unspeakably beautiful and glorious treasures Thou dost confer upon those who put their trust in Thee. Here in this life Thou dost load our souls with Thy boundless goodness. Forgiveness of sins is ours, and joy, and peace, and assurance that no one can pluck us out of Thy hand; and there is the delight of worshiping Thee, and of serving Thee; the thrill of growing more and more into Thy likeness; the happiness of unselfish ministry to others. All these Thou hast prepared for them who love Thee; all these are ours here in this present time, as we go down the vale of tears, amid the toil and dust of life's burdens, amid the smoke and shouting of life's battle fields. Truly, it is good to belong to Thee, to be joint heirs of Thy numberless mercies. How tawdry the world's bright things seem to our eyes, how shallow its music tinkles in our ears, how dully its allurements appeal to our hearts, when we have Thee. Only, dear Savior, keep us so constantly near Thy side that we may never lose our contentment with the delights of Thy Word and Thy Church. May the sweetness that is Thine never cloy our minds and hearts. *Amen.*

Read Matthew 9: 27-38

VERSE 36 — *He was moved with compassion on them, because they fainted.*

O THOU who didst call Thyself the Good Shepherd, and who desirest to make us all lambs and sheep of Thy fold, our hearts are warmed by the knowledge that there is One who careth for us, who pitieth us, who understandeth our troubles, who doth sympathize with us, who doth comprehend just how sorely we need help and heartening. It is precious to know not only that Thou art the all-seeing, all-knowing God, but that Thou wast actually among us on earth in human form, Thyself didst suffer human needs and wants, Thyself didst bear the very burdens which afflict our shoulders and break us down as we struggle on with our loads of sin and wo. How well Thou didst make Thyself understood when Thou didst confide to Thy hearers that the Good Shepherd layeth down His life for His sheep. Thou didst lay down Thy life, not only when death overcame Thee on Calvary, but also when Thou didst go about doing good, rendering redeeming ministry, pouring Thy very existence into the fervor of the messages Thou didst carry to the needy men and women of the ancient days. Look, Lord: we too are weary, and blind, and hungering, and fainting, and leaderless. With all earth's boasted accomplishments, we have nothing wherewith to solace our hearts and the hearts of our fellows. We need Thee. We need Thee as the Shepherd who layeth down His life for the sheep. Be Thou evermore our Redeemer, our Savior from sin. *Amen.*

JANUARY 24

Read Second Corinthians 1: 3-12

VERSES 3, 4 — *The God of all comfort, who comforteth us in all our tribulation.*

GOD of all comfort, Father of mercies, cheer us on our way; for, truly, the way is long and hard and beset with many dangers. Again and again we have felt that we must give up life's combat. Again and again it hath seemed to us as though we had reached places where there was no way through to deliverance. Then Thou didst come to us, and all was well. But new troubles assail us with every new day, and whenever darkness falleth we dread the defenseless hours of the night. Rather than need Thee less as we gain more and more experience, we find that we need Thee more and more. Somehow, having had Thy comfort, we yearn for it more eagerly when new distresses come upon us. Thou art ready, we know, to comfort us in all our tribulations. None of them can come upon us without Thy will. In them Thou dost conceal wise purposes which Thou hast toward us. The little vexations which annoy us, the awful calamities which sometimes appall us, Thou hast comfort for us in them all. No worry of ours is too insignificant for Thine attention. No doom is too terrible for Thy saving might. Continue to comfort us. When sin oppresseth our hearts and consciences, comfort us with new assurances that the blood of Thy Son is the propitiation which availeth in Thy sight. As Thou dost grant us abounding comfort, speed our steps to the side of those who need us, and enable us to comfort them in Jesus' name. *Amen.*

JANUARY 25

Read Romans 13: 8-14

VERSE 14 — *Put ye on the Lord Jesus Christ, and make not provision for the flesh, to fulfil the lusts thereof.*

O LORD, Thou who dost never sleep, whose watchful eye is ever open, how sorely we need Thy warnings. How greatly we need Thine admonitions that we be watchful, that we arm ourselves for the certain attacks of our foes, the devil, the world, the flesh. We are so much inclined to slumber. We love ease, and it is our habit to be free of thoughtfulness for our souls. So indolent do we grow that we often delude ourselves into the belief that danger is far away, that the enemy hath lost his cunning, that he will come against us no more. Do Thou rouse us from our stupor, even though Thou must deal vehemently with us. Send us whatever visitations we may need to make us watchful. When Thou hast aroused us, grant that we may not put our trust in our own craft and courage. Make us humble enough to know that we must put on the armor of Jesus; yes, that we must put Him on, for in Him alone is our salvation and our strength. Give us the will to crucify our own flesh with its pampered desires. Deaden in us the lusts of our corrupt nature. Show us that to be minded as Jesus was, with perfect trust in Thee and with unselfish love for all our fellow men, is our only escape from the unprofitable works of darkness. Lord, we know that it is day. Thou hast brought light into the world. Make us true children of the day. And in the end save us from the horrors of the eternal night, through Christ Jesus. *Amen.*

JANUARY 26

Read Second Corinthians 4: 1-10

VERSE 6 — *God, who commanded the light to shine out of darkness, hath shined in our hearts.*

O CHRIST, who art the Image of God, what brightness shineth forth from Thy glorious gospel. When Thou didst come into our world, born at Bethlehem, it was because our God was again saying, "Let there be light." How dark it was in this world before Thine incarnation. How terribly the god of this world had blinded men's minds. It is with terror we think of this world deprived of Thee, under the rule of its own gods. What wretched masters this world's gods are, without exception. How dost Thou shine in comparison with them. We thank Thee for laying bare to us their misery; for it is only when Thou dost shine in our hearts that we can rightly estimate their vanity. Thou art better than the god of sensual pleasure, the god of worldly gain, the god of bodily passion, the god of idle ease, the god of intellectual pride. We know and understand, it is true, that in following Thee we must take up Thy Cross and bear it after Thee; but always, when our strength might fail and our shoulders yield, underneath are the everlasting arms. The severest troubles can not distress us. The deepest perplexities can not make us despair. Still dost Thou shine in our hearts; and we, bearing Thy treasures in weak earthen vessels, but magnify Thee the more because our weakness is so plain to view that the glory of our ministry is seen to be Thine and Thine alone. Thanks be to Thee, that Thou hast condescended to let us bear about in our bodies Thy dying. *Amen.*

JANUARY 27

Read Genesis 28: 10-22

VERSE 15 — *Behold, I am with thee, and will keep thee in all places whither thou goest . . . I will not leave thee.*

MERCIFUL GOD, what infinite tenderness is Thine. With what patience Thou dost bear us wilful erring mortals. With all Thy goodness, we allow ourselves to be ruled by our love of selfish gain. We forget Thy words, "The soul that sinneth, it shall die." We forget Thy revelation, "The way of the transgressor is hard." Childish and headstrong, we go our way of disobedience. When it is too late, we see what folly we have committed. But it is never too late for Thy forgiving grace. Thou hast no pleasure in the death of the wicked. Thy pleasure is to have him repent of his wickedness and live. Thy yearning is to restore him to Thy favor. In the gray and the damp after the set of sun Thou dost come, pitying Thy wayward child, with tenderness like that of a parent's heart. Like as a father pitieth his children, so Thou dost pity them who stray from Thee into sin. Hosts of Thine angels stand ready to bridge the spaces between the prodigal and the home from which he hath stolen away. Preserve us, O God, from further error and waywardness. If we should again stray far from Thee, follow us with the love of Thy paternal heart. Be near us, even when we transgress. Keep us, even in the places where our rebellious footsteps may sometimes lead us. Surely, Father, Thy love will win us back to Thee, and we will pledge Thee our vows of greater faithfulness. We know Thou wilt hear us because of the intercession of Thy Son's blood. *Amen.*

JANUARY 28

Read Revelation 1:1-8

VERSES 5, 6 — *Unto Him that loved us and washed us from our sins in His own blood . . . be glory and dominion.*

JESUS, Thou who art called the Faithful Witness and the First-begotten from the dead and the Prince of the kings of the earth: to us Thy greatest beauty is this, that Thou dost love us. Although Thou art the Alpha and the Omega, who wast, who art, who wilt be forever, and who wilt appear with clouds and in great glory at the last day, yet, with all Thy majesty, Thou didst humble Thyself, didst take upon Thyself our nature, didst clothe Thyself with flesh and blood of our race, and didst shed Thy priceless blood, in order that Thou mightst wash us from our sins. Glory and dominion be unto Thee forever and forever. May our own hearts and voices vie with those of angels, of cherubim and seraphim, in magnifying Thy name. Grant that, when Thou comest with clouds, and we are caught up into the air to meet Thee, we may enter into Thy joy, endlessly to serve and worship and exalt Thee. But let us not, in looking forward to that day, neglect to give Thee glory and dominion here in this life. Make us now valiant champions of Thine honor. As we in this life enjoy the full bliss of Thy cleansing blood, let us in this life earnestly contend for Thy kingship. Let us as Thy chosen priests be tireless in showing the world that Thou art the only Offering for sin. Make us undismayed builders of Thy throne among men, not wearying until Thou Thyself dost call us to eternal rest. *Amen.*

JANUARY 29

Read Matthew 11:1-10

VERSE 6 — *Blessed is he, whosoever shall not be offended in me.*

LORD CHRIST, mighty Worker of signs and wonders, Bringer of relief to the afflicted and of life to the dead, Herald of good news to those who are oppressed and lost: we know Thou art indeed He who should come, fulfilling the prophecies of the Father, satisfying the longings of those who were waiting for the Messiah of God. Not only Thy works in days far past prove Thou art the Christ indeed. In our own day Thy deeds are seen on every hand. It is because of Thee that the world still standeth. It is through the good news which Thou hast preached to the poor that our earth to-day possesseth good tidings still. We rejoice in Thy presence, and we sing Thy praises unashamed and unafraid, even though others may forsake Thee, even though some may denounce Thee as the hinderer of progress and the cause of sorrow and privation. Lord, we are willing to deny our flesh the sinful amusements of the world, we are willing to go into what men consider captivity, for Thy sake. We desire to be Thy messengers, by Thine almighty help preparing the way for Thee to ride prosperously. We know true blessedness cometh to those who refuse to be offended in Thee. Grant us new courage to go and tell the wavering, the disheartened, the rebellious, that Thou alone art He who can lead our souls to the true and abiding joys. *Amen.*

JANUARY 30

Read Psalm 34: 11-22

VERSE 18 — *The Lord is nigh unto them that are of a broken heart and saveth such as be of a contrite spirit.*

LORD, our Lord, whose eyes are ever upon the righteous, whose ears are open to the cry of all who put their trust in Thee: look down upon us in mercy, for we come to Thee with broken hearts and contrite spirits. We are ashamed, O Lord God of Truth and Righteousness, because we have so often grieved and offended Thee. With Thine eyes upon us, we have transgressed Thy holy laws. With Thine ears open to our cries, we have cried out in murmuring and impatient frowardness. Have we offended Thee beyond forgiveness? Have we trifled too long with Thy grace? Is the day of our finding the things which belong to our peace gone by? Dear Lord, forbid that we should come short of the salvation Thou hast provided for us. Surely, Thy Spirit hath stirred within us, to bring us to Thee with broken hearts and contrite spirits. None of them, not one, who trusteth in Thee shall be desolate. We know Thou art very near us now, as we lay our penitent hearts at Thy feet, beseeching only that Thou wouldst not turn from us. We will not let Thee go unless Thou bless us. Thou canst not deny Thyself. Thou hast Thyself made us righteous by Thy shed blood. Thanks be to Thee for Thine unspeakably great mercy and gifts. We shall go forth into a better life, assured that all is well with us, Thy loving eye upon us, Thy listening ear open to our cries, because Thou art our Lord and Savior. *Amen.*

JANUARY 31

Read Psalm 25: 12-22

VERSE 14 — *The secret of the Lord is with them that fear Him, and He will show them His covenant.*

BLESSED GOD, our heavenly Friend, closer than brother, or father, or mother, or son, or daughter: we prize the intimate relationship which doth exist between Thee and us. We can not fully comprehend the greatness of the price Thou didst pay to adopt us as Thy children and to make us accepted in Thy sight; but this we know, Thou didst not spare Thine only-begotten Son, in order that we might be Thine, and live under Thee in Thy kingdom and serve Thee in everlasting righteousness, innocence, and blessedness. O God, how good it is to have the unshaken assurance that we are Thine; so truly Thine that Thou dost confide Thy secrets to us; so inseparably Thine that Thou hast made an inviolable covenant with us, receiving us through Baptism into Thy household, teaching us in the way we are to choose, plucking our feet out of the tempter's nets, striking our enemies down before our faces. But see, even with Thy covenant ever unbroken by Thee, we yield to foolish fears, and often cry out as though Thou hadst forgotten us. Free us from this folly, the imagination that we are lonely and forsaken. Strengthen our childlike trust in Thee. Draw us closer into the intimacy with which Thou dost let us penetrate into the inmost secrets of Thy heart. We come to Thee, holding our Savior by the hand, pleading our case because of His perfect righteousness. *Amen.*

FEBRUARY 1

Read Galatians 2: 11-21

VERSE 20 — *The life which I now live in the flesh I live by the faith of the Son of God, who loved me, and gave Himself for me.*

O CHRIST, Thou Son of God, who didst love us and didst give Thyself for us, what blessedness Thou hast brought into our lives by coming into our hearts and making us children of the Father in heaven. Thou hast made our lives new lives. Hadst Thou left us unloved, we would be under the power of sin and our lives would be led for the pleasures which sin affordeth and would be filled with the hopelessness with which sin rewardeth. Thanks be to Thee that Thou hast so drawn us to Thyself that we were crucified with Thee; and that Thou dost possess us so wholly that now it is not we who live, but Thou; and that through Thee, who art the Son of God, the life which we lead will not end when we leave this world, but will continue in the presence of our heavenly Father. Remain with us, Lord, and within us, purifying us more and more from the works of the flesh. Grant that we may never be found among those for whom Thou hast died in vain. As we lead the life which Thou dost work within us, preserve us from pride and self-sufficiency. Keep us mindful of the fact that it is not our obedience to the law which maketh us acceptable in God's sight. When our lives here on earth are ended, in Thy good pleasure take us into the perfect holiness of eternal life. We ask it for Thy love's sake. *Amen.*

FEBRUARY 2

Read Hebrews 13:1-9

VERSE 6 — *The Lord is my Helper, and I will not fear what man shall do unto me.*

LORD JESUS, Thou changeless Christ, the same yesterday, and to-day, and forever: it is the knowledge that Thou art our loving Helper which maketh our hearts established; and oh, what blessedness hath come to us because Thou hast established our hearts by the power of Thy grace. How little do the cares and fears of this world mean to us, how small do the hatred and threats of men seem to us, as long as we have Thee for our constant Companion and Helper. How sure we are of escaping the eternal night, with its terrors and alarms for the guilty soul, because Thou art our Savior even from sin's curse. Lord, do Thou in Thy great mercy make our hearts day by day more firmly established in faith and trust. Sometimes we still fear the ills and slights which come to us from the world, and we know it is the weakness of our faith which maketh us afraid. Pity us, dear Savior, and remain close by us. Make us strong enough in the faith to know that the wealth prized by this world is poor and perishable. Save us from our natural inordinate love for earthly things. Rescue us from the idolatry of covetousness whenever we are in danger of falling into it. Let our trust in Thee be so strong that we may never hesitate to share with others what we may have. Plant our feet firmly upon Thee, the everlasting Rock, who art the same yesterday, to-day, and forever. *Amen.*

FEBRUARY 3

Read Ephesians 2: 1-10

VERSE 10 — *We are His workmanship, created in Christ Jesus unto good works.*

FATHER IN HEAVEN, again the thought of Thine endless grace and goodness filleth our hearts with thankfulness and reverence toward Thee. So deep had we sunk into sin and wrong, we were in truth dead in trespasses, astray from Thy paths of holiness, under Thy wrath and displeasure from our very birth. Thou hadst made us in Thy perfect image, and we had permitted Satan to mar the work of Thy hands, the work of which Thou didst say it was very good. No life stirred within our hearts until Thou in mercy didst have compassion on us, and didst save us through Christ. Ah, what price Thou didst pay to redeem us from our just doom. We need but survey the terrible cross on which Thy Son bled His life away, and we must understand that Thy grace is infinite. And, now that we believe in Him, we are again Thy workmanship. What folly, when we forget that it is solely by Thy love and by Jesus' merits and by the Holy Spirit's breathing upon us that we are no longer dead in sin but are alive in Thee. What folly, when we think we are the architects of our own spiritual fortunes. Father, we give all the praise to Thee. It is Thou who workest within us both to will and to do. In our flesh dwelleth no good thing. There is among us by nature not one that doeth good, no, not one. Let us not fail of the good works unto which Thou hast new-created us. Fill us with love and kindness toward all who may need our service. We ask it in Jesus' name. *Amen.*

FEBRUARY 4

Read Luke 10:25-37

VERSE 25 — *"What shall I do to inherit eternal life?"*

LORD GOD, Thou who art the Author of all life, Thou who art the Giver of our souls' life, Thou from whom alone we can inherit eternal life: only if Thou dost make our lives profitable will they be worth living. When Thou dost come into our lives, how rich and complete Thou dost make them. There is a fulness and a happiness in life when Thou dost dwell in the heart which maketh every day of our lives a song and a sweet delight. We come to Thee to ask Thee for the abundance of trust and service which Thou art pleased to nourish within us. Thou hast called us out of the service of sin and hast made us new creatures in Christ, our Lord. Grant that our faith in Him may be a living faith. May it be living in its confidence that He doth redeem from all guilt, but living likewise in its willingness to offer itself to Him in tender ministry to our fellow men. We know we can not be Thy true children unless we bear in mind those who are in want, and, bearing them in mind, prove willing to deny ourselves in order to save them from their distress and danger. We must confess that we are still far off from the whole-hearted love which hath learned the Second Great Commandment, "Thou shalt love thy neighbor as thyself." Help us, Lord God, as we contemplate Thy boundless love, to grow in purity and strength of love to others. Hear us, for our Savior's sake. *Amen.*

FEBRUARY 5

Read Matthew 14: 22-33

VERSE 27 — *Jesus spake unto them, saying, "Be of good cheer; it is I; be not afraid."*

DEAR LORD CHRIST, what joy to know that Thou art everywhere, and that Thou art ever ready to save. Up in the silent solemn mountain wilderness Thou wast, in the dark hours of the night. Out on the boisterous sea Thou didst walk, when wind and wave were making strong men afraid. Teach us to feel Thy presence wherever we are. Make us convinced we are never alone; that Thou art nigh unto all them that call upon Thee, to all that call upon Thee in truth; that Thou wilt fulfil the desire of them that fear Thee; that Thou wilt also hear their cry and save them. Our frightened troubled hearts need often to hear Thy calm and untroubled voice, saying, "Be of good cheer — it is I — be not afraid." How mighty Thou art, O Christ! Why should we ever tremble? Even though we be called out upon the bosom of the rolling waters, why should we ever, no matter how boisterous the wind may be, lose our trust in Thee and begin to sink? Many are Thine enemies to-day. It is their will to cast Thee from Thy throne, to take from Thee Thy beauty, to rob Thee of Thy name as the eternal Son of the living God, as the Son of Man, truly born of the Virgin, our only Redeemer and Savior. The fury of their warfare against Thee is like the raving of mad storms. Yet Thou wilt triumph. O our Christ, keep us serene in our confidence that Thou canst overcome even the storms of unbelief, the noise of the many waters of whole nations' godlessness. *Amen.*

FEBRUARY 6

Read Genesis 41: 38-49

VERSE 39 — *"Forasmuch as God hath showed thee all this, there is none so discreet and wise as thou art."*

GOD of all wisdom, Thou who knowest the secrets of all eternity, Thou who dost read men's inmost thoughts, Thou who dost stir up the hearts of kings and princes: do Thou lead us daily in the paths which direct us to the fountain of Thy wisdom. It is Thou who must show us what we must know for this life and for the life to come. The fear of Thee is the beginning of all wisdom. We can not be truly wise unless we permit Thee to counsel and guide, to control and command us. How often and how sorely we need Thy wisdom as we try to make our way through life. How many perplexing times there are for us, even though we occupy only humble stations in this world. Make us discreet and wise to know Thy will, to discover the secrets of Thy love. May our eyes turn always to the pages of the sacred revelation which Thou hast given us in the Word. In this day, when many have begun to doubt the wisdom of the Scriptures, when many are walking in the pitiful light of their own conceits, strengthen in us the confidence which we have in Thy holy Book. Help us to see the weakness of the human understanding. Make us brave enough to confess our delight in Thy wisdom before those who call themselves learned and scholarly. Ever grant us Thy Spirit's guidance. We ask it in Jesus' name. *Amen.*

FEBRUARY 7

(In 1940 omit pages 42 to 73 inclusive)

Read Philippians 1: 19-30

VERSES 20, 21 — *Christ shall be magnified in my body, whether it be by life or by death. For to me to live is Christ, and to die is gain.*

BLESSED JESUS, Thou didst die for us, for all lost and condemned creatures. Thou didst truly taste of death, for Thou art truly man, of our own human race, even though Thou art God, begotten of God, the Father, from eternity. Thy death was real, the sundering of the ties which bound Thy body and Thy soul together. From Thy riven side flowed forth water and blood. For Thou hadst been made to be sin for us, and the wage of sin is death. God laid upon Thee the iniquity of us all. How nobly Thou didst die! And oh, how truly Thou hast taken the power of death away! How different death now is to the eyes of them who believe in Thee. For us, to die is gain. As we live on in faith in Thee, we look forward to the hour of our deliverance from the ills and pains of this mortal body. Often we hardly know which to choose, whether rather to desire to depart and be with Thee, or to wish to live on and serve Thee on earth a while longer. But we believe Thou knowest best, and we commit ourselves and all that we are and have into Thy safe keeping. Our times are in Thy hands. Whether we live many years longer or die to-day or to-morrow, it shall be ours by Thy grace to magnify Thee, to prove to the world Thou hast indeed entered into our hearts, and dost make Thy service a blessed joy, and hast taken from death its cruel sting, and from the grave its victory. No enemy, no danger, shall terrify us. We are happy in Thee, and will consecrate our every moment to Thy glory, whether we live or whether we die. *Amen.*

FEBRUARY 8

Read Matthew 6: 2-13

VERSE 6 — *Thy Father, which seeth in secret, shall reward thee openly.*

DEAR LORD, who hast taught us to say, "Our Father," we are glad Thou hast drawn us so close to our God that we enter His presence without fear, without reluctance, as dear children come before a dear father. Thou dost in all tenderness invite us to believe it doth please God to have us come to Him with all boldness and confidence. Thou hast indeed made our prayers a wondrous privilege. Touch us again and again with the wooing power of the Holy Spirit, and make our lives to be lives of prayer. Guard us against thoughtlessness and hypocrisy when we pray to Thee. Drive from these curious hearts of ours the coldness and the hardness. Grant that we be not of them who draw nigh unto Thee with their mouths and honor Thee with their lips only, while their hearts are far from Thee. Show us the folly of the vain repetitions with which some come to Thee, believing they will be heard for their much speaking. Keep us likewise from the sin of making a boast of our service and our worship of Thy great name. May we come humbly, with no thought of show, believing that our Father, who seeth in secret, will reward us openly. Help us to find quiet hours and places apart from the world, where we may often meet Thee in meditation and supplication; yet having Thee with us always, no matter where we may be. And do Thou grant us grace to adorn the prayer life with many deeds of holiness and sweet charity. *Amen.*

FEBRUARY 9

Read Deuteronomy 8: 10-18

VERSE 10 — *When thou hast eaten and art full, then thou shalt bless the Lord, thy God.*

DEAR HEAVENLY FATHER, how bountifully Thou dost always provide for Thy children. Thou dost fill the land with Thy goodness. The earth is Thine, and the fulness thereof; the sea, and they that dwell therein. Thou openest Thy hand and satisfiest the desire of every living thing. We eat of Thy bounty and are filled. In body and in soul Thou dost grant us abundance. Through seas and wildernesses Thou dost lead our feet secure and unharmed. It is by Thy grace we are still among the living, and that we dwell in a land blessed with peace and plenty. Yet how often we forget that every good gift and every perfect gift cometh down from the Father of Lights, with whom is no variableness nor shadow of turning. Thou art constant, but we are inconstant. Forgive our forgetfulness. Open our eyes to behold what multitudes of blessings Thou dost shower upon our way. Ofttimes our forgetfulness ariseth because we have lifted up our hearts in the vain imagination that our prosperity is due to our own desert and effort. Give us Thy Holy Spirit to keep us wise and humble always. We do not pray for riches, yet we ask Thee to deliver us from poverty. If it please Thee to grant us wealth, preserve our hearts in true faith, and lead us first to seek the kingdom of God and His righteousness. Whatever earthly possessions Thou mayest entrust to us, let Jesus and His blood always be our highest treasure. We ask it in His name. *Amen.*

FEBRUARY 10

(In 1932 and 1937 omit pages 45 to 73 inclusive)

Read Matthew 15: 21-28

VERSE 22 — *"Have mercy on me, O Lord, Thou Son of David."*

LORD JESUS, Thou Son of David, we cast ourselves entirely on Thy mercy. We realize better than ever before it is by Thy pardoning blood we still stand within the favor of our God. We know that in us, that is, in our flesh, dwelleth no good thing. We are all as an unclean thing, and all our righteousnesses are as filthy rags. If we say we have not sinned we deceive ourselves and the truth is not in us. We can not even call Thee our Lord, except by the working of the Holy Spirit within us. Dost Thou wonder, Lord, that with all our infirmities and shortcomings we have courage to come to Thee? Ah, Thou Thyself dost bid us come. Nothing in our hands we bring, simply to Thy Cross we cling. Just as we are, without one plea save that Thy blood was shed for us and that Thou bidst us come to Thee, O Lamb of God, we come. So unworthy are we that we will prize even the smallest crumbs which fall from Thy table. For the least of Thy gifts we will be thankful. Only, do not forsake us utterly. Do not pass us by when Thou goest to others. Perhaps, dear Master, perhaps, after Thou hast given us Thy grace for a season, our unworthy faith may grow stronger. Wilt Thou not help us forward to a day when Thou mayest say to us, "Great is thy faith, be it unto thee as thou wilt?" Even this Thy mercy can bring to pass. Hear us now, dear Lord. Do not put us away from Thee. We ask it, trusting in Thy love. *Amen.*

FEBRUARY 11

(In 1948 omit pages 46 to 73 inclusive)

Read Colossians 2: 6-15

VERSE 14 — *Blotting out the handwriting ... against us, ... He took it out of the way, nailing it to His cross.*

LORD CHRIST, in whom dwelleth all the fulness of the Godhead bodily, Thou hast done wondrous things for us. Great are the mysteries of Thy coming into our flesh and taking upon Thyself the burden of all our guilt. Stern, indeed, was the handwriting which stood against us: "The soul that sinneth, it shall die." Thus spoke the voice of God's justice. Of every sin committed we were to give account. Then Thou didst come, and with Thee came deliverance. All that was written against us Thou didst take out of the way, nailing it to Thy cross on Golgotha. Nor didst Thou fail to provide a way for us to enter with Thee into deliverance. We are buried with Thee in Baptism, into Thy death. Thy death hath been made our death, and all the demands of justice have been satisfied for us. What unspeakable merit there is in Thy blood, what unspeakable loving-kindness in Thy heart. And should we, whom Thou didst take unto Thyself in Thy death on the cross, deny Thee Thy heart's desire, that we in our lives be rooted in Thee, be built up on Thee, walking in Thee day by day, walking so truly in Thee and with Thee that men, seeing us, must think of Thee and Thy saving power? Lord, let the fulness of Thy redeeming power be found in us. As Thou hast died for us, give us courage to suffer and die, if need be, for Thee. And may it never be said of us that we, remembered by Thee, have forgotten the pleading of other perishing souls. *Amen.*

FEBRUARY 12 (National Holiday)

Read Deuteronomy 17:14-20

VERSE 15 — *Thou shalt in any wise set him king over thee whom the Lord, thy God, shall choose.*

O GOD, Thou supreme Ruler, King of kings, Lord of lords, who hast divided unto the nations of the world this earth which is Thine and Thine alone: we thank Thee to-day for the blessings of the ordinances which Thou hast enacted so that we may lead a quiet and peaceable life, in all godliness and honesty. We thank Thee for the prosperity and the civic order which our fair land doth enjoy. We thank Thee for raising up men among us, whenever there is need, who, guided by Thine unerring hand, are ministers of God unto us for good. We know there are many in our land who deny Thy goodness and who disown Thy name. We know in our councils Thy will is often forgotten. Yet we know that, for the sake of Thy children, who cry to Thee daily for the continuance of Thy blessing, Thou wilt not condemn our land. As Thou hast made us members of Thy kingdom of grace through the blood of our Savior, do Thou make us better citizens of this great commonwealth by reason of our citizenship in Him. Keep every foreign foe from our borders. Frustrate the designs of traitors who may be among us. Thwart the plans of evil-minded men who disregard the sacredness of their citizenship. Vouchsafe wisdom and honest purpose to our law-makers and executives. Above all, charge us with our responsibility to spread the truth of Christ's gospel everywhere in our land, at all times, undismayed and unfatigued. We lay this prayer before Thee in His name. *Amen.*

FEBRUARY 13

(In 1929 omit pages 48 to 73 inclusive)

Read John 5: 36-47

VERSE 39 — *Search the Scriptures . . . They are they which testify of me.*

HEAVENLY FATHER, since Thou art indeed our Father Thou must assuredly reveal Thyself unto us. How strange it would be to think that Thou, loving and caring for us, desiring our welfare, wouldst not make known to us who Thou art and what Thy gracious purposes are toward us. It is not hard for us to believe that the Holy Scriptures are Thy message to us, telling us whatever we need to know for our temporal and eternal welfare. And of whom should they bring us messages rather than of Thine only-begotten Son, who was with Thee in eternity, and who, fulfilling Thy will, came here on earth in our flesh to make us again Thy children? What we could not learn in the great book of nature, what neither sky nor earth nor sea could tell us, Thou hast made clear upon the pages of Thy Word. Thy Scriptures are they which testify of Thy Son and His love. We know that He who came born of Mary at Bethlehem is Thy Son, our Lord. How else could He have done the mighty works which bear record of Him? How else couldst Thou have honored Him so highly, even though He did not seek honor, but made Himself humble even unto the death on the cross? Do Thou kindle and keep in us a more fervent love for Thy Word. May its perplexing passages not deter us from rejoicing in its beauty and in its power to save us. Silence the voice of our natural reason when we read Thy revelation, and show us our Savior's glory shining from every page. *Amen.*

FEBRUARY 14

(In 1934 and 1945 omit pages 49 to 73 inclusive)

Read Matthew 15:29-39

VERSES 29, 30 — *He went up into a mountain and sat down there; and great multitudes came unto Him.*

SAVIOR, we adore Thy love once more to-day, as we think of Thy tender ministry to the souls of those who were as sheep without a shepherd. How gracious Thou wast to them all. There was not one in the vast companies which came to Thee whom Thou didst not seek to save. How sorely they needed Thee. How fully Thou couldst satisfy their every want. How different was Thy message from that which earthly-minded teachers had brought to them. What a fulness of God there was in Thee as Thou didst live and move and have Thy being, One of our own race, among mortal men. How clearly Thou didst unfold, as the days went on, that Thou wast indeed that Christ who should come into the world. Were men sick, Thou couldst heal them. Were they hungry, Thou couldst feed them. Were their souls weary and heavy laden, Thou couldst give them rest. Thou art the same dear Savior to-day, and wouldst gather us about Thee as truly as Thou didst gather the needy multitudes in Galilee long years ago. Savior, lead us to feel our need of Thee. Prevent the influence of our times, the spirit of the world to-day, from filling us with imaginations of our own sufficiency. Keep before us the fact of our sinfulness and weakness. We do need Thee. No other can feed us, no other can heal us, no other can bring us pardon and peace. We come to Thee. Receive us, and let us receive from Thee grace for grace. *Amen.*

FEBRUARY 15

Read First Thessalonians 4: 1-7

VERSES 3, 7 — *This is the will of God, even your sanctification . . . God hath not called us unto uncleanness but unto holiness.*

O GOD, Thou dwellest in holiness and righteousness and purity. Thou hatest all manner of iniquity. He who doeth evil shall not dwell with Thee. Thy face is against them that do evil. And behold, we are all impure and evil-minded, unable to stand in Thy presence. The lust of the flesh and the lust of the eyes and the pride of life attract us, although we know full well they are not of Thee. But Thou hast in mercy called us, not unto uncleanness, but unto holiness, unto pure and clean life; and Thou hast given us power over our fleshly nature through the transforming blood of our Savior, Thy dear Son, Jesus Christ. Keep us, we pray Thee, under the power of His blood. Bring all our passions and feelings into subjection to Him. Sanctify us wholly. Help us bring our bodies as living sacrifices to Thee. May we not be satisfied with half-hearted surrender to our Lord, but grant that we may abound more and more, even in the midst of great temptations walking so that we may please Thee. Give us wisdom to avoid those companions and those places in which impurity reigneth. Make us loathe that which might weaken us. To this end fill us with devotion to Him who gave His life for us, seeking not pleasure and delights, but choosing the Cross, with its pain and sacrifice. We ask it in His pure name. *Amen.*

FEBRUARY 16

Read Romans 10: 9-18

VERSE 10 — *With the heart man believeth unto righteousness, and with the mouth confession is made unto salvation.*

DEAR FATHER IN HEAVEN, how blessed we are because we have knowledge of Thee. Give us the mind always to remember Thou didst send us this knowledge by the faithful preaching of Thy Word. Thou hast sent forth men to testify and bear witness of the life and death of our Savior. With Thy Word Thou dost send forth Thy Holy Spirit, to work upon our hearts and to open our understandings and to implant faith within us. Thou didst not ask who we were, of what race or in what station. We were lost sinners and we needed Thee, and in Thy love Thou didst come to us. How unthankful we would be if we could forget this Thy mercy. But how shall we thank Thee for this boundless goodness? How show our gratitude to Thee for rescuing us from the curse and the ills of sin? Ah, Thou dost ask us to become Thy witnesses to others. As Thou hast led us to faith, Thou wouldst move us to confession of our Lord's dear name. We offer ourselves to Thee, wholly, with all our powers, with the new powers Thy grace hath given us. Take our hearts, our lips, our eyes, our hands, our feet, take us and possess us so wholly that we may never lack in our bold confession of Jesus and His saving blood. Give us courage to risk our earthly welfare, or even our lives, if need be, for love to Him who gave His all for us. Make us faithful, our Father, unto the end, and grant that many may be led aright through our confession of His name. *Amen.*

FEBRUARY 17

(In 1926 omit pages 52 to 73 inclusive)

Read Nahum 1: 1-10

VERSE 3 — *The Lord is slow to anger, and great in power, and will not at all acquit the wicked.*

ALMIGHTY GOD, how apt are we to forget what power and majesty are Thine. They who do not love Thee desire to have us doubt Thy great might. They ask us to believe we live in a world which came into being without Thy will and Thy Word. And, because by nature we are rebels against Thy throne, our hearts sometimes still incline to listen to the denials of the unbeliever. Convince us anew of Thy kingship over all things in heaven and on earth. We know Thou art jealous of Thine honor. Thou wilt not give Thy glory to another, neither Thy praise to graven images, nor wilt Thou acquit him who robbeth Thee of Thy glory as the Maker of all things. How can we doubt Thine almighty power? Do not the mountains quake before Thee? Do not the sun and the clouds and the winds obey Thy command? Restrain the wiles of them who dishonor Thee. If we have withheld our worship from Thee, forgive us. Thou art slow to anger, even though Thou couldst consume us. Thou knowest them who trust in Thee. We know Thou wilt avert Thine anger from us, because Thou didst make it all to rest upon our Savior when He suffered and died for us. We plead His blood and His merits. We know they avail in Thy sight. We know His kingdom will stand secure when all the rebellious imaginations of men and nations have been destroyed. We will abide in Him, and Thy favor will be ours eternally. *Amen.*

FEBRUARY 18

(In 1931 and 1942 omit pages 53 to 73 inclusive)

Read Mark 9: 30-40

VERSE 35 — *If any man desire to be first, the same shall be last of all and servant of all.*

O LAMB OF GOD, Thou didst come to be the Servant of God and the Servant of all Thy fellow men. Although Thou wast eternal God, Thou didst make Thyself of no reputation, and didst take upon Thyself the form of a servant, and didst humble Thyself and become obedient. By Thy deep humiliation Thou hast highly exalted us, lifting us up from the shame and death of sin into the very presence of our God, and into the endless happiness of everlasting life. Never once didst Thou waver as Thou wast journeying the way of sorrows. Not one item didst Thou omit of all the obedience which perfect righteousness required. When at the last the cross was laid upon Thee, Thou wast humble enough to bear it without murmuring. Now Thou dost ask of us to be like Thee, to be the least and the last of all, to be the servants of all. Thou hast asked us to be like little children: not to strive for earthly honor and place, but to commit our destiny to Thy keeping, confidingly following in Thy footsteps. We need all Thy grace to enable us to heed Thy commands. Our pride and selfishness contend against the new spirit Thou hast given us. Strengthen us, dear Lord, in our faith and trust in Thee, and in our resolves to follow Thee, bearing the Cross as Thou didst bear it. And do Thou richly bless us as we strive to serve all other men. We ask it for Thy love's sake. *Amen.*

FEBRUARY 19

(In 1947 omit pages 54 to 73 inclusive)

Read Second Thessalonians 2: 13-17

VERSE 13 — *God hath from the beginning chosen you to salvation.*

MERCIFUL GOD, even in eternity Thou didst plan our redemption from sin and our salvation from sin's curse. If we are rescued from its peril, it is because Thou didst choose us. Thy loving heart went forth to us, Thy tender mercy yearned for us, Thy pitying grace searched us out. We can not understand why Thou shouldst consider us in our wilful turning from Thee, except as we try to understand it in the light of Thy divine nature. Thou hast no pleasure in the death of the wicked, but that the wicked turn from his way and live. Thou art not willing that any should perish, but that all should come to repentance. Whatever lay within divine power and love Thou hast planned and performed to save us. Oh, how highly should we prize the salvation worked out for us in the sacrifice of Thy dear Son. With what fear and trembling should we hold fast what we have been taught of Thy goodness and kindness. Send us new strength from on high, this day and all the days to come. With Thy help we can stand firm, without Thee we can do nothing. Surely, Thou wilt not permit us to perish and to have our Savior die for us in vain? Draw us to Thee and place round about us the armor of Thy truth. Incite us too, dear Father, to serve Thee in bringing other lost souls to a knowledge of Thy love for them. We bring this prayer to Thee, confiding in Thy love, because Jesus, Thy Son, died for us according to Thine eternal counsel. *Amen.*

FEBRUARY 20

Read Revelation 2: 1-11

VERSE 10 — *Be thou faithful unto death, and I will give thee a crown of life.*

O FAITHFUL GOD, Thou hast never, not even in the least degree, left Thy words in our behalf unfulfilled. Always we can trust Thee. Always we can boast before the world that Thou art a God of inviolable honesty, that Thou hast never permitted any soul which trusted in Thee to be put to shame. We will, no matter what dark night of trial or tribulation may come, both lay us down in peace and sleep; for Thou, Lord, only makest us dwell in safety. We know Thou art with us at this hour, and also with all the suffering, the distressed, the erring, the fatherless, the widowed, the wanderers; because Thou art ever faithful. Should not Thy faithfulness move us to be truer to Thee? With all Thou hast done for us in Jesus, can we do otherwise than keep our pledge of faithfulness to Him and Thee? Yet — how often we forsake our first love. Be merciful to us, lest we lose the crown of life. How glorious it is, this crown of life, which Jesus merited for us when He wore the crown of thorns. What joy will be ours when we stand before Thy throne, crowned with the life which can never end, where all our tears are wiped away, where sin and sorrow and death are unknown. Truly, the sufferings of this present time are not worthy to be compared with the glory which shall be revealed in us. And yet, O God, we desire to be faithful, not because Thou wilt so richly reward us, but because the love of Christ constraineth us. *Amen.*

FEBRUARY 21

Read Matthew 16: 13-20

VERSE 16 — *"Thou art the Christ, the Son of the living God."*

CHRIST, Thou Son of the living God, in our day, too, the question of all questions is, who Thou art. All through the years, since Thou didst join Thyself to our humanity, the men and the nations of the world have asked concerning Thee. For those who have refused to listen to flesh and blood, who have permitted the Father in heaven to reveal Thy secrets to their inquiring hearts, there can be but one answer. Thou art indeed the Christ, the Anointed; anointed without measure, to be the Prophet of infinite knowledge, the High-priest of the priceless sacrifice, the King of a dominion which will never end. Who can hear Thy saving words, who can view Thy sacrifice of Thy sinless guiltless self, who can behold the power with which Thou hast gone throughout the world in Thy kingdom, without acknowledging Thee the Christ, the Son of the living God? We accept Thee, O Savior, just as Thou art in the pages of that sacred story of old. Now do Thou accept us, weak, sinful, guilty, as we are, and make us unafraid confessors of Thy name. Help us to answer the cry of the world for deliverance by testifying of Thy salvation. Make us steadfast as the very rock, unmoved by the storms which rage about Thy Cross. Convert many hearts to Thyself, their only Help and Hope. Hear us, Lord, and let this our believing prayer be acceptable in Thy sight for Thy great mercy's sake. *Amen.*

FEBRUARY 22 (National Holiday)

(In 1928, 1939, and 1950, omit pages 57 to 73 inclusive)

Read Deuteronomy 20: 1-9

VERSE 4 — *The Lord, your God, is He that goeth with you, to fight for you against your enemies, to save you.*

GREAT GOD, how often Thy people have failed to see that Thou art with them in all their battles against those who rise up to war with them. Thou hast asked us to cast all our cares upon Thee, for Thou carest for us. Thou dost send Thine angel, and he campeth round about them that fear Thee, and delivereth them. Thou hast bidden us to be anxious in nothing. Thou, the mighty God of numberless victories, art with us, and Thou hast promised that not any man shall be able to stand before us. Yet, in every new distress we cry out in fear, as though Thou hadst never fought for us, as though the enemy would surely overwhelm us. Give us greater assurance. O Thou strong Son of God, who didst come upon earth to destroy the works of the devil and who didst triumph over him openly in our behalf, give us wise and understanding hearts to know that, since Thou didst not forsake us when we were yet in our sins, Thou surely wilt not forsake us, now that we are Thine by the redemption of Thy blood. We ask Thee to lead on in every battle, in our warfare against Satan, against the wicked men of this world, against the evil in our own sinful nature. Fight for us, fight with us, fight in us, O mighty Captain of our salvation. With Thee nothing is impossible. May we grow into a perfect trust in Thee, and, fighting under Thy banner, go from victory to victory, until at the end we overcome the last enemy, death, and enter with Thee into eternal triumph. *Amen.*

FEBRUARY 23

(In 1944 omit pages 58 to 73 inclusive)

Read Habakkuk 2: 12-20

VERSE 14 — *The earth shall be filled with the knowledge of the glory of the Lord, as the waters cover the sea.*

LORD GOD most glorious, who coverest Thyself with light as with a garment, who ridest upon the clouds, who hidest Thyself in thick darkness: what majesty, what infinite splendor, is Thine. What glory Thou hast brought into our own hearts and lives and homes and lands, by revealing Thyself as the God of long-suffering and compassion, yet as the God of righteousness and holiness. Throughout this world the preaching of Thy great name hath gone. Thou dost ride prosperously, making the nations bend before Thine awful throne. As the waters of the vast seas cover the face of the earth, the story of Thy love for sinful men hath flooded the world with blessing. May this Thy liberal provision for our welfare not remain unused by us. Let the wealth of Thy gospel flood our hearts as the waters cover the sea. In the new life which cometh to us by its regenerating power, may we destroy every idol which would usurp Thy place within our hearts. May we give ourselves so fully to Thee that covetousness and intemperance and uncleanness may be far from us. May there be no soul in all our human race which doth not feel the flood of Thy divine knowledge. Make the preachers of Thy Word true to Thee, and render their ministry resistless, like the tides of the swelling seas. Receive us, as we bring Thee this our unworthy prayer, for the sake of Jesus Christ, our Lord. *Amen.*

FEBRUARY 24

Read First Timothy 1: 12-20

VERSE 17 — *Now, unto the King eternal, immortal, invisible, the only wise God, be honor and glory forever and ever.*

HOLY, HOLY, HOLY, Lord God almighty, adored by angels, worshiped by cherubim and seraphim; teach our reluctant lips to sound Thy praises on all our ways through life. Thou art the King eternal, immortal, invisible. Thou art the only God, infinite, all-wise, ruling everywhere, merciful, full of truth. Thou dost richly and daily provide us with all that we need to support this body and life; dost defend us against all danger; dost guard and protect us from all evil. Thou hast redeemed us, lost and condemned creatures, purchased and won us from all sins, from death, and from the power of the devil; not with gold or silver, but with Thine own precious blood, and with Thine innocent sufferings and death; only that we may be Thine own and live under Thee in Thy kingdom. All eternity will not be sufficiently long for us to praise Thee as we should for all Thy care over us. Vile and wretched as sin may make us, Thou dost forgive and reclaim. Enable us to bring Tnee more than the idle praise of lips which may not mean what they say. Enlist us in Thy gracious cause, and make us valiant soldiers of the faith once for all delivered unto the saints. Assure our hearts that whatever in our past hath been amiss Thou hast so truly borne away, that our praise and service of Thee is acceptable. Hold us in Thy hand, lest we fall from Thee. Make us, Thy subjects, so humble, so persevering, that Thou mayest indeed, after our life here on earth, be our King eternal. We ask it of Thy mercy. *Amen.*

FEBRUARY 25

(In 1925 omit pages 60 to 73 inclusive)

Read Matthew 6: 19-25

VERSE 21 — *Where your treasure is, there will your heart be also.*

GRACIOUS GOD and Father, preserve us from the unhappiness of divided hearts. It is our weakness of faith which moveth us to try to serve two masters, to give Thee a portion of our devotion and to bestow another portion on things which become idols because of our affection for them. Thou wouldst have our whole hearts. Thou wouldst be our highest Treasure. Thou wouldst deliver us from that love of earth's good things of which even our own experience teacheth us that it only maketh us unhappy and anxious. Make us remember that the treasures of this earth are all perishable, and that, if we set our hearts' affections upon them, we will be filled with anxiety whenever they show their changeableness and corruptibleness. When Thy Son came into our flesh He cared little for this world's good things. He had not where to lay His head. In poverty and self-denial He went His way, content that He had Thee and that He was doing Thy will. Show us the wisdom of laying up treasures for ourselves in heaven. Give us the treasures of sin's forgiveness, of reconciliation with Thee, of assurance that eternal life is ours through Christ. If it doth please Thee to endow us with earthly goods, bestow upon us willing minds to deal with them as Thy stewards, who must one day render account to Thee. Make us happy in Thee, content in unselfish service, and sure of eternal blessedness through Christ. *Amen.*

FEBRUARY 26

(In 1936 and 1941 omit pages 61 to 73 inclusive)

Read Matthew 16: 21-27

VERSE 26 — *What is a man profited, if he shall gain the whole world, and lose his own soul?*

LORD JESUS CHRIST, how precious our souls were in Thy sight. It was for them Thou didst look forward, submissive and patient, to the dread hours when Thou wouldst be made to suffer many things at the hands of them who would not receive Thee, when Thou wouldst be made to suffer even unto death. No power could restrain Thee from pursuing Thy set purpose to the bitter end. Thou knewest that to seek comfort and freedom from the cross would be to listen to the temptation of Satan. Oh, canst Thou not make these wavering hearts of ours understand that we must deny ourselves and take up our crosses and follow Thee? How often, dear Savior, do we give proof that we have not yet learned how precious our souls are, and how little value the things of this world possess. How often we forget that even the gain of the whole world is as nothing compared with the saving of one single soul. Open our eyes, that we may see as Thou didst see. Give us power to put the suggestions of Satan behind us. Give us courage to withstand him. Thou hast said he will flee from us if we resist him. Be mighty within us, that we may manfully resist. Lend us wisdom to value other men's souls as Thou hast valued ours. Let no price be too great for us to pay to save one soul from eternal death. Banish our sluggishness in the work of missions. Make us see the need of safeguarding the souls of our children. Do this for Thy mercy's sake. *Amen.*

FEBRUARY 27

Read Revelation 3: 1-12

VERSE 5 — *He that overcometh, the same shall be clothed in white raiment.*

O CHRIST, our mighty Savior, Thou didst overcome, and Thou art clothed in white garments. With Thee in that life of bliss there are thousands of our fellow believers, who remained steadfast in Thy strength, to whom Thou hast kept the glorious promise that they should be with Thee. It is Thy gracious will that where Thou art there shall Thy servants also be. Wilt Thou be gracious unto us and favor us with Thy gifts, so that we may endure unto the end and overcome? Wilt Thou fill our hearts with the gladness of them who wear the garments of white in the life beyond? Thou, the Son of Man, didst not come to destroy men's lives, but to save them. As our High-priest Thou hast passed into the heavens, and Thou didst say Thou wouldst go to prepare a place for us. But the time is not yet for us to pass into the heavens. Thou hast left us here upon earth, to do Thy will. Thou dost bid us be watchful, lest we fall into temptation. Loving Savior, Thou knowest our infirmities. Thou seest how much inclined we are to sleep. Rouse us to greater watchfulness. Remind us that the enemy is ever at hand to take advantage of our remissness. Thou Thyself wilt appear without warning when Thy good time hath come. Should we not watch, our lives might prove sad failures. Save us from such fate. To this end make us diligent to hear and heed Thy words, and draw us often to the communion of Thy body and Thy blood in Thy Holy Supper. We ask it, resting in Thy grace. *Amen.*

FEBRUARY 28

Read Matthew 17: 1-13

VERSE 5 — *Behold, a bright cloud overshadowed them, and, behold, a voice out of the cloud.*

SAVIOR, who didst make Thyself so lowly that Thou wast the least esteemed among men, we know that throughout the years of Thy lowliness Thou didst still possess the fulness of that glory which the Godhead alone can have. Thou hadst not lost Thine eternal majesty, Thou hadst not forfeited Thy power. Whenever Thou didst so will, it broke through the poor garments of Thy lowly humanity and shone with blinding splendor. How often we need the cheer which can come to us only through the knowledge that Thou art the omnipotent God. Keep our faith bright and shining, even when clouds come and hide Thee and Thy glory from our eyes. Keep fresh in our minds the glory which always shineth from Thy Word, even though it be so despised by the learned of this world that they call it foolishness. Impress upon us that the simple preaching of Thy gospel, the simple bearing of Thy Cross to the souls of men, doth spread in our world the only true light. Make us, Thy followers, feel the rapture of Thy presence. It is truly good to be with Thee, whether Thou art shining in glory so that men may see, or whether Thou art hiding Thyself in the quiet influence of the still small voice. Flood our hearts with the glorifying light which we know Thou alone canst send forth. Help us through the dark days, comfort us in the dreary nights, breathe true consolation into our souls through the written Word of Thy revelation. We know Thou canst do all things, and we confide in Thee. *Amen.*

FEBRUARY 29

Exodus 3: 1-10

VERSE 5 — *Put off thy shoes from off thy feet, for the place whereon thou standest is holy ground.*

LORD GOD, what lack of reverence doth afflict the world to-day. How few there are, even among those who call themselves Thy children, who feel the dread responsibility of being Thy stewards. It is Thou hast given us this life. The gifts and powers we possess are all from Thee, and it is only through Thy sufferance we continue in their possession. Thou hast said we must give account for every idle word we speak. Oh, grant us a keener sense of Thy sovereignty over us and of our entire dependence upon Thee. Enlighten us so that we may comprehend Thou art with us everywhere, and in everything we do and everywhere we go we are beheld by Thine eyes, which look upon us to approve or to condemn. Show us Thy providences in the little things which form our daily experiences. Make us conscious of the fact that Thou knowest our down-sitting and our up-rising; that Thou understandest our thoughts afar off; that Thou compassest our paths and art acquainted with all our ways. We can not hide from Thee. We can not hide even one of our many transgressions from Thee. Yet we need not fear Thee with fear which hath pain. Through Thy Son Thou hast been reconciled with us. Thou hast pardoned us freely, and when Thou dost come to us it is only to bless us. We thank Thee in His name, and in His name beseech Thee to show Thyself to us step by step as we go on our way. *Amen.*

MARCH 1

(In 1933 omit pages 65 to 73 inclusive)

Read Psalm 26

VERSE 8 — *Lord, I have loved the habitation of Thy house, and the place where Thine honor dwelleth.*

MERCIFUL FATHER in heaven, Thou canst not be made to dwell in houses built by men's hands; yet art Thou willing to hallow our sacred places and to make them holy temples, where Thou art pleased to grant us a special dispensation of Thy divine presence and communion. Oh, that we might be able to say we love the habitation of Thy house above all other places. Oh, that we might be more willing to honor Thee by diligently seeking the places where Thine honor dwelleth. Father, Thou knowest how wayward we, Thy children, are. Thou seest how slow our feet are to journey toward Thy house, how slow our hearts are to flame with zeal for Thy dwelling-place among us. Take our hearts into the care of Thy chastening love. Teach us the virtue of sincere self-examination. Test us by Thy judgments and try us by Thy disciplines. Grant us so true a love of Thy house that we may sacrifice our all to found it firm in our community. Let the beloved ordinances of Thy temple be so dear to us that we may not rest until Thy temples have been built everywhere throughout the earth. When Thy Word is proclaimed, when Thy sacraments are administered in Thy house, may we receive them into hearts which are like the good soil, bringing forth fruit a hundred-fold. Preserve the pure preaching of Thy Word to us and to all men, for only through its power can salvation come. Hear us for Jesus' sake. *Amen.*

MARCH 2

(In 1927. 1938, and 1949, omit pages 66 to 73 inclusive)

Read Hebrews 13: 11-21

VERSE 14 — *Here have we no continuing city, but we seek one to come.*

O JESUS, Thou great Shepherd of the sheep, whom God hath brought again from the dead, who art ascended up on high after leading captivity captive: how real, how near, Thou hast made the city which is to come. Hadst Thou not revealed unto us that there is a city in the heavens, what uncertainty would be ours. But now we know our life here upon earth is not our abiding life. We are only sojourners here, strangers and pilgrims, who seek the bright glorious city to come. Help us as we pursue our way to its glories. The way Thou didst go was a way of suffering and shame. Reproach was heaped upon Thee. Thou wast not permitted to die within the gates of the holy city, but Thou wast led without the gate, there to bear the shame, there to die for us, because sin had made us outcasts from God's presence. Lord, we are willing to bear Thy reproach with Thee. We are willing to give ear to Thy Word, as Thou dost send it to us through Thy chosen ministers. We are willing to lead the life of prayer and unselfishness. But we need Thy strength. We need Thee every hour, every day, to the very end. Do not forget us or forsake us on our way. Be our Shepherd and our Guide. When death cometh to us by Thy providence, grant us to die in faith, and lead us out of death, even as Thou Thyself didst rise from its embrace, into the new life of the continuing city above. Hear us in mercy. *Amen.*

MARCH 3

Read Exodus 4: 1-14

VERSE 12 — *I will be with thy mouth, and teach thee, what thou shalt say.*

LORD, ALMIGHTY GOD, in whose hands we are but as clay in the hands of the potter: fashion us as Thou seest fit. Take us wholly into Thy direction, and let Thy Spirit control us in soul and mind and body. The longer we live, the clearer it becometh to us that we are but dust beneath Thy feet. What is man that Thou art mindful of him, or the son of man, that Thou visitest him? There is not one thing which we could do except for Thy presence with us. Even the movements of our bodies are accomplished through strength which Thou dost provide. And when our souls are to do the things which are pleasing in Thy sight, we find they are powerless, paralyzed by the sickness of sin. But we have Thy promise that, whenever Thou wouldst have us serve Thee, Thou wilt vouchsafe Thine aid. If we are to speak for Thee, Thou wilt teach us what to say. If we are to labor for Thee, Thou wilt give us wisdom and strength. If we are to suffer for Thee, Thou wilt grant us patience and fortitude. If we are to die for Thee, Thou wilt make us brave and strong to the uttermost. Oh, convince us of our entire dependence on Thee, but comfort us with a faith which is persuaded that Thou wilt not, canst not, leave those unaided who put their trust in Thee. How clear Thou hast made Thy care for us in sending Thy Son into our flesh. Thou wilt, we know, in Him freely grant us all things. Help Thou our unbelief, banish our doubts, remove our fears — we ask it in His name. *Amen.*

MARCH 4

Read Mark 1: 21-31

VERSE 22 — *He taught them as One that had authority.*

ALMIGHTY CHRIST, what blessedness cometh to us in the feeling of Thine authority. Not one of Thine adversaries was able to stand against Thy sublime majesty. When Thine enemies sent forth ruffians to take Thee into their power, they returned empty-handed, saying of Thee, "Never man spake as this Man." Of a truth, their witness could not be otherwise. We read the story of Thy teaching, of Thy journeys, of Thy control of evil spirits, of Thy command over the diseases which did afflict both souls and bodies, and we worship Thee as the Almighty One, the Sun of Righteousness, risen among men, with healing in Thy wings. O Christ, how many are the voices and the hands still raised against Thee. Yet how majestic Thou dost tower above all the tumult of men's hatred and disobedience of Thee. Fill Thou our souls with the great calm which did abide in Thine. Drive from our minds whatever doubts may find lodgment there. Lend to the preaching of Thy faithful ministers in this our day that authority which maketh the consciences of sinners and unbelievers bow before Thee, acknowledging Thine authority. Speak to our hearts in tones so persuasive that we may remain faithful to Thee. Heal our diseases, dear Master; cast out the evil within us; take away the weakness and the faint-heartedness. Make us and our fellow believers a conquering army, endued with Thy strength, resistless, victorious. Hear us in loving-kindness. *Amen.*

MARCH 5

(In 1930 omit pages 69 to 73 inclusive)

Read Psalm 29: 1-11

VERSE 11 — *The Lord will give strength unto His people; the Lord will bless His people with peace.*

GREAT GOD, who commandest, and Thou art obeyed, who speakest, and the universe hasteth to heed Thy voice: let Thy will be heard and heeded throughout our world to-day. Thy people wait upon Thee, looking to Thy hand for every good and every perfect gift, listening for Thy voice. They know Thou wilt give them strength, they know Thou wilt bless them with peace. Who can withstand Thy displeasure? Thy voice is upon the waters. Thy voice breaketh the cedars of Lebanon. Thy voice divideth the flames of fire. Thy voice shaketh the wilderness. God of might and glory, let Thy voice speak into the depths of our hearts. Let it make us still: let it be our law, our will. But always dearest to us be Thy voice as Thou hast spoken through Thy beloved Son in the last times, that Son whom Thou hast appointed Heir of all things, who by Himself purged all our sins. It is for His sake that we, with hearts and hands and voices, would give glory and strength unto Thee. It is in Him we would come and worship Thee. Because of His redeeming grace we dare approach Thee in all Thy greatness, knowing Thou wilt condescend unto us. Through Him Thou dost give Thy people strength, through Him Thou dost bless them with peace. Bring us more peace, O God. Let peace like a river attend our ways, and the ways of other men and nations. And at the end make us partakers of that eternal peace which Thou alone canst impart. Do this, for His sake. *Amen.*

MARCH 6

(In 1935 and 1946 omit pages 70 to 73 inclusive)

Read Matthew 6: 26-34

VERSE 33 — *Seek ye first the kingdom of God and His righteousness.*

BLESSED HEAVENLY FATHER, what numberless times Thou hast shown that Thou carest for us. What numberless times Thou hast shown that our whole world lieth in the hollow of Thy hand and is governed and preserved by Thee. Yet, in every new distress we are ready to despair, as though we had no God, as though Thou wert not our heavenly Protector and Preserver. We know wherein our weakness lieth. We fear for the safety of the body. The spirit is willing but the flesh is weak. We shrink from earthly pain and want. We grow anxious for bodily comfort and safety. Sometimes it is our envy on account of the seeming better fortune and greater wealth of others which maketh us concerned about the things of this life. Send Thy Spirit into our hearts, to make us prize the heavenly treasures higher. Bestow upon us the wisdom which seeketh first Thy kingdom and Thy righteousness, and the faith which trusteth that all other needful things will be added unto us. Dost Thou not show us in the fowls of the air, which sow not, nor reap, nor gather into barns, that Thou canst and dost provide food and drink for Thy creatures? Dost Thou not show us in the lilies of the field, which toil not, nor spin, that Thou canst and dost clothe Thy creatures? Hast Thou not sacrificed even Thine only-begotten Son, that our souls might have food, that our souls might be clothed with righteousness? Oh, we of little faith! Be merciful to us, pardon the slowness of our hearts, fill us with trust, for His name's sake. *Amen.*

MARCH 7

Read Mark 1: 35-45

VERSE 40 — *"If Thou wilt, Thou canst make me clean."*

HOLY GOD, how wretched and leprous we are in Thy sight. How Thou, in Thy perfect purity, must loathe our souls' diseases. What death must await our souls if no physician is found, if no healing is brought to us. Wretched creatures that we are — who will deliver us from the body of this death? We know what hath plunged us into our dire misery. It is our sin, our departure from Thy communion, our transgression of Thy holy laws. We have done those things which we ought not to have done, and we have left undone those things which we ought to have done. We have thought to find happiness and gain apart from Thee, only to discover that, unless we are with Thee, we can not be satisfied. We come to Thee, O God, humbled, cast down, penitent, throwing ourselves at Thy feet. If Thou wilt, Thou canst make us clean; and, if Thou dost make us clean, Thou canst take us into Thy joy and rest. Wilt Thou? Canst Thou pardon sinners who have transgressed as we have? Ah, why did Thy beloved Son come into our flesh, if not to raise us up from earth to heaven, from death to life? Thou wilt, Thou wilt; for Thou hast sworn in Thy holy Word that Thou hast no pleasure in our death. Forgive us through His blood. Cleanse us of this deadly leprosy. Purify us, make us spotlessly clean. And in our cleansing let us not forget our Healer, but let us proclaim His name and power to many who may yet be languishing in the grip of evil. We ask it for Thy love's sake. *Amen.*

MARCH 8

Read Psalm 11: 1-7

VERSE 1 — *"In the Lord put I my trust."*

GOD OF LOVE AND GRACE, we come to Thee distrustful of our own hearts. Truly, our hearts are deceitful and desperately wicked. Thou alone canst search them out. Thou alone canst try them. Thou alone canst establish them. We appear before Thee, bewailing our own uncertainty and infirmity. We know, dear Lord, that we need a Rock that is higher than we. We know we must have some One in whom to put our trust. But so many tempters come to us and so many deceivers speak fair words to us, that we are confused and scattered, and our minds forbid us to cast our anchor where it will hold. Thou dost not need us, O God; but we need Thee. We ask Thee to speak to these curious hearts of ours and teach them to be still. Why can we not compose ourselves in the arms of Thy loving mercy? Why can we not overcome the fears and foolish superstitions which afflict us? Lord, we are powerless. But Thou canst work within us. Thou, who didst make us living souls, canst move these souls of ours to content themselves, in heavenly love abiding. Be gracious to us. Show us the impotence of other helpers, the insecurity of other foundations. Impress us with a sense of the loveliness and safety of Thy hallowed mountain, the hill on which our Savior died. Turn our eyes to Golgotha, and, with the knowledge that He hath atoned for all our sins, bring a deep sense of security into our souls. We believe Thou wilt do this, for His sake. *Amen.*

MARCH 9

Read Psalm 18:1-12

VERSE 2 — *The Lord is my Rock, and my Fortress, and my Deliverer: my God, my Strength, in whom I will trust.*

MERCIFUL GOD, what destruction sin hath worked in our world and in our lives and in our hearts. As by one man sin entered into the world, and death by sin, so death hath passed upon us all, for we all sinned. What terrors death bringeth to our hearts. Its sorrows compass us about. Its shadows fall athwart our path, even when we are rejoicing in the brightest days of life. Always there is the fear that death may come; always the certainty that death will come. But, thanks be to Thee, Thou hast made a way of escape for us. Though death hath brought into our life's journey a deep dark valley, Thou dost remain our Rock, our Fortress, our Deliverer. Though Thou art angry with the wicked every day, Thou art a God of compassion, Thou art the Lord, the Lord God, merciful and gracious, long-suffering, and abundant in goodness and truth, keeping mercy for thousands, and forgiving iniquity and transgression and sin. Thou hast brought us to faith in our Savior, Christ. Thou hast implanted us firmly in Him. And now we are persuaded that neither death, nor life, nor angels, nor principalities, nor powers, nor things present, nor things to come, nor height, nor depth, nor any other creature, shall be able to separate us from Thy love, which is in Christ Jesus, our Lord. What a great Rock Thou art, what an impregnable Fortress! Oh, keep us safely shielded evermore from unbelief and error, even as Thou hast thus far held us safe, in Jesus, our Redeemer. *Amen.*

ASH WEDNESDAY

Read Isaiah 58: 5-11

VERSE 5 — *Is it such a fast that I have chosen — a day for a man to afflict his soul?*

SAVIOR, when in dust to Thee low we bend the adoring knee; when, repentant, to the skies scarce we lift our weeping eyes; oh, by all Thy pains and wo, suffered once for man below, bending from Thy throne on high, hear our solemn litany! We desire to commemorate with true hearts and sincere minds the days of Thy sufferings and death. We desire to bring Thee an acceptable sacrifice, a sweet savor, meet, right, and salutary. Truly, it is right that we should worship Thee, Lamb of God without blemish, who didst in Thine own body bear all the world's sins. What shall we render unto Thee? Shall we afflict our bodies with hunger and thirst, with self-inflicted pain, with self-planned hardship? What wouldst Thou be profited thereby? Wherein would our souls be blessed thereby? Thou hast other sacrifices which please Thee more truly. Thou askest that we spend ourselves in loosing bands of wickedness, which are destroying men's souls; Thou askest us to help undo heavy burdens which weigh down the oppressed; Thou askest us to lend our strength to the breaking of every unjust yoke which crusheth a fellow man. It is for us to deal our bread to the hungry, to bring the outcast poor beneath the shelter of a friendly roof, to clothe the naked. Serving Thee thus, our light shall break forth as the morning and our health shall spring forth speedily. Righteousness shall go before us, and Thy glory shall be our reward. Grant it, O Savior, for Thy sufferings' sake. *Amen.*

FIRST THURSDAY IN LENT

Read Matthew 23: 24-33

VERSE 25 — *Ye make clean the outside of the cup and of the platter.*

O THOU SINLESS CHRIST, how keen Thine eye is to discover all impurity and insincerity in the hearts of men. Thou knowest what is in us. Thou understandest our thoughts afar off. We can hide nothing from Thee. We can not deceive Thee with outward piety and religiousness. How Thou abhorrest all sham and hypocrisy! Knowing this, should we not hold all insincerity in abomination? Yet, so apt is our nature to practise pretense and deceit that we lead our own selves astray. We keep clean the outside of the cup and of the platter, and within we are unclean. Our fellow men are made to believe we are truly Thine, while Thou seest and knowest that with our hearts we are still attached to that which is sinful. How long, O Lord, how long? Canst Thou not awaken in us so true an abhorrence of hypocrisy that we will be free from its curse and shame? Make us sincere, above all else, in our trust in Thee and Thy redemption. Make us sincere in our confession of faith in Thee. Make us sincere in our service in Thy kingdom. Make us sincere in our love of our fellow men. Make us sincere in our lives, in all our words and deeds. Let all our promises be sacred to us. May we inwardly detest all forms of dishonesty. Make us true friends of those whom we profess to love. Give us grace to defy the opinion of the thoughtless world. Hear us, O Christ, because Thou art our Savior. *Amen.*

FIRST FRIDAY IN LENT

Read John 12: 20-30

VERSE 21 — *"We would see Jesus."*

LORD JESUS, who art called the Fairest of ten thousand, the Bright and Morning Star, the Rose of Sharon, and the Lily of the Valley: how wondrous fair Thou art. Although Thou wast despised and rejected of men, although Thou wast so uncomely that even Thy friends hid their faces from Thee, eternal glory and beauty are Thine. Oh, the beauty of Thy sinlessness, the glory of Thy redeeming power, the wonder of Thy suffering and death, the brightness of Thy resurrection, the transfiguration of Thine ascension! We would see Thee, Lord, every day. We desire to have the vision of Thy loveliness ever before us. Through the scalding tears of our griefs and sorrows, we would see Thee. Through the smoke and the dust of the battle, we would see Thee. Through the mists and the shadows of doubt, we would see Thee. Through the deep darkness of death, we would see Thee. Show Thyself to us, beautiful Savior, at every turn of the way. Bless us with seeing eyes, which will not lose sight of Thee, no matter what else may intervene, no matter what may befall. Let not the world's slander of Thee, let not the opinion of those who falsely call themselves Thy friends, distort for us the image of Thy loveliness. Shine Thou radiant as our God and Lord, as our Redeemer and Savior, on all our paths through life. And, when death cometh to seal our eyes, we will depart from this world, murmuring in sweet confidence as we go on our way, "We would see Jesus;" and, awaking yonder, shall see Thee face to face. *Amen.*

FIRST SATURDAY IN LENT

Read Romans 5: 3-11

VERSE 8 — *While we were yet sinners Christ died for us.*

LOVING SAVIOR, was ever love like Thine? How little we can comprehend its depths. In our own selfish experiences it is seldom one is found who will lay down his life even for a good man, although we know that greater love hath no man than this, that he lay down his life for his friends. But Thou didst come and Thou didst die for us, unasked and unsought, while we were yet sinners. Thus doth our God commend His love to us. Quicken our minds, lest we fail to accept the marvelous offering of Thy love. Remove the veil from our eyes, lest we fail to see how surpassingly precious Thy love is when compared with the rewards promised us by the flesh, the world, and the devil. We rebelled against Thee, but Thou didst love us rebels. We forsook Thy purity and steeped ourselves in the blackness of sin, but Thou didst love us, stained and polluted as we were. Savior, let the influence of Thy love grow strong in our hearts. Make us willing, because of Thy love, to bear whatever tribulation Thou mayest see fit to send us in this life. Let trials, bravely borne, work patience in our hearts; and let patience, gained through Thy love, deepen the blessedness of our Christian experience; and in our increasing experiences fix in us an abiding hope, a hope which can not be made ashamed. Thou didst die for us while we were yet sinners. Oh, withhold from us no good gift of Thy love, now that Thou hast won our hearts for Thyself. *Amen.*

FIRST SUNDAY IN LENT

Read Isaiah 53: 2-9

VERSE 4 — *He hath borne our griefs and carried our sorrows.*

JESUS, Thou wast stricken, smitten, and afflicted: it was the hand of Thy Father which rested heavy upon Thee when Thou didst endure the anguish and the shame of the cross. Thou hadst come to bear our griefs and carry our sorrows. The chastisement of our peace Thou hadst taken upon Thyself. With Thy stripes Thou didst purpose to heal us. Truly, we did need a Savior like Thee. No other could have borne the load Thou tookest upon Thyself; for our sins were grievous, and the wages of sin was eternal death. What love Thou hadst for us, what infinite love, surpassing the love of friend for friend — and, behold, we were Thine enemies when Thou didst show us this marvelous love. We look upon Thee in this holy lenten season, viewing Thy form robbed of all comeliness, like a root out of a dry ground. We listen as men despise and reject Thee, and heap upon Thee the curses of their rage. But as for us, our hearts yearn for Thee. We are weary of the burden of our sins, weary of the tortures of our consciences, longing for peace and rest; and we find relief and peace in Thee, O Lamb of God. Like sheep which have gone astray, we hear Thy voice, calling us to safety and plenty. We come, dear Lord, beseeching Thee to apply to us the full power of Thy redeeming grace. Make us Thine, wholly and solely. Through the influence of Thy constraining love make us patient, tender toward our fellow men, forgiving toward those who wrong us. Do this for Thy mercy's sake. *Amen.*

FIRST MONDAY IN LENT

First Peter 1: 13-25

VERSE 18 — *Ye were not redeemed with corruptible things, as silver and gold.*

O LAMB OF GOD, without blemish or spot, how precious was the price with which Thou didst redeem us. Not with gold or silver, which the children of this world prize above all else, were we purchased and won from our sins, from death, and freed from the devil's power; but with Thy holy precious blood, and with Thine innocent sufferings and death. Thus it is written in the holy Word, and this Word endureth forever. We, who are as grass, who live amid perishable things, who change from day to day, can not but be astonished at the unchangeableness of Thy holy Word. We praise Thy great name; and we worship Thine infinite wisdom in giving us this priceless gospel. Now, Lord, engrave on our hearts Thy will that we be holy; and let us not forget Thou hast purchased us in order that we may be Thine own, and live under Thee in Thy kingdom, and serve Thee in everlasting righteousness, innocence, and blessedness, even as Thou art risen from the dead, livest and reignest to all eternity. May we never forget what an infinite price Thou didst pay for our redemption. Direct our eyes toward the revelation which Thou wilt make of Thyself on that great day, in order that we may pass the time of our sojourning here in the fear of God and in the love of our fellow men. Make our hearts pure and fervent in this love. Let Thine infinite sacrifice move us to bring our very selves as holy offerings, to Thy glory and praise Accept this our supplication, for Thy mercy's sake. *Amen.*

FIRST TUESDAY IN LENT

Read First John 2: 1-11

VERSE 1 — *We have an Advocate with the Father, Jesus Christ, the Righteous.*

DEAREST LORD JESUS, Thou who art in Thyself so righteous that no man could convict Thee of a sin even in Thy direst temptations: what happiness is ours because Thy Word doth reveal to us Thou art our Advocate with the Father. Ah, how we had offended this loving Father with our sins. What grievous curse He was compelled to pronounce upon us because He is holy and can not overlook sin. Thou must come and propitiate His just and holy wrath. No one else could do this, for among men all are sinners, and even an angel from heaven could not have brought the precious sacrifice which Thou wast able to offer for us. So precious are Thy blood and death, Thou art the Propitiation for all the world's sins. Like a bright light Thou hast come into the gloom and distress of our lives, and hast banished the darkness. We thank Thee, O Lord, for this great mercy. We know our guilt hath been borne, fully, so that the Father's justice is satisfied. And, now that Thou hast procured for us His favor, and hast made us His children again, Thou desirest that we walk as Thou didst walk, in the way of Thy great commandment that we love one another with pure hearts fervently. Drive the darkness of lovelessness from our hearts. Fill us with true love to all men, even as Thou didst love them all. Remind us that we do not truly know Thee unless we heed Thy commands. Hear us, Lord, for Thy great love's sake. *Amen.*

SECOND WEDNESDAY IN LENT

Read Romans 8: 11-18

VERSE 17 — *If so be that we suffer with Him, that we may be also glorified together.*

DEAR LORD JESUS CHRIST, suffering hath a new meaning to us since Thou didst come into our flesh and didst bear our woes and sorrows. We read Thou didst despise the shame for the joy that was set before Thee, and that now Thou art set down at the right hand of the throne of God. We would indeed be wearied in our minds, and faint, if we did not consider how Thou didst endure contradiction of sinners. Beholding Thine exaltation in glory, we would rather suffer for Thee and with Thee than live after the flesh. Help us to be undismayed when sufferings come upon us. Bestow upon us the mind which seeth that the sufferings of this present time are not worthy to be compared with the glory which shall be revealed in us. Lead us by Thy Spirit, so that we may in all things give evidence that we are the children of God; that we have the true spirit of adoption, and not the spirit of bondage. Endue us with grace to help others bear their burdens. Bless our hearts with sympathy and understanding, so that we may assist others through the pain and the darkness. May it not seem strange to us that, while we are serving Thee, trials are yet sent to us. Should Thy mercy send us sorrow, toil, and wo, or should pain attend us on our path below, grant that we may never fail Thy hand to see; grant that we may ever cast our care on Thee. Shouldst Thou see us waver, with one look recall, nor for fear or favor suffer us to fall. We dare ask it, because Thou lovest us. *Amen.*

SECOND THURSDAY IN LENT

Read Hebrews 9: 6-15

VERSE 12 — *By His own blood He entered in once into the holy place, having obtained eternal redemption for us.*

O GOD, our Lord, to whom we can not come except we have a Mediator, for we have sinned against Thy majesty and have merited to be cast away from Thy communion forever: we approach Thee through the sacrifice and intercession of Thy Son, Jesus Christ of Nazareth. If Thou didst in olden times permit men to approach Thee through mediation of priests who themselves were laden with sin, how much more wilt thou allow us to draw near through the mediatorship of Him who by His own blood entered into the holiest place and, by reason of the perfect innocence which was His, obtained for us an eternal redemption. He is our Highpriest, delighting in taking upon Himself all our burden of guilt and despair, and fearless to the utmost in bearing the cross Thy justice laid upon his guiltless shoulders. Thou canst not cast us off when we come to Thee in His name. Thou canst not withhold any good thing from us. Thou must fully and freely grant us an eternal pardon, no matter what our sins may be. Though they be as scarlet, yet shall we be in Thy sight white as snow; though they be red like crimson, yet shall we be as wool before Thee. May His blood, which maketh us guiltless, likewise purge our consciences from dead works to render Thee living service. Give us power and willingness to love Thee with all our hearts, and to love our neighbors as ourselves. Enable us to put the spirit of Jesus into all we do and say and think. Hear us for His name's sake. *Amen.*

SECOND FRIDAY IN LENT

Read Romans 6: 3-12

VERSE 8 — *We believe that we also shall live with Him.*

JESUS, it doth not estrange us that Thou didst die in shame, disgraced and outcast, covered with mockery and scorn. It doth not affright us that Thou wast the Man of Sorrows and acquainted with grief. It doth not displease us that Thou hadst no form nor comeliness. All this Thou didst take upon Thyself in order to be our Savior and Redeemer from sin and eternal death. Though Thou wast the lowliest of men, yet Thou hast been so highly exalted, there is no other name than Thine given among men whereby we are saved, and in Thy name every knee shall bow, of things in heaven and things on earth and things under the earth, and every tongue shall confess Thou art Lord. In the wondrous life into which Thou didst enter we have entered with Thee. We are buried with Thee by Baptism into Thy death, and we have been raised up with Thee, so that now we live in Thee, with Thee, for Thee, like Thee. Death hath no more dominion over Thee, and sin hath no more dominion over those who live in Thee. Oh, watch over us with untiring eye, that we fail not of the new life into which Thy death hath planted us. Grant that, although we yet dwell in this sinful world and yet have sinful weaknesses within our hearts, sin may never again reign in our mortal bodies. Keep us in mind of our living connection with Thee and of Thy victory over sin and death, and in our communion with Thee let us find strength daily to put sin under our feet. Grant this through Thy grace. *Amen.*

SECOND SATURDAY IN LENT

Read Genesis 3: 14-21

VERSE 15 — *It shall bruise thy head, and thou shalt bruise His heel.*

MIGHTY GOD, sovereign Deliverer, and Thou, Jesus, Champion of our souls, we rejoice in the victory Thou hast given us over Satan, that arch-fiend, who at the first did lead our race into rebellion against Thee. What mercy was Thine, in that Thou didst promise Thy deliverance in the very hour in which Thou didst visit the curse upon them who had sinned against Thee. Lord Jesus, Thou art the Seed of the woman. Thy work of redemption was a warfare against Satan for the freedom of our souls. When Thou wast crucified, the power of the evil one did bruise Thy heel. But, oh, the ecstasy of the thought — when he did bruise Thy heel Thou didst crush his head. Thy death on Calvary was Thy victory over death and hell, over Satan and damnation. We sing the songs of Thy triumph. We laud Thy great and mighty name, and magnify the love which made Thee faithful unto death. But, dear Savior, we desire likewise to follow Thine example. Clothed with Thy strength, we wish to battle against Satan and his hosts. We have Thy promise that, if we resist the devil, he will flee from us. In prayer and watchfulness Thou canst make us able to overcome all his assaults. Do Thou make us as watchful against his wiles as against his power. May we look for his approach in whatever guise he may assume to take us unawares. Anoint us with Thy Spirit, root and ground us in Thy Word, with which we shall be able to quench all his fiery darts. We ask it for Thy mercy's sake. *Amen.*

SECOND SUNDAY IN LENT

Read Second Corinthians 5: 17-21

VERSE 19 — *God was in Christ, reconciling the world unto Himself.*

DEAR LORD, again we contemplate the mystery which is so deep and great, that Thine eternal Son was manifested in our human flesh. We know and believe the Man, Christ Jesus, was more than man. In Him God was. For the Word was made flesh and dwelt among us; and we beheld His glory, the glory as of the Only-begotten of the Father, full of grace and truth. Thou wast in Christ, reconciling the world unto Thyself. In Him there is redemption for every sin of every soul in past and present and future of our human family. Forbid that His redemption of us should prove in vain. Thou didst make Him to be sin for us; make us now to be righteousness in Him. For His sake impute to us that perfect righteousness which we must possess to stand before Thy judgment. Declare us free from the punishment of all our sins because our sin hath already been punished in Him. In Him impart to us also that righteousness which showeth we have been made new creatures, all the old nature passing away, our thoughts and feelings and wills being made new. Give us deep joy in the ministry of His saving gospel, so deep a joy that we will heed His command and help to have it proclaimed to all nations. Let the newness of our lives be shown in the kindnesses which we are ready to do, without wage or reward, to any of our fellow men who may be in need. We ask it in His name. *Amen.*

SECOND MONDAY IN LENT

Read Galatians 3: 6-14

VERSE 13 — *Christ hath redeemed us from the curse of the law.*

O GOD, righteous, holy, sinless, Thou just Judge, Thou Avenger of the wrong, do Thou hold sin before us in its ugliness and deadliness, lest we forget from what depths we have been drawn up by the redeeming blood of our Savior. In His awful sufferings and death we behold the terribleness of our sin, and the dreadfulness of the curse we had brought upon ourselves by our transgression of Thy holy law. He was made a curse for us because the curse rested upon us. How can we doubt the destroying power of sin when we see its curse all around us? It is by sin that sickness and pain and weakness and all the other afflictions of soul and body came into our world. And there would be no help for us if He had not come to be made a curse for us. None of our race could by any means redeem his brother, nor give to God a ransom for him; for the redemption of their soul was precious. But the Christ hath come, He who was true God from all eternity, who became true man, born of the Virgin Mary, the God-man, and He took upon Himself our curse. Now is fulfilled Thy comforting promise, "The just shall live by faith." Thou dost account faith unto us for righteousness; for by faith are we made one with Him, so that His merit is accounted ours. Nothing in our hands we bring, simply to His cross we cling. Blessed be Thy compassion and forgiving love. Accept our broken hearts and contrite spirits, and establish us in the faith in Him, unto a peaceful end. *Amen.*

SECOND TUESDAY IN LENT

Read Psalm 18: 13-24

VERSE 16 — *He sent from above, He took me, He drew me out of many waters.*

GOD IN HEAVEN, who dost see and know the wretchedness of us sinners here below, we rejoice this day in Thy tenderness and goodness. Passing all understanding, exceeding all expectation, is Thy delight in us. No merit or worthiness had we. No service had we rendered Thee. Yet Thou didst send from above, Thou didst take us, Thou didst draw us out of many waters. Lord Jesus, Thou Thyself didst need to go out into the dark waters in order to draw us forth from their destruction. Thou didst need to rob Thyself of all Thy bliss and glory in order that Thou mightst bring us forth into the large place of Thy kingdom of grace. When the fulness of the time had come, God sent forth Thee, His Son, made of a woman, made under the law, to redeem them that were under the law, that we might receive the adoption of sons. Surely, Thou hast borne our griefs and carried our sorrows. What gratefulness should be ours for This Thine infinite salvation. Constrain us by Thy love to walk worthy of our new calling in Thee. Hast Thou brought us forth into a large place — enlarge our hearts, our sympathies, our kindnesses. Let our love go out into all the world. Make us a blessing to our fellow men, in our homes and the circle of our near friends, but farther also, out in the great world. Make us bearers of Thee to the dying souls of others. Help us draw them out of many waters, help us bring them forth into large places, for Thy name's sake. *Amen.*

THIRD WEDNESDAY IN LENT

Read Colossians 1: 12-20

VERSE 14 — *We have redemption through His blood, even the forgiveness of sins.*

JESUS, REDEEMER, who didst assume our human nature in order that Thou mightst shed Thy precious blood for us, and we might have forgiveness of sin through Thee: we thank Thee that Thou hast made us meet to be partakers of the inheritance of the saints in light. We know how unworthy we are of Thy sacrifice. The longer we enjoy the liberty which Thy blood hath purchased for us, the clearer doth it become to us that our lot was indeed a desperate one. Thou didst draw us up out of a horrible pit. We had erred and strayed from the ways of our God like lost sheep, and in the wilderness of God-forsakenness we had sunk into abject misery. We lay in the power of darkness. The image of our God, which He had given to us at our creation, was distorted, disfigured, lost. The punishments of His righteous wrath lay upon us, crushing us into eternal damnation. But Thou hast made peace between Him and us by the blood of Thy cross. We have been snatched from the snares of the dark powers of hell, and have been translated into the kingdom in which Thou art sovereign Lord. Thou, who art the Image of the invisible God, the First-born of every creature, hast made it possible for us, by new creation in Thee, to bear once more the image of our Father in heaven. Bless us as we endeavor to contemplate the infinite pity which Thou didst show us in shedding Thy blood in our stead. Hinder all thoughts of worldly affairs from crowding Thee out of our hearts. Be Thou All-in-all to us. *Amen.*

THIRD THURSDAY IN LENT

Read Genesis 22: 1-12

VERSE 8 — *"God will provide Himself a lamb for a burnt offering."*

GRACIOUS FATHER, how wonderful are Thy ways and purposes. How strange they sometimes seem to us. How far past our understanding they sometimes lie. Father, often it seemeth to us as though Thou hadst changed Thy countenance, as though Thou didst deal with us in hatred and not in love. Yet, we know that perfect love is over all Thy ways with us, although far above our sight. As high as the heavens are above the earth, as far as the East is from the West, so high are Thy thoughts above our thoughts. How strangely Thou didst lead the saints of old; yet always for their own profit and our edification. How strangely Thou didst order the life of our dear Lord; yet in every step of His journey it was for our salvation. In Him Thou didst provide a Lamb, to be offered up for the sins of the world. In Him Thou didst, for us all, work deliverance from the vanity of sin and from our impotence to serve Thee in the beauty of holiness. In Him Thou didst find the Lamb without blemish, pure, spotless, undefiled. Worthy is He to receive power and riches and wisdom and strength and honor and glory and blessing, for He hath redeemed us unto Thee by His blood. Draw our hearts, by the working of Thy Holy Spirit, into a deep and unwavering trust in His sacrifice. May it justify us in Thy sight; and may we, following His example, be ever found willing to bring sacrifices of praise and obedience to Thee. Grant this for His sake. *Amen.*

THIRD FRIDAY IN LENT

Read John 12: 1-11

VERSE 3 — *Then took Mary a pound of ointment, very costly, and anointed the feet of Jesus.*

SAVIOR, Thou who wast called the Christ because Thou wast anointed with the Holy Spirit and with power: we, too, desire to anoint Thee with our love and devotion. We know Thou art pleased to have us come to Thee, although we are poor and weak and sinful. The sacrifices which please Thee are humble and contrite hearts, hearts which have learned to hate their sin and to love Thee, hearts which are willing to serve Thee and to sacrifice whatever they possess for Thine honor and glory. We know that, when we devote our love to Thee, a fragrance ariseth which is acceptable to Thee. We know, too, that, the more devotedly we serve Thee, the more openly we show our love for Thee, the greater displeasure will be awakened in the hearts of those who are Thine enemies and in the hearts of those who are only outwardly attached to Thee. Nevertheless, we will serve Thee. We draw near to Thee and to Thy cross in this solemn season, and our hearts glow with sympathy and love for Thee. Show us, dear Master, what we may do for Thee. Let no murmuring arise in our flesh against our spirits' devotion to Thee and Thy Church. Remind us that we may serve Thee in those who are the least of Thy brothers here on earth. Make this lenten season very fruitful in good works and offerings on our part. Purify us of unholy motives in what we do. We ask it for the sake of Thy shed blood. *Amen.*

THIRD SATURDAY IN LENT

Read John 12: 31-37

VERSE 32 — *I, if I be lifted up from the earth, will draw all men unto me.*

O CHRIST, who wast lifted up from the earth because Thou hadst taken upon Thyself the office of our High-priest, who hadst purposed to let Thine enemies lift Thee up from the earth upon the cross in order that Thou mightest draw us all upward to Thee: we know that by Thy sacrifice of Thyself Thou hast drawn us out of the depths of sin's curse and away from the lust of the flesh and the lust of the eyes and the pride of life. By Thy death Thou didst overcome the prince of this world, to whom we had become subject in our sins. Thou hast judged this world in its wickedness, and in its powerlessness to afford happiness to men's souls. From the darkness and the disgrace of the cross Thou didst come forth as the victorious Redeemer, the only Savior of souls. We come to Thee with our sin and guilt and lay our whole burden at Thy feet. Lord, without Thee we would long since have perished. Without Thee we would have no hope. It is Thy cross which lifteth us up from earth to heaven, from wretchedness to God. Give us grace to thank Thee as we should. Help us learn that true gratefulness will lead us to walk in Thy light. Save us from hardening our hearts. Frighten us by the example of those who, in spite of all Thy seeking love, have turned from Thee and against Thee. Preserve us from falling again into error and distrust after Thou hast raised us up into the light. Do this, although we have deserved nothing but punishment, for Thy mercy's sake. *Amen.*

THIRD SUNDAY IN LENT

Read John 13: 1-17

VERSE 1 — *Having loved His own which were in the world, He loved them unto the end.*

O MASTER, precious Savior, whom, yet unseen, we love — O Name of might and favor, all other names above: we worship Thee, we bless Thee, to Thee alone we sing. We praise Thee, and confess Thee our holy Lord and King. How can we do otherwise, viewing the wondrous love which Thou didst display when Thou hadst gone forth on Thy way of suffering and death? Thou hadst loved Thine own throughout the distressing days of their weakness and their slowness of heart to believe and trust Thee; and Thou didst love them even unto the end. Although Thou knewest the Father had given all things into Thy power, yet didst Thou humble Thyself in order to render unto Thine own the lowliest service, that they might learn of Thee the grace of true humility and self-sacrifice. Make clear to us, here in the somber shadows of this mournful season, the beauty and happiness of heeding Thy commands and following Thine example. We feel the power of sin still in our members; but the power of Thy gospel is mightier. Constrain us by Thy love to imitate Thee in all things. Break down within us the remnants of fleshly pride which remain. Let the delights of the world lose their attraction for us. Impress upon us that we, Thy servants, can not be above our Lord. Bring humility and harmony into Thy Church. May we in honor prefer one another. Purge out all thoughts of hatred and revenge. May no service for Thy sake be too lowly for us. We ask it for Thy dear name's sake. *Amen.*

THIRD MONDAY IN LENT

Read John 14: 1-11

VERSE 1 — *Let not your heart be troubled.*

LORD JESUS CHRIST, true Man and God, who borest anguish, scorn and rod, and diedst at last upon the cross to bring Thy Father's grace to us: we pray Thee through Thy bitter wo, let us poor sinners mercy know. Cometh the hour of failing breath, and we must wrestle, Lord, with death; then come, Lord Jesus, come with speed, and help us in our time of need; lead us from this dark vale beneath, and shorten then the pangs of death. Thou who hast bidden us not to let our hearts be troubled canst comfort us in our deepest distresses. It is Thou who hast prepared the many mansions in the heavenly world, and it is Thou through whom we can journey thither. Thou didst go the way of the cross because Thou didst purpose to be in truth the Way on which our feet, in spite of our iniquities and transgressions, might be led to the shining house of our Father on high, where Thou art, and where Thou desirest Thy servants should be. Though Thou didst die for us, the blackest death in human history, yet art Thou the Life, and through faith in Thee we may have eternal life and be raised up to glory at the last day. Though Thou wast accused and condemned, yet art Thou the Truth, and there was no guile found in Thee, no sin, no blemish. We feel Thy presence with us, O our Savior, and we know that, when the hour of our departure from this world cometh, Thou wilt make Thy presence felt to us. Thanks and eternal praises be to Thee and the Father, and the Spirit, who bringeth us Thy truth. *Amen.*

THIRD TUESDAY IN LENT

Read John 14: 15-24

VERSE 18 — *I will not leave you comfortless: I will come to you.*

JESUS, Name all names above; Jesus, best and dearest, Jesus, Fount of perfect love, holiest, tenderest, nearest; Jesus, Source of grace completest; Jesus, purest; Jesus, sweetest; Jesus, Well of power divine; make us, keep us, seal us, Thine. Jesus, crowned with thorns for us, scourged for our transgression, witnessing through agony yet a good confession; Jesus, clad in purple raiment, for our evils making payment: let not all Thy wo and pain, let not Calvary, be in vain. It was all because Thou didst not wish to leave us comfortless that Thou didst endure the dread suffering of the burden of our sins. Thou knewest, if Thou didst not go this way, Thou couldst never prepare our hearts to become dwelling-places of the Spirit, and Thou and Thy Father could never make an abode with us unless our sins were atoned. It was Thy good pleasure to lay down Thy life, for Thou hadst power to lay it down and power to take it up again. Thou art still the Lord and Giver of life, and, because Thou livest, we shall live also. Grant that we may not come short of the blessings of Thy sufferings and death. May we not be like the world, which can not receive Thee and Thy Spirit. Fill our penitent hearts with undying love for Thee, and in this love lead us on the way of Thy commandments. Come to us every day, Lord. We will not be ashamed of Thee. Thou art our Honor, our Glory, our Crown. Bless us always, in Thine unspeakable grace. *Amen.*

FOURTH WEDNESDAY IN LENT

Read John 16: 1-15

VERSE 7 — *It is expedient for you that I go away.*

LORD, Thou who art our Light and our Salvation, how often Thy thoughts are far too high for our weak understanding. If we had had Thy life and work to plan, we would have ordered it otherwise. If Thy followers, when Thou wast here, visible in the flesh, had had their will, Thou wouldst have been dissuaded from Thy divine work of redemption. They did not know what was expedient, nor do we now know what is wisest and best. Grant us ready minds to commit the keeping and the conduct of all our affairs into Thy hands. Thou wast in all things true and steadfast, even when the way led into the agony and terrible wo of the last hours of Thy deep humiliation. Thou didst see and know the way to its very end, and beyond the cross Thou didst behold the kingdom and the power and the glory. Guide us, dear Lord, by Thy Holy Spirit into a knowledge of the truth. May we not only be willing to trust Thee to choose our ways for us, but may we learn to see beyond the present sufferings and view the glory which awaiteth us, according to Thy promises. Though the time may come when we are for Thy sake persecuted, though men may think they are doing Thee a service if they take our lives, bestow upon us grace sufficient still to confide in Thee and in the wisdom of Thy providences. In our faith and life may we always glorify Thee before men, until at last we share with Thee the unending glory of eternity. We believe in Thee. Help us, for Thy great love's sake. *Amen.*

FOURTH THURSDAY IN LENT

Read John 17: 1-17

VERSE 3 — *This is life eternal, that they might know Thee, the only true God, and Jesus Christ, whom Thou hast sent.*

LORD JESUS, Thou Sun of Righteousness, shine through the gloom of this vale of tears, and bless us with Thy heavenly light; even as Thou didst seek to bring light and comfort into those desolate hours when Thy loved ones were filled with dread forebodings because Thou wast about to leave them and to be delivered into the hands of sinners. Our life is not true life unless we know Thy Father and Thee, and we can not know Thee or Thy Father except by Thy grace and the working of the Holy Spirit, whom Thou dost send. We know Thy love is so true and strong, Thou dost never lose one of those who cling to Thee in true penitence and abiding trust. In the face of the hatred of all the world Thou dost hold us secure. It is not Thy pleasure now to take us out of this wicked world. Thou wouldst have us sojourn here, to work Thy will and to strive to bless men's souls. To this end do Thou sanctify us through Thy truth, the truth of Thy Word. Make this holy season a time of quickening and refreshing throughout Thy Church upon earth. Lead those who profess to be Thy followers into closer unity, the unity of the faith; so that they may be bound together to spread that precious Word which, sown like seed, springeth up into everlasting life. May our contemplation of Thine amazing sacrifice spur us on to greater zeal in the work of missions. May every day of our lives be hallowed by the companionship which Thou affordest us. We ask it for the sake of Thy suffering and death. *Amen.*

FOURTH FRIDAY IN LENT

Read Matthew 26: 14-25

VERSE 24 — *The Son of Man goeth as it is written of Him.*

DEAR LORD CHRIST, Thou who didst come into our flesh not to judge and condemn, not to cast away and destroy, but to seek and to save, to heal and to bless, to redeem and to forgive: can it be there were hearts so base that they rejected Thee in Thy loveliness and tender ministry? Can it be that those who enjoyed Thy friendship thought more of earthly pelf than of Thy companionship? Can it be that human heart can grow so debased that it lifts up its treacherous self against Thee in dastard betrayal? Can it be that Thine own familiar friend, whom Thou didst trust, who did eat of Thy bread, did lift up his heel against Thee? Ah, thus it was written of Thee, and thus Thou didst go, walking the way of sorrow, uncomplaining, unresisting, for thus Thou knewest the way must lead which would end in our deliverance from the curse and the depths of sin. Accept our offering of grateful homage, dear Master, as we come to Thee with repentant hearts, knowing the sacrifices which please Thee are humble and contrite spirits. Lord, we know Thou hast rescued us from the power of sin and the danger of damnation. Yet we tremble, lest we might perhaps again fall from Thee. Oh, watch over our faith, that it may never fail. Create in us clean hearts, and renew right spirits within us, lest we, after we have tasted of Thy goodness, rise up against Thee to betray Thee. Search our hearts and steady them, as Thou alone canst, O Lord, our Strength and our Redeemer. *Amen.*

Read Matthew 26: 26-35

VERSE 31 — *I will smite the Shepherd, and the sheep of the flock shall be scattered abroad.*

SAVIOR, how can we ever be offended because of Thee? Art Thou not our good Shepherd, smitten for us, because Thou wast willing to leave Thy life for Thy sheep? Was ever love like Thine? What couldst Thou have done more for us sinners than what Thou didst in humble service and obedient suffering and unselfish sacrifice? What love Thou didst show Thy followers all through the weary days of Thy pilgrimage in this mortal flesh. How Thou didst love them even to the end, knowing that death lay in wait for Thee. What unbounded love Thou didst display on that last night, when Thou didst break the bread with Thy disciples, and didst institute for them and for us the mysterious sacrament of Thy body and Thy blood. What love Thou didst exercise when Thou didst, aware of all the danger, proceed to Gethsemane, where Thou wast willing to agonize under the dread burden of our hideous sin, and to be betrayed into the hands of ruffian Gentiles. Can we ever be ashamed of Thee, when Thy love was so great and so true, so complete and so enduring? Dear Savior, uphold Thou our footsteps, that we slip not. We feel the will within us, to be faithful to Thee, no matter what betide; yet we know our own weaknesses. Compass us with Thy saving strength, that we may have boldness in the day of temptation to confess Thee. Guard Thy whole Church, that Thy sheep be not again scattered because Thine enemies smite Thee. We ask it for Thy mercy's sake. *Amen.*

FOURTH SUNDAY IN LENT

Read Matthew 26: 36-46

VERSE 39 — *Not as I will, but as Thou wilt.*

JESUS, beloved Son of the Father, in whom He was ever well pleased: we follow Thee this day into the shadows of the garden, where in the stilly night Thou didst agonize, because the wretched burden of our sin's guilt weighed heavy on Thine innocent shoulders. We can not fully comprehend Thine agony; but this one thing we know, that Thy suffering was well nigh beyond endurance, that it did make Thee exceeding sorrowful unto death. So dreadful was the torture Thou didst undergo, that Thou didst implore frail men to watch with Thee, that Thou mightest gain courage from their presence and their prayers. Lord, it is too wonderful for us, Thine agony in the night of Thy betrayal. How couldst Thou, the glorious Lord of all, become a worm, trodden to earth? How couldst Thou, sinless and guiltless, become the guiltiest of all — how couldst Thou be made to be sin? We gaze upon Thee, lost in astonishment that such things could be — yet, O Christ, lost in love and praise that they were. Now, do Thou take our whole selves under the guidance of Thy saving blood. Break the stubborn wills within us, and bend them into compliance with Thy holy will. Save us from our own undoing. Drive the sleep of carelessness and worldliness and foolish anxiety from our hearts, and render us watchful, prayerful, sober, strong; and renew our faith in Thee from day to day, that Thine agony be not suffered in vain in our behalf. We pray this, relying upon Thy grace. *Amen.*

FOURTH MONDAY IN LENT

Read Matthew 26: 47-58

VERSE 50 — *Jesus said unto Him, "Friend, wherefore art thou come?"*

LORD JESUS CHRIST, glorious God from all eternity, existing with the Father and the Spirit before the foundation of the world; equal with them in power, in majesty, in wisdom; Ruler among the angels, commanding them in mighty legions to work Thy sovereign will: what mockery, that mortal men, armed with swords and staves, should take Thee into their power, should bind Thee, should lead Thee away to Thy doom! Was there none to deliver Thee? Was there none to stand by Thee? Ah, Thou hadst not come to be ministered unto, but to minister, and to give Thy life a ranson for many. Thou hadst not come to reign on earth and to overwhelm men with Thine omnipotent power, but Thou hadst come that the Scriptures might be fulfilled. Thou didst not ask Thy disciples to fight for Thee with carnal weapons. Thy kingdom was not to be of this world, founded upon bodily force. In eternity Thou hadst planned Thy kingdom, a realm of the spirit; wherein men would, under the persuasion of the Holy Spirit, render willing subjection to their God. It was of this kingdom Thy holy prophets had spoken; and Thou alone couldst come and found it. It is in this kingdom alone we find rest for our souls, the rest which we must have for our happiness. We thank Thee for Thy submission, Lord. Do Thou work in us the mind which can not betray Thee, but which will make us Thy constant friends; that we may abide with Thee here amid all wicked opposition, and be with Thee in eternity in Thy glory. *Amen.*

FOURTH TUESDAY IN LENT

Read Luke 22: 39-51

VERSE 44 — *Being in an agony, He prayed more earnestly.*

LORD JESUS CHRIST, our minds fail us as we look into the shadows of Gethsemane and see Thee, prone on the earth, Thy soul sorrowful unto death, Thy sweat as it were great drops of blood; and as we hear Thy voice pleading with the Father because the cup Thou wast made to drink was so exceedingly bitter. Thine agony is too deep for us. We can not comprehend what depths stirred in Thy soul as Thou didst pray more earnestly. Only, we know God could not spare Thee, because Thou hadst been made to be sin for us. We know perfect love was working out our redemption when Thou didst suffer and pray in the garden. Oh, how Thou didst love, healing even the wound which one of Thy captors had received. Dear Lord, we thank Thee for Gethsemane. When the tempter's power assaileth us, we go thither in our thoughts, and Thy conflict maketh us brave. When griefs grow so heavy that we feel we can not bear them longer, we seek refuge in prayer, and we think of Thy pleading in the garden. When sin promiseth us happiness and success in its service, we turn to Thy dark hours and learn anew that sin can only curse us. Savior, be not far from us when our times of suffering afflict us. Help us learn the lesson of ready submission to the will of the Father in heaven. Teach us to subdue all our desires to His wise purposes. Make us willing to endure suffering for others. Keep us ever sober and consecrated because of Thy marvelous love, for Thy mercy's sake. *Amen.*

FIFTH WEDNESDAY IN LENT

Read John 18: 1-9

VERSE 4 — *Jesus, therefore, knowing all things that should come upon Him, went forth.*

LORD CHRIST, of whom it was foretold that Thou wouldst go as a lamb to the slaughter, we stand in awe, beholding the calm with which Thou didst go forth to meet the terrifying experiences of Thy betrayal, Thy capture, Thine illegal trial, Thy condemnation, and Thy death. Thou knewest all things which were to come upon Thee. Thou hadst known them from eternity as the Son of God, Thou didst know them as the God-man, who hadst chosen to take upon Thyself all that the justice of God must visit upon the human race. Nevertheless, Thou didst not turn back, but didst pursue to its end the path of suffering, the like of which no man had ever known. We know Thou didst not fall into the hands of Thine enemies because Thou hadst lost Thy divine power. Hadst Thou chosen, Thou couldst have put them all to flight, even as Thou didst fell them to the ground by one word. But there were prophecies to fulfil, and there was a world to redeem, and there were souls to save. It was not possible that the bitter cup should pass from Thee unless Thou wert willing to forsake us in our dire need. We can not understand how Thou couldst love us so. Oh, help us to be more thankful for Thy great sacrifice. Move our hearts to truer repentance and turn us more firmly away from all evil desire. Increase our powers of perseverance. Cheer us when the way is hard and we must suffer because of our trust in Thee. We ask it for the sake of Thy perfect obedience and love. *Amen.*

FIFTH THURSDAY IN LENT

Read Matthew 26: 59-68

VERSE 63 — *Jesus held His peace.*

O THOU PATIENT SAVIOR, meek and unresisting even though Thou wast falsely accused, even though Thou wast tortured beyond human endurance: we would beseech Thee for a portion of Thy spirit, that we may be quiet before our God, that we may be patient under trials, that we may be self-controlled, even when we are innocently condemned. Truly, Thou wast without guilt or stain. Thy holiness is perfect. Not one evil word didst Thou ever utter, not one unholy deed didst Thou ever commit. Not even Thy bitterest enemies could justly accuse Thee of any sin. Never, even in a single thought, wast Thou impure or unrighteous. Well couldst Thou hold Thy peace before the false witnesses, before the unjust accusers, before the unrighteous judges. There was nothing for Thee to confess, and Thou hadst not in mind to resist. By Thy silence Thou didst atone for the many words of sin which have passed our lips. By Thy calm Thou didst atone for the fret and unrest which our anxieties bring forth in our lives. By Thy meek acceptance of the sentence of death Thou didst atone for all our guilty deeds. O Thou who couldst hold Thy peace in the presence of that awful hour, grant us the peace which passeth all understanding. Lay the quieting influence of Thine atonement upon these fearful hearts of ours. Keep us in perfect peace when the dread of death affrights us. We ask it of Thy love. *Amen.*

FIFTH FRIDAY IN LENT

Read Mark 14: 66-72

VERSE 72 — *Peter called to mind the word that Jesus said to him . . . and he wept.*

DEAR SAVIOR, how faithfully Thou dost always warn us when Thou seest we are in danger. What true friendship is Thine, in that Thou dost warn us even against our own selves. Help us to understand that it is always in love and care for us Thou dost speak Thy solemn words of warning. Guard us against the folly of thinking that when Thou dost bid us beware of certain things it is because Thou wouldst deprive us of life's enjoyments. Make us see ourselves as Thou seest us, weak, unstable, not dependable; and keep down within us the pride which doth resent Thy words of caution. Deepen the love which we profess to have for Thee. Purify it. Send us through the fires which will purge away the dross from our faith and bring us forth from the furnace like refined silver and gold. Preserve us from heedless and thoughtless endeavor in Thy cause. Forbid that we should choose our own ways of serving Thee. Remove the earthly mind from us, and fill us with heavenly-mindedness. Let the deepening shadows of this holy season make us feel our need of Thee and of Thy light upon our path. When we do err again, look upon us with gracious love and tenderness, which will melt our obdurate hearts and work in us true repentance. Happy we, that Thy pardoning love is so constant and so willing to forgive us, even when we have sinned most grievously. Keep us under its influence, dear Savior. We ask it for the sake of Thy shed blood. *Amen.*

FIFTH SATURDAY IN LENT

Read Luke 23: 1-12

Verse 1 — *The whole multitude of them arose and led Him unto Pilate.*

LORD JESUS CHRIST, innocent Lamb of God, who didst remain blameless even throughout the godless persecution of Thy trial before the high court of Thine own people: in thought we attend Thee on Thy way to the judgment hall of the Gentile governor. We desire to follow with Thee to the bitter end, for we know it is our sin which sent Thee to Thy doom. We listen as Thou dost proclaim to the scoffing governor that Thou art indeed a King, and we know Thou dost speak truth. O Master, how kingly Thou didst bear Thyself, though all the mockeries and temptations which Hell could invent were thrust upon Thee. Thy holy calm in the midst of Thy trial cometh to us as a solemn rebuke when we, beneath the lightest burden, before the attack of the slightest annoyance, lose our self-control and commit the sins of impatience. How couldst Thou be thus perfect? Nay, let us rather ask how Thou couldst have been otherwise. Thou art our God, the Sinless One, without fault or weakness. Not all the guile of Herod and of Pilate could swerve Thee from Thy course, when Thou hadst determined Thou wouldst bear our burden unto the death of the cross. Precious Savior, help us to endure when we are led into danger and temptations. Only Thy mighty grace can strengthen us so that we will win victories in the time of trial. We look to Thee with thankful hearts, because Thou didst not waver. We look to Thee, pleading that Thou wouldst help us stand. *Amen.*

FIFTH SUNDAY IN LENT

Read Matthew 27: 11-23

VERSE 22 — *"What shall I do, then, with Jesus, which is called Christ?"*

LORD, OUR SAVIOR, at Thy birth it was said of Thee Thou wast set for the fall and rising again of many in Israel, and for a Sign which should be spoken against, that the thoughts of many hearts should be revealed. When Thou didst behold how the rulers of Thine own nation set themselves in array against Thee, Thou didst warn them, calling Thyself the Stone which the builders rejected. Thou didst say unto them that whosoever would fall upon this Stone would be broken; but on whomsoever It would fall, It would grind him to powder. With all Thy yearning love Thou couldst not reclaim them. Thou wast the King of the Jews; but, when Thou camest unto Thine own, Thine own received Thee not. A vile murderer was preferred before Thee. Thy people were moved with less justice and compassion than the Gentile governor. Oh, do Thou safeguard our souls, lest we, too, reject Thee when we are asked, "What shall I do, then, with Jesus, which is called Christ?" Shield us against the wiles of these deceptive hearts of ours, which might lead us to prefer vile things and men of earth to Thee, the King of Heaven. Watch over our passions and appetites, lest we, blinded by their inordinate vehemence, crucify Thee afresh. Protect us against hidden insidious sin, and against lurking evil habits which have not yet been drowned out of our nature by daily contrition and repentance. Bind us to Thyself with a faith which can not be made to waver. *Amen.*

FIFTH MONDAY IN LENT

Read Matthew 27: 24-31

VERSE 29 — *When they had platted a crown of thorns, they put it upon His head.*

LORD JESUS, our King and our God: we see Thee wearing the crown of thorns, Thee, who from eternity hast been the Monarch of all, the omnipotent Ruler of all the heavens and all the worlds. It was sin which planted thorns in this earth, and it was sin which platted yon crown of thorns and planted it on Thine innocent brow. What depths of human depravity were in the hearts of those who thus dishonored Thee. Yet, O King of our hearts and lives, we can not wish Thou hadst not worn the thorns. Are they not the royal signs that Thou didst become our King by Thy seeking and saving love? Thou art delectable to our eyes, despite the thorns, despite the cast-off scarlet robe, despite the reed placed in Thy hands in jeering mockery as a scepter. Thou art fair to our hearts, despite the wales and the wounds, despite the dust and the blood, which befouled and tortured Thee. Oh, piteous sight, which greeteth us as we look toward the judgment hall of Pilate! Oh, sorrowful journey, out to Golgotha! Would, we might have been there, Lord, to serve Thee, to relieve Thy sufferings. Yet, can we not serve Thee now? Wilt Thou not be pleased if we bring Thee hearts of faith and lives of obedience? Take us and all we have, and command us, as our King. Possess our hearts for Thyself alone. Be Thou our only Hope, our highest Joy, our worshiped Leader, our unfailing Comforter, our unerring Guide, and our God forever and ever, world without end. *Amen.*

FIFTH TUESDAY IN LENT

Read Luke 23: 26-37

Verse 28 — *Jesus, turning unto them, said, "Daughters of Jerusalem, weep not for me."*

BLESSED LORD AND SAVIOR, how easily our hearts respond in pity as we consider the story of Thy terrible humiliation and disgrace, and Thine awful suffering and anguish as Thou wast led out to the Place of the Skull. Yet, what do all our tears avail, unless they be tears of penitence because of our sins rather than tears of compassion for Thee? Thou dost not need that any should mourn for Thee. It is we who need to be mourned over. Work in us day by day the repentance without which we can never be saved from our sins. Though Thou must lay a heavy cross upon us, as Thy cross was laid upon the shoulders of Simon of Cyrene, we welcome it, dear Lord, if it be needed to bring us to Thee and to keep us with Thee. Ah, how far we still are from that new life which Thou desirest to create in us. How far we still are from likeness to Thee. Thou wast willing to die among malefactors, that Thou mightest fulfil the Word of Thy God. Thou hadst grace of heart to pray for those who nailed Thee to the cross. Thou hadst courage to suffer and die when Thou couldst with ease have saved Thyself. Come to us, mighty Savior, and work Thy gracious will in our hearts. Influence us so that we may weep for ourselves, on account of our sin and unworthiness. Cure us of the feverish desire always to save ourselves from suffering. Let Thy Cross lift us up into closer likeness of Thee. Do this for Thy great love's sake. *Amen.*

SIXTH WEDNESDAY IN LENT

Read Matthew 27: 35-44

VERSES 35, 42 — *They crucified Him . . . "He saved others, Himself He can not save."*

JESUS OF NAZARETH, King of the Jews, who didst say that Thou, if Thou wert lifted up, wouldst draw all men unto Thee: Thou dost today draw our eyes and minds to Calvary, where Thou wast hanged upon the cruel cross. There they crucified Thee! Oh, terrible words — oh, fateful story! There they crucified Thee! There they nailed Thee, the Sinless One, upon the cross accursed! There Thou didst suffer, and there was none to save Thee. Thou hadst saved others, Thou didst purpose to save all men. Yet Thou couldst not be saved. They called to Thee to come down from the cross. Angels would have delighted to come to snatch Thee from that disgrace and shame. Thou and Thy Father had willed otherwise. God spared not His own Son, but delivered Him up for us all. It was because of this Thou didst bleed Thy life away. It was because of this Thou didst not come down and save Thyself. Yet Thou wast God, though Thou didst hang powerless there, though Thou wast numbered with the transgressors, though even Thy poor garments were taken from Thee and divided among Thine executioners. We preach Thee crucified, and we preach none other. Thy cross is our salvation: it is our badge of honor. Thou wast wounded for our transgressions, Thou wast bruised for our iniquities. The chastisement of our peace was upon Thee, and by Thy stripes we are healed. All hail to Thee, King of the Jews, Jesus of Nazareth, our King and our God, our Joy, and our Boast to endless ages! *Amen.*

SIXTH THURSDAY IN LENT

Read Luke 23: 39-43

VERSE 41 — *"We receive the due reward for our deeds, but this Man hath done nothing amiss."*

O CHRIST, Thou Lamb of God, that takest away the sins of the world, what amazing wonder is this, that Thou, suspended on yon terrible cross, abandoned by the prophets and priests of God's chosen people, outcast and forlorn, on the threshold of defeat by Hell and Satan, canst lift up Thy voice in comforting promise and assure a poor dying soul that it shall, within not many hours, be with Thee in the glories of Paradise? Can it be that those hands, outstretched in the pain and shame of crucifixion, held the keys of heaven in their grasp? Can it be that after all Satan had not overpowered Thee? Even so, O Christ; for the sins which oppressed Thee and crushed Thy heart into death were not Thine. Thou wast the one Man who had done nothing amiss. Had we hung upon that cross, had we been consigned to everlasting damnation, we would have received only the due reward for our deeds. Thou dost indeed hold in Thy hand the key which openeth the gates of heaven. Thou art the eternal Son of the living God, with power to open, and no man can shut; with power to shut, and no man can open. We draw near to Thee again, unashamed of Thy cross and death, knowing our hope of heaven hereafter is all in Thee, and loving Thee because Thou didst not despise the shame and the cross, because Thou knewest our liberty could not be bought except by Thy condemnation. Endless thanks and praise be to Thee for Thy marvelous goodness to us. *Amen.*

SIXTH FRIDAY IN LENT

Read John 19: 19-27

VERSE 25 — *Now, there stood by the cross of Jesus His mother.*

JESUS OF NAZARETH, King of the Jews, all hail be unto Thee from our inmost hearts, which Thou hast won unto Thyself by Thine unbounded love and tenderness. It was in mockery Thou wast crowned by Thy tormentors; yet no king hath ever worn so glorious a crown as was the badge of shame which was wound about Thy brow. It was in fiendish hatred the superscription was placed over Thy head on the cross; yet no truer epitaph hath ever been written than were the lines which proclaimed Thou wast Jesus, the Savior, and that Thou wast King. Thou wast despoiled of all Thy garments, and rude soldiers divided them as their rightful reward; yet Thou didst in Thy nakedness and exposure weave for us the impenetrable garment and armor of righteousness, arrayed with which we can stand in God's presence, and protected by which we can meet all the assaults of the wicked one. With no thought of Thyself or the easement of Thy pains, Thou didst give thought to Mary, who had given birth to Thee, and Thou didst provide for her, lest loneliness and poverty be her lot; and in that very hour Thou didst provide for us all, uniting us with Him who alone can ward off from us eternal loneliness and poverty. Jesus, King, we stand at the foot of Thy cross, subdued, astonished, repentant, pleading with Thee to give us in full measure all the blessings which Thou didst gain for us there. May we not fail of accepting Thy redemption. We ask it for Thy name's sake. *Amen.*

SIXTH SATURDAY IN LENT

Read Matthew 27: 45-49

VERSE 46 — *"My God, my God, why hast Thou forsaken me?"*

O OUR GOD, how couldst Thou forsake Thy Best-beloved, Thine Only-begotten, who was in Thy bosom from all eternity? How couldst Thou deny Him the love and the fellowship which had bound Thee unto Him through everlasting ages in the holy Trinity? How canst Thou bid our understandings comprehend what happened there on Calvary? God forsaken by God! What wonder the earth shook in terror! What wonder the sun lost its splendor! What wonder the graves were opened and the dead came forth! What wonder the veil in the temple was divided! God forsaken by God! It could not be! Yet it must be! For He who hung upon the cross, very God of very God, had taken us to Himself, with all our sins and guilt, and He who forsook Him must forsake Him, because He was made to be sin, and the God of holiness and righteousness can not withhold His punishment from sin. Blessed mystery, which bids us dare to hope! Blessed gospel, which holds out pardon and reconciliation to us! Blessed truth, that God died to save us from God's avenging justice! Dread tragedy, joyful message! Dark deed of Hell, bright gift of Heaven! Father, we come to Thee, hushed and subdued, lost in the wonder of it all, pleading only that we be of those who, repentant and believing, childlike and trusting, shall always be true in faith, in confession, and in life, to Him who was forsaken by Thee on Calvary. *Amen.*

PALM SUNDAY

Read Mark 11: 1-11

VERSE 9 — *Hosanna! Blessed is He that cometh in the name of the Lord!*

LORD CHRIST, Thou Son of David, yet at the same time David's Lord and God: hosannas and hallelujahs are sung unto Thee this day throughout the world. Wherever men have hopes and fears in this whole world the story of Thy triumphal entry into the city of Jerusalem is this day being retold; and wherever it is being retold human hearts are strewing palms in Thy way and spreading their garments in Thine honor, in token that they subject themselves to Thee as King and God. Our hearts beat high with joy. We see in Thee Him who hath come in fulfilment of the prophecies of the Old Testament, who was to be the almighty Son of God, yet meek and lowly, taking upon Himself the sins of us all. But with the joy in our hearts there is mingled sadness; for this day is the threshold of that holy week in which Thou didst show Thy faithfulness unto death, the awful death on the cross. We pause with Thee as Thou lamentest over Jerusalem, the city which would not consider the things which belonged to its peace. Lord, grant that we to-day may not seek to satisfy our hearts with hollow hosannas. Make this a day of earnest prayer and self-examination for us. Preserve us from the error of accepting Thee outwardly, while our hearts are untouched by Thee. We cast ourselves upon Thy mercy. Rule Thou unchallenged in our hearts. Bring every thought and emotion in us into humble subjection unto Thyself. We ask it of Thee in Thy great goodness. *Amen.*

MONDAY IN HOLY WEEK

Read John 19: 28-30

VERSE 30 — *He bowed His head and gave up the ghost.*

GRACIOUS LORD AND SAVIOR, we have entered into the week in which Thou didst go the way of sorrows to its dread end. In thought we go again to Calvary to see with eyes of faith all that was there performed, as purposed and planned by our Father in eternity, in order that we might have the forgiveness of all sins and be reconciled with Him. In thought we try to fathom Thy holy mind, O Jesus, to comprehend how Thou couldst, pure and stainless as Thou wast, accept the part of the vilest sinner and take upon Thyself the experiences and the doom of the foulest transgressor. What yearning for our souls must have possessed Thee, to enable Thee to go the bitter way to its black end. We hear Thee cry, "I thirst," and our hearts tell us it was for us Thou didst thirst, for our souls and their happiness. It was because Thou knewest Thou hadst redeemed us that Thou didst cry in triumph, "It is finished!" It was because Thou didst see the host of the ransomed entering into happiness and peace eternal that Thou couldst so peacefully bow Thy head on the racking cross and give up Thy spirit. Oh, what love, what pity, and what desire to save! Still dost Thou yearn over us and for us. Take us, O Savior, take us wholly unto Thyself. We will not withhold from Thee our hearts and souls and minds. Thou hast purchased us. Thou hast fully paid the price. We are Thine. Do with us as it pleaseth Thee. We trust Thee fully, for this life and for the life beyond. *Amen.*

TUESDAY IN HOLY WEEK

Read Luke 23: 44-49

VERSE 46 — *When Jesus had cried with a loud voice, He said, "Father, into Thy hands I commend my spirit."*

FATHER IN HEAVEN, we know Thou didst forsake Thy Son when He hung upon the cross. We know Thou couldst not do otherwise, for He had been made to be sin in our stead. Thou in Thy perfect holiness couldst not but condemn Him, burdened with all the world's sin. But we rejoice as we hear Him, when death cometh upon Him, commend His spirit into Thy hands and again call Thee Father. We know Thou didst accept His sacrifice, as also that Thou Thyself hadst prepared this, the only Sacrifice for sin which could be acceptable to Thee. We thank Thee for the impressive evidences of Calvary: for the deep darkness which shrouded the earth when the Sun of Righteousness was sinking into death; for the rending of the temple veil, and the proof that henceforth there should be no veil of partition between Thee and us. We can not, no matter how skeptical our hearts might by nature be, withhold the tribute given to Him who died on Golgotha by him who was His executioner, "Verily, this was the Son of God!" With all the people whom Thou didst terrify by the dread spectacle of Thy Son's death, we smite upon our breasts and go our way — but only to come back to the cross on which He died and lay down the burden of our sins, and with it all our pride and self-sufficiency, begging Him to apply to our salvation the precious blood of His guiltless death. Father, what a Savior Thou didst send us! Forbid that we should ever put His love to shame. *Amen.*

WEDNESDAY IN HOLY WEEK

Read Matthew 27: 50-56

Verse 52 — *The graves were opened, and many bodies of the saints which slept arose.*

JESUS, OUR SAVIOR, as we see Thee hanging dead on the cross, our minds go back to that early day on which God said of the forbidden fruit in Eden, "In the day that thou eatest thereof thou shalt surely die." Impress upon us once more the truth which we must know and often consider, that sin brought death into the world. Had we not sinned, there would have been no death for us. Hadst Thou not taken our sins upon Thyself, Thou wouldst not have died on Golgotha. What dread power death hath, to take away the life of the very Son of God! But O our Savior, by suffering death Thou hast robbed death of its power. Well may the earth quake when Thou passest into the dark realm of death; for Thou didst go down to meet death in order to rob it of its terrors and of its power to hold us captive forever. When Thou didst die, the graves of many were opened, and the bodies of those who slept in them went forth, restored to life again. Because Thou didst die, our own graves shall one day be opened, and we shall go forth into new life. So death hath become the gate-way of life by the wondrous working of Thy might and mercy. For this we thank Thee, even while we sorrow because Thou must die. Help us, dear Master, to face the thought of death without fear. Strengthen in us the faith which overcometh every terror of the enemy. Keep living within us the glad conviction that the death of all Thy saints is precious in Thy sight. Hear us in mercy. *Amen.*

MAUNDY THURSDAY

Read First Corinthians 11: 23-32

VERSE 28 — *Let a man examine himself, and so let him eat of that bread and drink of that cup.*

BLESSED JESUS, as Thou hadst loved Thy disciples, Thou didst love them to the end. As Thou didst love them, Thou didst love us. Our generations, yet unborn, were the objects of Thy tender solicitude when Thou wast here upon earth, visible in our flesh. Because Thou didst love us so, because Thou didst yearn to draw us so close to Thee that we might verily be one with Thee, Thou didst institute the holy Supper of Thy body and Thy blood. Thou desirest to have our eyes see and our tongues taste Thy goodness. Thou didst give us a sacrament by which we may show forth, vividly and impressively, to our own souls and to the world, Thy death, until the great day when Thou comest again, visible in the clouds of heaven. Thou dost purpose by this holy feast to feed our souls, giving Thy very Self unto us, for the strengthening of our faith in Thee, and of the bond of fellowship which uniteth us with each other in Thy Church. Preserve unto us the full benefits of Thy holy Supper. Remind us of the words in which we are adjured to examine ourselves, and thus to eat of the bread and to drink of the cup which are the communion of Thy body and Thy blood. Let us approach Thy table often; and, when we approach, may it be with hearts which yearn to find Thee, which hunger and thirst after the righteousness Thou alone canst impart. We ask this, relying solely upon Thy love and merits. *Amen.*

GOOD FRIDAY

Read John 19: 31-37

VERSE 34 — *One of the soldiers with a spear pierced His side, and forthwith came there out blood and water.*

LORD OF LIFE, Thou wast truly dead. It had been written concerning Thee, "I will smite the Shepherd;" and Thou wast so sorely smitten that Thine own word was fulfilled, "The Good Shepherd giveth His life for the sheep." This Thou couldst truly say, though Thou wast the eternal God. Help us to believe the mystery of Thy death, though we may not with our puny minds be able to understand or comprehend it. Our souls, amazed and stupefied, cry out, "How could God die? How could death have power over the Almighty?" Our groping minds can find no answer. Yet we know these things came to pass. Thy side was pierced with the spear, and there flowed forth water and blood. So truly wast Thou dead that no bone of Thee was broken to hasten the flight of Thy soul from its tortured body. Oh, mystery of all mysteries! Our Lord and God dead on the cross! The Giver of life, the Maker of all things, fallen a victim to the great enemy of all life! Only in Thy wisdom, O God, could such things come to pass. Only because there was no other way to bring about our rescue did such things come to pass. Can we ever, throughout the endless cycles of eternity, sufficiently thank and praise Thee for Thy wondrous salvation? Help us to thank Thee now, in this present life. Make us so devoted to Thee that life will mean to us only our opportunity to serve Thee. Make our contrition for sin sincere and lasting. Make our faith in Christ mighty and enduring. *Amen.*

SATURDAY IN HOLY WEEK

Read Matthew 27: 57-66

VERSES 59, 60 — *When Joseph had taken the body, he wrapped it in a clean linen cloth, and laid it in his own new tomb.*

GREAT GOD, Giver of Life, who hast visited death upon our race because of our transgressions, because we chose the way of death rather than the path of life: we thank Thee that in the person of our dear Redeemer Thou hast hallowed the abode of death. Lord Jesus, who wast dead for us upon the cross, Thou wast borne to the tomb, wrapped in fine linen, and laid to rest in the bosom of the earth. We are thinking to-day of Thy consoling words, "I am the Resurrection and the Life; he that believeth in me, though he were dead, yet shall he live; and whosoever liveth and believeth in me shall never die." We believe, dear Lord. Do Thou keep this Thy promise to us, and convert our death into that which is not death. In thought we follow Thy bruised body to the tomb to-day, and our hearts are silent and oppressed, because it was our sin which made it needful for Thee, the Prince of Life, to taste of death and to be entombed. We follow Thy body to Joseph's garden, we stand with the women, beholding, and sweet peace cometh into our souls; because we know we are buried with Thee by Baptism into death, that, like as Thou wast raised up from the dead by the glory of the Father, even so we shall walk in newness of life: the life of reconciliation with God, the life of regeneration and sanctification. Now, Lord, do Thou hallow the resting-places of our dead, and watch over our dust when we are gathered unto them, against the great day of Thy coming again. *Amen.*

EASTER SUNDAY

Read Matthew 28: 1-15

VERSE 6 — *He is risen, as He said.*

ALMIGHTY CHRIST, death could not hold Thee in its power. Thou wast willing to pay the price of our ransom from sin and sin's curse, though the price might be Thine own life; but when Thou hadst satisfied all the demands of justice it was not possible Thou shouldst be holden of death or Thy body should see corruption. This day we celebrate Thy rising from the tomb, Thy taking up of Thy life again. Truly as Thou wast dead, so truly didst Thou come back into life again. It needed not the coming of angels and the rolling-away of the stone. Thou didst come forth from death's dark chamber by no other power than Thine own. Yet we thank Thee for the angel, and for the rolling-away of the stone; for thus Thou didst show Thine own that Thy grave was empty and didst lead them step by step to believe Thou hadst truly triumphed over death. Even Thine enemies were compelled to acknowledge Thy bodily resurrection, for their keepers at Thy sepulcher were witnesses of the glorious truth. We ask Thee now to work in our hearts joy and peace, and in our consciences rest and confidence, because Thou hast proved Thyself to be indeed He who could deliver us from sin and death and from the power of the devil. Open our eyes to see the folly of those who deny Thy resurrection. Make this a glad day for all who are in doubt or other distress. Embolden us to be courageous witnesses of the power of Thy grace in our hearts. We ask it all for Thy glorious name's sake. *Amen.*

EASTER MONDAY

Read Mark 16: 1-14

VERSE 6 — *"Be not affrighted. Ye seek Jesus of Nazareth, which was crucified. He is risen."*

DEAR LORD, Thou didst through the mouth of Thy holy angels bid the trembling hearts of those who were astonished because of Thine empty grave not to be affrighted. Verily, there was ever enough of joyful news to drive all fear and fright from their hearts. They had mourned Thee as dead, and all their hopes which had centered in Thee were being put to shame. Then came the tidings of the empty tomb, then the vision of angels, then Thine own appearances. How could they longer fear when Thou hadst performed all these mighty miracles? How can we ever fear anything, knowing the story of Thy gospel is true, knowing it hath been the world's sufficient refuge for many centuries? Yet, how apt we are, with each new danger or distress which cometh into our lives, to grow alarmed. Do Thou grant that Thine Easter story may make us bolder and stronger. Let us grow stronger in our faith, and may our faith prove the victory which overcometh the world for us. Let us grow stronger in our love, and may our love to Thee impel us to serve Thee faithfully. Let us grow stronger in our powers of mind and soul, and may we place them all at Thy disposal. Let us grow stronger in our confession of Thee, and may our courage in witnessing for Thee impress and win our fellow men. Let us grow stronger in our hope, and may our hope lift us up over all the temptations and hard places, and point the way to eternal rest and joy. We ask it for Thy love's sake. *Amen.*

TUESDAY AFTER EASTER

Read John 20: 1-10

VERSE 6 — *Cometh Simon Peter . . . and went into the sepulcher, and seeth the linen clothes lie.*

O HOLY SPIRIT, Spirit of Truth, how slow we are to accept the messages which Thou art pleased to bring unto us. With many infallible proofs Thou dost make plain to us Thy revelations, and still we are slow of heart to accept what Thou revealest. Our natural man receiveth not the things which are Thine. Thou must enlighten us before we can accept what is heavenly truth. We know how reluctant the apostles of our Lord were to believe He had truly risen from the dead. Even when they had beheld the empty sepulcher, and the idle grave clothes, and the napkin, folded and laid in a separate place by itself, they believed only that His body was no longer in the tomb. It seemed too great for them, the truth that He had kept His promise and had taken up His own life in the body again. Do Thou have mercy upon us when we are inclined to doubt. Multiply the proofs of the truth of Thy holy Word to us. May nothing be too wonderful or too mysterious for us. Should anything be impossible for God? Did it not behoove Christ to suffer and die, but to rise from the dead again? Could any other be the Christ? Was not all that transpired in His life and at His death and thereafter spoken of by the prophets of old? Hath not His power in our hearts given infallible proof that He is indeed risen, that He liveth forevermore? Ground us firmly in our faith, and help us lead doubters to Him. Hear us, in His name. *Amen.*

WEDNESDAY AFTER EASTER

Read John 20: 11-18

VERSE 18 — *Mary Magdalene came and told the disciples that she had seen the Lord.*

JESUS, REDEEMER AND LORD, how good and kind Thou art, knowing the needs of every suffering heart, understanding with wise and loving sympathy every need of ours, and willing to consider all our circumstances. May we never think Thou art unmoved by our tears and insensible to our sufferings and griefs. We love the story of Thy tender kindness toward Mary Magdalene, to whom Thou didst first appear after Thy rising from the dead. What relief came to her mind, what happiness filled her heart, when Thou didst show Thyself to her as she stood by Thine empty sepulcher. With what eagerness she went forth, when Thou hadst vanished from her sight, to tell the others she had beheld Thee with her own eyes. Lord, we have not seen Thy bodily form; but we know Thee and Thy power, and we have felt the influences of Thy presence time and again. Our minds also Thou dost satisfy with sweet relief, our hearts also Thou dost fill with abounding joy. Let our feet be swift to carry the gospel of Thy love and Thy power to others who need Thy comfort. Banish all doubts from our minds. In days when Thy resurrection is denied or misinterpreted, help us to speak convincingly of its reality and its meaning. Flood the world throughout its length and breadth with the brightness of the Easter truth. Drive away the shadows of death and the fear of death by the story of Thy mastery over death and its curse. We pray this for Thy love's sake. *Amen.*

THURSDAY AFTER EASTER

Read Luke 24: 13-24

VERSE 15 — *While they communed together and reasoned, Jesus Himself drew near and went with them.*

DEAR HEAVENLY FATHER, lighten our eyes, lest we sleep the sleep of death. How often our vision is holden, so that we fail to recognize Thy greatness and Thy grace. How many eyes to-day are still closed to the precious truth that Jesus is risen, that He is risen indeed, and that He hath taken away the victory of the grave and the sting of death; and that He willeth to save all those who will but come to Him and put their trust in Him. We, too, who love Him and confide in Him — how often He walketh close by our side, and we know it not. Increase the light in our hearts and the brightness on our path. Cheer us on our way by granting us not only the reality of Jesus' presence but the realization of it and its power to help us on all our ways through life. Quicken the slowness of our spirituality. Instruct our foolish hearts. Convince us that our risen Lord is with us in our humblest occupations, breaking bread with us no matter how lowly our circumstances, taking pains with us no matter how dull our perceptions. Grant that the truth of His rising from the dead may be to us the key for all the Scriptures. If He is not risen, then is our faith vain, then are we yet in our sins; but, since He is risen, we shall live also, and we shall be where He is, in glory; and our bodies, subject to corruption though they be, shall partake of the unspeakable glory of the life in heaven. Bind us closer to Him, for His dear name's sake. *Amen.*

FRIDAY AFTER EASTER

Read Luke 24: 25-36

VERSE 29 — *"Abide with us, for it is toward evening, and the day is far spent."*

LORD CHRIST, how often it is evening in our lives. How often the shadows fall, and the darkness doth drape deep folds about us. How often the darkness hideth shapeless dangers and mysterious enemies. How often we are afraid, because the light hath vanished and the gloom hath enveloped us. Abide with us, fast falleth eventide; the darkness deepeneth; with us abide. When other helpers fail, be Thou near by, to comfort and to guide us, and to assure us that Thy death hath not plunged the world into hopelessness, but hath brought life and immortality to light. We do not ask Thee to appear in visible form, to cheer us with the sight of Thy bodily presence. It is enough if Thou wilt be with us in Thine invisible presence, attending us on our ways through both the gloom and the glare. It is enough if Thou wilt send us Thy Holy Spirit, to convince our hearts every day that Thou didst indeed rise from the dead and will one day appear in the clouds, so that our eyes may behold Thee. It is enough if Thou wilt expound Thy holy Word so unto us that we may feel our God is speaking to us, guiding us wherever He may call us to go, and making clear to us the purposes of our journeyings. We would constrain Thee, blessed Lord, to enter our homes with us, to sup with us, to tarry for a season, to be our daily guest. Give us ready minds, to believe, and then to see, what wisdom there is in all Thy ways and purposes. Hear us in Thy great mercy. *Amen.*

SATURDAY AFTER EASTER

Read John 20: 9-29

VERSE 19 — *Came Jesus, and stood in the midst, and said unto them, "Peace be unto you."*

O HOLY GHOST, who pourest sweet peace into the heart; who all our souls restorest: Thy comfort ne'er depart. The peace which Thou dost bring is the peace of our Lord and Savior, Jesus Christ. He Himself said of Thee, "He will take of mine and give it unto you." We know our peace resteth solely upon the merits of Him who died and rose again for us. He was delivered for our offenses, and raised again for our justification. The chastisement of our peace was upon Him, and with His stripes we are healed. We beseech Thee to come to us with the full power of His precious gospel, the story of His birth, His life, His suffering, His death, His resurrection from the dead. Through Him we shall have peace indeed. Bring Him into the midst of us, and let us consider His pierced hands and feet, and His riven side. Possessed of His peace, make us a blessing unto all with whom we come into contact day by day. Ah, how this world and its many hearts stand in need of peace. Make us bearers of true peace to the souls of our fellow men. Help us teach those of our own households and those far away that there can be no peace except by the answer of a good conscience, cleansed by Jesus' blood. Bring the peace of the Christ to so many thousands that its blessedness will be felt everywhere, in city and nation and world. Grant us, when the restless journey of this life is ended, abiding peace, eternal peace, in the world to come. We ask it all for Jesus' sake. *Amen.*

MARCH 31

Read Psalm 25: 1-11

VERSE 7 — *Remember not the sins of my youth, nor my transgressions.*

LORD, if Thou shouldst mark iniquities, O Lord, who shall stand? But there is forgiveness with Thee, that Thou mayest be feared. Our fear of Thee is not the fear which hath pain, for perfect love casteth out fear, and Thy love toward us is perfect. We stand before Thee in childlike fear, reverencing Thy holy name, yet drawing close to Thy merciful heart, as we ask Thee not to remember our sins against us. All Thy paths are mercy and truth unto such as keep Thy covenant and Thy testimonies. Hast Thou not made an inviolate covenant with us in the blood of our Redeemer? It is because of this covenant we cast ourselves upon Thy mercy. From childhood we have transgressed Thy commands. Thy ways have not been our ways. But even then Thou wast our God. Ever of old Thy loving-kindnesses have been. Lift our souls up from all hopelessness on account of sin. Show us Thy ways, teach us Thy paths, lead us in Thy truth. Be with our youth to-day, in these times when strong temptations are their daily experience. Claim them as Thy children, bought by the blood of Thy Son. Let Thy paths seem pleasant to them, pleasanter than the paths of the pleasures which the world affords. Fashion our homes into pious households, where Jesus is a constant guest. Bless all our daily intercourse with each other and with our fellow men. Save us from hidden sin. Send us daily power to keep thy covenant unbroken. We ask it, without merit of our own, for Thy name's sake. *Amen.*

APRIL 1

Read Exodus 14: 5-14

VERSE 14 — *The Lord shall fight for you, and ye shall hold your peace.*

ALMIGHTY GOD, no power can avail before Thee. The mighty ones of this earth, with all their engines of warfare, are but as the puniest creatures before the sweep of Thine almighty arm. As often as human power hath measured its strength with Thine, it hath been humbled into the dust. The mighty hosts of Satan's realms believe in Thy terrible power, and they tremble at Thy approach. We, Thy children, ask Thee to convince our doubting hearts that, with Thee defending us, we need never fear. How quick we are to lose heart. How little is required to make us cry out in alarm. Whatsoever things were written aforetime were written for our learning, that we through patience and comfort of the Scriptures might have hope; yet we fail to receive it. Impress upon us the comforting truth that Thou, who wast with Thy people in days of old, hast not changed, but art with us, Thy people, as truly as Thou wast with them. Let us hold our peace, while Thou fightest for us. Expel all fears from our hearts. Often have we stood in the presence of some great salvation which Thou hast worked. Correct us of our forgetfulness. When Thou dost try our faith, grant that we may stand unmoved. Above all else, do Thou fight for us and with us against the sins which beset us. Grant us full remission through our Lord Jesus Christ, and strengthen us in His grace, so that we may prove more than conquerors and in the end gain the everlasting victory. We ask this in His name. *Amen.*

APRIL 2

Read Luke 11: 5-13

VERSE 9 — *Ask and it shall be given you; seek, and ye shall find.*

GRACIOUS GOD, kind Father in heaven, Thou who art the Maker and Preserver and Ruler of all; Thou who dost possess all the gold and the silver; Thou whose are the cattle upon a thousand hills: have mercy upon us, Thy little children, who so often conduct themselves as though they were the offspring of a father stricken with poverty and impotent to save. We realize, O God, that our besetting weakness is weakness of faith in Thee. We are afraid to trust Thee fully. We are afraid to commit ourselves wholly into Thy keeping. It often seemeth to us as though, in spite of Thy many promises, and in spite of the fact that Thou dost always keep Thy promises, help must after all come to us through our own efforts. Thou hast indeed commanded us to labor and pray. Thou hast said that, if we refuse to work with our hands, we shall not have meat to eat. Yet Thou dost desire that we ever bear in mind that all our good things come from Thee, and that we can not have unless we ask. Pour into our hearts the spirit of true prayer. We know that, even though we ask and seek and knock at the door, Thou wilt not, Thou canst not, give us that which will harm us. Teach us to ask aright, so that we may not ask in vain. Regenerate our souls so completely into the likeness of our Savior, that we may pray as He prayed. Then wilt Thou give us above that we are able to ask or think, for Thou wilt grant us the Holy Spirit, and, with Him, all things needful. Let this our prayer be acceptable to Thee in Christ. *Amen.*

APRIL 3

Read Exodus 14: 15-22

VERSE 15 — *Speak unto the children of Israel, that they go forward.*

LORD, Thou unconquerable Leader of Thy hosts, Thou who dost marshal companies and legions of angels at Thy good pleasure: Thou hast by the blood of Jesus translated us from Satan's domain and service into the ranks of the soldiers of the Cross. It is Thy will that we carry forward the great cause of our Savior's kingdom. All we need to insure victory Thou hast given to us, and Thou hast promised to be with us in all we undertake in His name. Thy Son, whose every word is truth and whose every promise is sure, hath said that where but two or three of us are gathered together in His name He will be with them. He hath said He will be with us always, even unto the end of the world. Never, when we have gone forward in His name, have we lacked anything needful. Cheer us, almighty Lord, as we go forward with the battle against sin. Be our Leader against the foes which assail us from within our own evil nature. War with us against the world with its seductive lusts. May our eyes ever look to Thee for Thy pleasure in the warfare committed to us. May we not fight with carnal weapons, but only with the sword of the Spirit. When we come to Red-Sea places in our journey, drive far from us dismay and perplexity. Lead us forward, ever forward. We are Thine, bought with the precious blood of Thy dear Son. We know Thou wilt not fail us. *Amen.*

APRIL 4

Read Exodus 15: 22-27

Verse 25 — *The Lord showed him a tree, by which, when he had cast it into the waters, the waters were made sweet.*

FATHER, the way Thou leadest us is a weary way, and we are frail and helpless, and our hearts are distressed, and the burden lieth heavy on our shoulders. Often Thou dost lead us where the waters are bitter and the wilderness is bleak. All the while our future is unknown to us, and the cloud which veileth it from our eyes may hide dangers and terrors, which we can not but fear. We can not go our way unless Thou wilt instruct us that Thou hast wise purposes in every step Thou bidst us take, and that Thou hast deliverance from every evil. Forgive us the slowness of heart with which we learn the lesson of Thy constant presence and love. Forgive us the blindness which maketh us unable to see Thy footprints on the wilderness way. Forgive us the unfaith which keepeth hidden from us the wells of sweet water and the palm trees which are just beyond, to refresh and cheer us at the end of the day. Father, there is no bitterness in our lives which Thou canst not sweeten. Even the bitter disappointments which we bring upon ourselves by our disobedience and wilfulness Thou art willing to overrule for our good. Thou, who hast taken the curse away from sin by the tree on which Thy Son was crucified, canst surely save us from every evil of body and soul, property and honor; and finally, when our last hour hath come, Thou wilt grant us a blessed end, and graciously take us from this vale of tears to Thyself in heaven — and this all through our Savior's blood. *Amen.*

APRIL 5

Read Exodus 16: 14-26

VERSE 15 — *This is the bread which the Lord hath given you to eat.*

DEAR LORD JESUS, when Thy disciples did ask Thee how Thou wouldst have them pray, Thou didst not forbid them to ask for the bread which doth nourish the body; but Thou didst bid them ask that it be given to them day by day, for each day only its portion, trusting to Thy goodness to have bread in store for them when the morrow might come, and believing that all through their lives Thou wouldst day by day have ample supply for their wants. Thy servant, David, saith, "I have been young, and now am old; yet have I not seen the righteous forsaken, nor his seed begging for bread." We know that we, in ourselves, are far from being righteous. We have not deserved even the crumbs which fall from Thy table. Yet Thou dost not measure Thy bounty toward us by our own deserts. Thou hast bread for us, day by day, unworthy as we are. It is Thy will always to bless us, but always to grant us only that which will truly bless us. Quicken our slow senses to see in whatever manna Thou dost provide for us that which is for our highest good. Help us learn the hard lesson that sometimes bodily hunger and poverty are the food which we need for our souls' welfare. Feed us evermore with the manna of life, that true manna of which Thou didst say, "Your fathers did eat manna in the wilderness, and are dead: this is the Bread which cometh down from heaven, that a man may eat thereof and not die: I am the living Bread which came down from heaven." We ask it, trusting in Thy love. *Amen.*

Easter Sunday – 1947

APRIL 6

Read Mark 3: 20-35

VERSE 35 — *Whosoever shall do the will of God, the same is my brother, and my sister, and mother.*

BLESSED LORD AND MASTER, who hast made us sons and daughters of the Father in heaven: we thank Thee that Thou by Thy love hast drawn us into Thy kinship. Thou didst become our very Brother in the flesh in order to reclaim us from the fatherhood of the devil and make us children of God's household, heirs with Thee of eternal life. So wonderful wast Thou that Thine own people could not comprehend the mystery of Thy person. So wonderful art Thou that at this day, when much learning hath filled the minds of men, Thou art still misunderstood. Lord, let not our reasoning powers move us to reject Thee. If we can not comprehend Thee, we can not but love Thee. Forbid that, having come to Thee, having tasted and seen Thy goodness, we should permit the old nature again to triumph in us and to make us sin against Thy Holy Spirit, who hath worked faith in Thee in our hearts. We can not love the world again, nor the wisdom of the world. We desire to have Thee to be our Brother, our Closest of Kin. We have heard Thee proclaim, "This is the will of Him that sent me, that every one which seeth the Son and believeth on Him may have everlasting life." Continue us in the faith in Thee. Make our faith so fervent and devout that we may feel Thy nearness, that we may be conscious of our close relationship to Thee; and that others, seeing our life in Thee, may know that we belong to Thee. Hear us in mercy. *Amen.*

APRIL 7

Read Deuteronomy 9:1-6

VERSE 3 — *The Lord, thy God, is He which goeth over before thee as a consuming Fire.*

LORD, OUR GOD, glorious in holiness, fearful in praises, doing wonders, who is like unto Thee? Thou art a consuming Fire to them who fight against Thee. Thou breakest the bow, and cuttest the spear in sunder; Thou burnest the chariot in the fire. Thou wilt be exalted among the heathen, Thou wilt be exalted in the earth. Thou didst go before Thy people of old, when Thou didst lead them into the land of Thy promise. Neither sea nor river, neither giant nor strong-hold, could resist the march of Thine armies, because Thou didst lead them. Many a Jordan lieth in our path as we go our ways at Thy bidding; and there are giants in the land, who endeavor to strike terror to our hearts, who tempt us to doubt Thy might. We know Thou wilt not fail us nor forsake us. Whenever we must go at Thy behest, Thou wilt go over before us, preparing the way for us, putting dismay into the hearts of our foes, and assuring to us the lands of promise. Keep us humble, Lord God, when Thy blessings come to us. Keep from our minds thoughts of pride and reliance on ourselves. May we always acknowledge Thee as our Helper. It is not our righteousness which moveth Thee to be our Strength. It is only Thy mercy. May we be mindful that pride goeth before destruction, and a haughty spirit before a fall. For all our conquests, praise and honor and thanks and service be unto Thee, now and evermore, through Jesus Christ, our Lord and Savior. *Amen.*

APRIL 8

Read Exodus 17: 8-13

VERSE 9 — *"I will stand on the top of the hill with the rod of God in my hand."*

ALMIGHTY GOD, great Deliverer, what shall we do in the presence of the numberless enemies who rise up against us? Knowing us to be Thine, they attack us all the more frequently, and with all the greater hatred. They fear neither us nor Thee, in their blind enmity against Thy holy name. Each new victory we win but seemeth to lead us into new danger. Each enemy we overcome but seemeth to raise up others in his stead. Where shall we flee in our distress? For this thing we have besought Thee thrice; but Thou hast said unto us, "My grace is sufficient for thee, for my strength is made perfect in weakness." Place Thy rod within our hands, as we stand on the hill-tops of life's struggles. Place into our hands the rod of Thy Word, which is quick and powerful, and sharper than any two-edged sword, piercing even to the dividing asunder of soul and spirit, and of the joints and marrow. Place into our hands the rod of faith; for our faith is the victory which overcometh the world. Place into our hands the rod of hope in Thee; for hope maketh not ashamed. Place into our hands the rod of Thy righteousness; for they that hate the righteous shall be desolate. Mighty God, build us up in strength against the foes of Thy Word and of the Cross of our Savior. Great is their pride; and we are so few and weak. But we know unto Thee belongeth the victory, and in Thy name we will set up our banners. Be with us, for Thy mercy's sake. *Amen.*

APRIL 9

Read Mark 9: 41-50

VERSE 50 — *Have salt in yourselves, and have peace one with another.*

LORD JESUS, we know Thou didst not come into our flesh in order to preach the law unto us. Thou didst come to bring the message of Thy gospel, the good news that there is salvation for our souls through Thy life, Thy suffering, Thy death, Thy resurrection from the dead. Thou didst come to be our Mediator, reconciling God with us and us with God. Thou didst come to atone for our sins, to bear the penalty which our sin had merited at the hands of an outraged God. Yet Thou art also our example, showing us the way in which we must go in order to prove that our faith in Thee is indeed worked by the Spirit of God. Do Thou make our religion a matter of our daily life. Make us the salt of the earth, but grant us grace first of all to have salt within ourselves, that seasoning force which purifieth and keepeth from corruption. Impress upon us the worth in Thine eyes of the little kindnesses which our fellow men so sorely need. Impress upon us the worth of every immortal soul in this great human family. Let us pass no one by; let us despise none of Thy children, whatever their earthly rank or station. Embolden us to lay stern hands upon the faults we find within ourselves, and upon the inclinations of the fleshly nature which still clingeth to us. Incline us to have peace with our fellow believers and all others, rather suffering unrighteousness than insisting upon our own rights. Thou, Lord, wast lowly. Draw us into the likeness of Thy beauteous image, for Thy love's sake. *Amen.*

APRIL 10

Read Psalm 33: 6-18

Verse 9 — *He spake, and it was done: He commanded, and it stood fast.*

MIGHTY MAKER of all things, what wisdom and skill, what might and power, we see displayed throughout Thy universe, the work of Thy hands, the creature of Thy mind. Day unto day uttereth speech, and night unto night showeth knowledge. Nature, which Thou didst not endow with our speech, hath myriads of voices, extolling Thy goodness and Thy providence. Thou didst but speak, and whatever Thou hadst willed was done. Thou didst but command, and whatever Thou hadst ordained stood fast. By Thy words were the heavens made, and all the host of them by the breath of Thy mouth. Still dost Thou care for Thy creation, for Thou lookest from heaven and beholdest all the sons of men. What dost Thou see in us, almighty Maker? Weak, erring mortals, unable to exist except by Thy will; weak, erring sinners, who have gone astray from Thee. There is no king saved by the multitude of a host: a mighty man is not delivered by much strength. We must all come to Thee, laden with our sins, to plead Thy mercy and Thy pardon. Speak, O God, that our salvation may be done. Command, O God, that our deliverance from eternal death may stand fast. Look from Thy heaven in infinite pity, and bless our souls with life. Have pity also on our nation. Let its rulers and citizens be subject to the King who died on the cross. Hear our supplication, for His dear name's sake. *Amen.*

APRIL 11

Read James 1: 2-12

VERSE 12 — *Blessed is the man that endureth temptation.*

O CHRIST, Thou who wast in all points tempted even as we are; Thou who didst bear the attack of Satan's most powerful allurements; Thou who didst endure the charge of Satan's most cunning wiles: we know temptations must come to us in this earthly life. The devil, like a roaring lion, goeth about, seeking whom he may devour. Every man is tempted when he is drawn away by his own lust, and enticed. As the world hated Thee, so it doth hate us, and doth attempt to seduce us into misbelief, despair, and other great shame and vice. Thou, too, who dost never tempt us to sin, dost come and test us unto the strengthening of our faith. Oh, favor us with the endurance which we need in order not to yield to evil when we are tempted. Render us so steadfast that we may count it all joy when we fall into divers temptations. Deliver us from the doubts which make us waver like a wave of the sea, driven with the wind, and tossed. In Thy good providence the trial of our faith worketh patience; and, if we but let patience have its perfect work, we will be perfect and entire, wanting nothing. Thou hast also promised Thou wilt not suffer us to be tempted above that we are able, but wilt with the temptation also make a way to escape, that we may be able to bear it. Fulfil this promise to us, whatever temptations may assail. Let nothing in our lives, our stations, our possessions, weaken us in the hour of trial; and unto Thee be glory for the victory. *Amen.*

APRIL 12

Read Mark 5: 35-43

VERSE 36 — *Be not afraid: only believe.*

GLORIOUS SAVIOR, mighty Christ, ever ready to help, able to save to the uttermost: how many thousands of suffering ones have come to Thee in their distresses, crying for consolation and liberation. Not one who sought Thee in faith and hope hast Thou denied. Him who cometh unto Thee Thou wilt in no wise cast out. All they who labor and are heavy laden are bidden come to Thee, and Thou hast promised to give them rest. No distress is too dire for Thee: thou wilt deliver us in six troubles — yea, in seven there shall no evil touch us. Thou hast power even over death, that dread enemy, of whom our timid human nature is strangely afraid. Thou knowest what fear there is in our hearts at the thought of death. Thou knowest what sorrow is ours when death taketh one of our loved ones. But in the presence of death Thou dost still cheer us with Thy greeting, "Be not afraid, only believe." Mighty Savior, Thou art Lord even over death. At Thy command life came forth at the Creation, for without Thee was not anything made that was made. At Thy command life cometh again to those whom death hath claimed. Convince these questioning minds of ours that Thou art of a truth the Almighty. Bring into our hearts a confidence which will enable us in death both to lay us down and sleep, knowing Thou dost still watch over us and wilt bestow the resurrection life upon us. Pity us in our fears, for Thy name's sake. *Amen.*

APRIL 13

Read Exodus 34: 1-7

VERSE 6 — *The Lord God, merciful and gracious, long-suffering, and abundant in goodness and truth.*

HOLY GOD, with Thee is perfection, and there is no variableness nor shadow of turning in Thy perfect righteousness and purity. At the beginning Thou didst implant Thine eternal law into the hearts of the man and the woman whom Thou didst fashion in Thine own image. When sin had come into their hearts, and in their offspring the remembrance of Thy holy will had grown dim, Thou didst send to Thy people those ten great words, which Thy Son hath summed up in the two commandments, "Thou shalt love the Lord, thy God, with all thy heart and with all thy soul and with all thy mind, and thy neighbor as thyself." Thou art not a God that hath pleasure in wickedness, neither shall evil dwell with Thee. We praise and extol Thee for Thy holiness and righteousness. Though we know we have not kept and can not keep any one of Thy commandments, yet we rejoice in Thee as a God who hateth sin and all manner of evil. But we rejoice in Thee with all the greater joy because Thou hast revealed Thyself to us as a God who is merciful and gracious, long-suffering, and abundant in goodness and truth, keeping mercy for thousands, forgiving iniquity and transgression and sin. It is upon Thy mercy we rely, mercy so great that Thou didst not spare Thine only Son, but didst send Him to destroy the works of the devil and win us back to the righteousness which availeth before Thee. Let Thy goodness still be abundant in our behalf, for His blessed name's sake. *Amen.*

APRIL 14

Read James 1: 16-25

VERSE 17 — *Every good gift, and every perfect gift, is from above.*

DEAR HEAVENLY FATHER, it is to Thee we look for every good thing. Thou art the Fountain of all blessings. Thy store-houses are never empty, Thy resources never exhausted. The trees of the Lord are full of sap, and they bear fruit every month. He that planted the ear, shall He not hear: He that formed the eye, shall He not see? Assure us, our Father, of the living truth of these words, and direct our hearts and minds upward to Thee in every want which we may feel. We do covet the best things, the good gifts and the perfect gifts. They can come only from above, from Thee, who art the Father of Lights. Preserve us from the error which doth imagine there may be other providers of good and perfect gifts. Work in us the childlike confidence that Thou art pleased to have us turn to Thee for our supplies. We did not choose Thee, but Thou hast chosen us. Of Thine own will Thou hast begotten us with the Word of truth. Now, Father, we look to Thee above all else for the gifts which will make us pleasing in Thy sight: that we may be swift to hear Thy Word when it is preached to us; that we may be slow to speak words of murmuring and doubt; that we may be doers of the Word, and not hearers only; that we may intelligently look into the perfect law of liberty and continue therein, and be blessed in our deeds. Hold us in Thy safe keeping as a kind of first-fruits of Thy creatures in Jesus, our Savior. *Amen.*

APRIL 15

Read Matthew 7: 12-20

VERSE 13 — *Enter ye in at the strait gate.*

LORD GOD, we know Thou art a jealous God, visiting the iniquity of the fathers upon the children unto the third and fourth generation of them that hate Thee. Thou desirest truth in the inward parts of our nature. Into the holy Jerusalem whither Thou wouldst lead us there shall in no wise enter anything that defileth, neither whatsoever worketh abomination, or maketh a lie; but they which are written in the Lamb's Book of Life. We yearn to be of Thy people, we yearn to enter that holy city. Wilt Thou not strengthen and keep us, so that we may enter in at the strait gate? Wilt Thou not vouchsafe to us the mind to crucify the flesh with the affections and lusts? The broad way inviteth us so constantly, and so many there are who travel upon it. The shout of their pleasures and the jeer of their contempt for us is loud. Hold Thou the Cross of our dear Lord steadfastly before our eyes, lest we go astray. May we look unto Him, the Author and Finisher of our faith; who, for the joy that was set before Him, endured the cross, despising the shame, and is set down at the right hand of Thy throne. Enfold us so completely in His love that we, too, may despise the world's sinful pleasures and may ignore the shame which is fastened upon us because we do not walk in the world's ways. Point us to the end of the narrow way, which leadeth unto life. Though there be few that find it, make us to be of those few. Do this for our Savior's sake. *Amen.*

APRIL 16

Read Isaiah 8:16-22

VERSE 20 — *To the law and to the testimony!*

GRACIOUS LORD, who hast not left Thyself unwitnessed, but hast given us the sure testimony of Thy holy Word, preserving it in all times against the wickedness of those who willed to destroy it: we thank Thee for its light and life. Thy Word is a lamp unto our feet and a light unto our path. In Thy divine revelation we have a more sure word of prophecy, whereunto we do well that we take heed, as unto a light that shineth in a dark place, until the day dawn, and the day-star arise in our hearts; for the prophecy came not in old time by the will of man; but holy men of God spake, as they were moved by the Holy Spirit. Alas, that we so little heed Thy holy Word! Alas, that other voices so often lure us into the charm of their destructive sounds! Why should we listen for the voice of the dead, why should we incline our ears to them who make pretense of having familiar spirits, why should man's vain imaginings cause us to follow, when we have Thy glorious revelation of Thyself, of Thy gracious purpose to save us, of Thy sacrifice of Thy Son for our salvation? O Holy Spirit, give us deeper reverence for the law and the testimony. Let it be our delight, our guiding star, our sure foundation. Make clear to us the vanity of all else. Let our boast be that Word which can not pass away, even though heaven and earth vanish. We ask it for Thy mercy's sake. *Amen.*

APRIL 17

Read Mark 5: 24-34

VERSE 28 — *"If I may touch but His clothes, I shall be whole."*

MERCIFUL CHRIST, potent Physician of our bodies and of our souls, willing to let Thy virtue stream forth to every poor sufferer: we draw near to Thee to-day to touch the hem of Thy garment and to be made sound of all our diseases. What a Helper Thou hast ever been to them who put their trust in Thee. How freely and how abundantly Thou hast fulfilled the desires of them who feared Thee, who believed that with Thee nothing is impossible. We do not know, dear Master, whether it is best for us to be relieved of this or of that bodily affliction. Often the chastening and the testing of pain and burden-bearing is better for us than would be relief from the trial. This we leave to Thy pleasure, saying, as Thou didst say in Gethsemane, "Not my will, but Thine, be done." But this we know, that, when Thou dost not free us from certain earthly ills, it is not because Thou dost not love us, nor yet because Thou hast no longer power over disease and sickness. It is only that Thou wouldst grant us greater good. So we come to Thee, nothing doubting, firmly believing, and we touch Thy seamless robe, knowing that virtue will come to us from Thy bounty. Maintain, we pray Thee, in our souls the deep, abiding trust we have in Thee and in Thy saving power; above all else, the faith we have in Thy blood, which can cleanse us from all sin and heal us of every infirmity of the soul. We know that finally Thou wilt deliver us from every evil of life, and wilt grant us eternal bliss. *Amen.*

APRIL 18

Read First Peter 1: 3-9

VERSE 6 — *Now for a season, if need be, ye are in heaviness.*

JESUS, OUR SAVIOR, who didst bear the heavy cross of the guilt of all the world; whom, having not seen, we love more than all besides: look upon us with understanding pity, as Thou seest us in heaviness of heart because of the tribulations of this present state. Keep us mindful of the fact that our heavinesses are but for a season, and that we need them for our perfecting. Let us not grow discouraged, for Thou hast begotten us unto a lively hope, and Thou dost hold before us an inheritance incorruptible. A little while only dost Thou ask us to bear the cross. Even while we bear it Thou wilt glorify it and make us strong enough to bear it without falling beneath its weight. Are we not kept by the power of God? Would He not send us all the hosts of heaven if they were needed to safeguard us against evil and loss? Thou wouldest have us know that the faith which the Holy Spirit hath kindled in our hearts is very precious to Thee. Thy will is to establish us in the faith, making it more precious than gold. O Thou unseen Christ, make Thyself plain to the vision of our faith. Show us Thy radiance as we toil in heaviness. Take us by the hand, and lead us through these dark days. Shine into our night with the brightness of that incorruptible crown which we are to receive by Thy mercy. Make our deepest sorrows the sources of our highest joys, for the sake of Thy redeeming grace. *Amen.*

APRIL 19

Read Leviticus 10: 1-11

VERSE 3 — *I will be sanctified in them that come nigh me.*

O HOLY GOD, whose majesty is so great that earth is but Thy footstool, the heaven of heavens being Thy throne: how can we mortal men venture to approach Thee? Thy holiness doth overwhelm us, so that, with Simon, we fain would cry out, "Depart from me, for I am a sinful man." We tremble at Thy presence, O God most holy. We hide our faces from Thee in confusion. Yet we hear Thy loving voice, calling us to Thee, bidding us come home to our Father, saying to us, "Return unto me, for I have redeemed Thee; I have blotted out, as a thick cloud, thy transgressions, and as a cloud thy sins." So earnestly dost Thou desire our return that Thou hast made a way for us in Thy Son, our Savior, Jesus Christ. In Him Thou dost call us all, whatever our sins may be, to Thee. But we beseech Thee, when we come, guard us against coming to Thee and Thine altars with strange fire. Thou desirest to be sanctified in them who come nigh Thee. Thy Son is the Way, and the Truth, and the Life; no man cometh unto Thee but by Him. By grace are we saved, through faith; and that not of ourselves; it is Thy gift — not of works — lest any man should boast. Purge from our hearts all thought of self-righteousness. Fashion our hearts like those of servants, whose eyes are ever toward their master, seeking to know only his pleasure. Let us experience the happiness of trusting Thee so completely that we renounce self and self-will throughout. Hear us, for our Savior's sake. *Amen.*

APRIL 20

Read Ezekiel 18: 19-27

VERSE 20 — *The soul that sinneth, it shall die.*

RIGHTEOUS GOD, for whom it is impossible to be unjust: we ask Thee this day to enlighten us so that we may always comprehend that Thou dost deal faithfully with all men. Our eyes are often holden, our sight is dim. The voice of the tempter doth whisper in our ears, "Yea, hath God said?" Thousands have forsaken Thee, and they murmur that, if they would have joy and pleasure, it must be by their own doing, because Thou hast unjustly denied them that for which they crave. Thousands have rebelled against Thee, because Thou didst seem to punish them when they had deserved rewards of good. Amid these temptations and seductions, do Thou give us clearness of mind to know the way of the Lord is always equal. Thou hast no respect of persons. With Thee there is no difference, for all have sinned and come short of Thy glory. When we accept Thy righteousness in Christ, Thou art ready to pardon; and Thou dost offer His righteousness to us all. Only the soul which persisteth in unbelief shall die. They who turn to Thy Son shall live. Thou hast no pleasure in the destruction of Thine own handiwork. Grant us also to see in the changing experiences of our lives the unchanging traces of Thy just and righteous will. Make our confidence firm and unshaken that Thou, the Judge of all the earth, always doest right. Preserving us in the true faith, do Thou save our souls from eternal death, through Him who suffered and died for us. *Amen.*

APRIL 21

Read Genesis 3: 1-13

VERSE 8 — *They heard the voice of the Lord God walking in the garden in the cool of the day.*

DEAR HEAVENLY FATHER, who didst create our human family, and who didst bless it with Thy choicest blessings: how blissful must have been the life our first parents led before sin came. How pleasant was the paradise into which Thou didst place them. How happy the days, as they passed, sinless and cloudless, without thorn or thistle to cumber the ground, without tears or toils. How intimate the communion which Thou didst have with them, every evening in the cool of the day. How happy we would deem ourselves, could that shining dawn of human history be brought back again. But Thou hast promised that it shall be so, even in spite of sin. If any man sin, we have an Advocate with the Father, Jesus Christ, the Righteous; and He is the Propitiation for our sins; and not for ours only, but for the sins of the whole world. In Him our fellowship with Thee hath been restored. In the faith worked in our hearts by Thy Holy Spirit we have been brought nearer to Thee again. Thou dost come into our lives, not only in the cool of the day, but at all times, and dost hold sweet communion with us. Thou art with us in the hour of prayer, when we enter into our closets and shut the doors and speak to Thee in the solitude of privacy. But Thou art with us just as truly when we are in the noise and press of the daily struggle for existence. May we not miss the sound of Thy voice when Thou speakest. May we never hide from Thee when Thou comest near. Grant this for Jesus' sake. *Amen.*

APRIL 22

Read Hosea 6:1-6

VERSE 1 — *"Come, and let us return unto the Lord."*

MERCIFUL HEAVENLY FATHER, whose patience is never exhausted, whose heart goeth forth to us sinners who, like sons leaving their father's house and squandering all their goods in riotous living, are perishing in a far country: incline Thine ear to us, and hear us as we bring Thee our praises for Thy constant mercy. With each new departure into sin, with each return to Thee in answer to Thy seeking, searching grace, we feel more unworthy of all the love Thou dost bestow upon us. We are not worthy of the least of all the mercies and of all the truth which Thou hast showed unto Thy servants. Even though we had done all those things which are commanded us, we could only say, "We are unprofitable servants: we have done that which was our duty to do." Should we stray from Thee again, do Thou in loving-kindness keep open the way for us to return. Let Thy voice reach us, wherever we may be. Send Thy Holy Spirit to lead us back to Thee, and grant that we may not strive against Him. And may Thy mercy so soften our hearts that we may offer Thee the service of kindness and pity toward our brothers. Thou desirest mercy, not sacrifice. Thou hast taught us to say, "Forgive us our trespasses, as we forgive those who trespass against us." Furnish our hearts with those good graces which will render us faithful keepers of our brothers. Let the pardoning love of Jesus constrain us to be very tender toward those who wrong us. We ask it for His sake. *Amen.*

APRIL 23

Read Mark 7: 31-37

VERSE 37 — *"He hath done all things well."*

LORD JESUS, who didst so willingly render obedience to the Father; who didst so perfectly trust Him in all things; who didst leave all to His will even when Thou wast well-nigh crushed beneath the burden of the world's sin: we see and know what wisdom was in the confidence Thou didst place in Thy Father. Grant us Thy Holy Spirit, in order that confident faith may be worked in our hearts. We know our God doeth all things well; but we do not yet have the joyful trust which would lead us so to act, so to suffer, that our conduct would give proof of our full surrender to Him. Anxious fears arise in our minds; discontented murmurings come into our thoughts; imaginings that we are forsaken afflict us; despair of our deliverance doth assail us. "What shall we eat, and what shall we drink, and wherewithal shall we be clothed?" So our hearts clamor. We fear poverty may come, or sickness, or death. We fear for ourselves, for our children, for our homes, for our country. How idle are all our anxieties, how vain our reliance upon self. Except the Lord build the house, they labor in vain that build it: except the Lord keep the city, the watchman waketh but in vain. It is vain for us to rise up early, to sit up late, to eat the bread of sorrows. Thou dost all things well. We will trust Thee. If Thou couldst work the redemption of our souls from eternal doom, surely Thou canst do all things well for us. Be with us in this our prayer. *Amen.*

APRIL 24

Read Second Peter 1:1-11

VERSE 3 — *His divine power hath given unto us all things that pertain unto life and Godliness.*

ALMIGHTY CHRIST, who didst seem to be the most infirm and helpless of men, but who wast in very truth the omnipotent God come into our weak flesh: Thy divine power hath worked marvelous things for us, whereof we are glad. All things which pertain to our eternal life Thou hast given to us. It is Thou who didst come to us, calling us to repentance, enlightening us by Thy Word, kindling faith in our hearts. It is Thou who didst lay before the justice of God the price without which we could not be ransomed. It is Thou who dost send the Comforter, the Holy Spirit, to preserve and strengthen faith within us. It is Thou who dost regenerate and renew us through and through, so that a new man daily cometh forth and ariseth, who shall live in righteousness and purity before God forever. Through Thee we have escaped the world's corruption. Through Thee an entrance hath been ministered unto us abundantly into the everlasting Kingdom. It is through Thee we are made partakers of the divine nature. Not one thing hast Thou omitted of all that was needed in order perfectly to accomplish our restoration to the Father's favor and glory. Happy we, that Thou, our own Brother, of the seed of David, born of the Virgin Mary, didst have divine power. We worship Thee, O Son of God and Son of Man. We thank Thee for the exceeding great and precious promises which we dare apply unto our own selves. Multiply grace and peace unto us, of Thine infinite abundance. *Amen.*

APRIL 25

Read John 6: 26-35

VERSE 27 — *Labor not for the meat which perisheth.*

O HOLY SPIRIT, Thou who art willing to dwell in our hearts if we by faith have received Jesus Christ into them; Thou who hast wisdom to enlighten human minds; Thou who hast life to infuse into human souls: do Thou instruct us in the art of valuing the unseen and eternal things at their true worth. We are of the earth, and we are earthy, and we are earthly minded. The body's senses and feelings usurp authority over the life of the spirit within us. We prize the meat and drink, the property and honor, the health and strength, the ease and comforts, of this present life above their true worth. So deceitful are our natures that we seek for worldly gain even from the kingdom of our Lord Jesus, although He hath so firmly proclaimed, "My kingdom is not of this world." When we are asked to choose between the perishable things and the imperishable, between the things which we see and the things which remain unseen, how apt we are to heed the promptings of the flesh and to prefer the bodily things. How we labor for these, and suffer, and sacrifice, and bleed. Ah yes, how many there are who barter away their virtue and their salvation for the meat which perisheth. We need Thine indwelling power, O spirit of Truth, to guide and control us aright. Leave us not, neither forsake us, for Thou art our only Hope. Our Savior hath promised us that He will give Thee unto us. We beseech this of Thee, trusting in His promises. *Amen.*

APRIL 26

Read Mark 9: 14-29

VERSE 23 — *All things are possible to him that believeth.*

BLESSED CHRIST, dost Thou speak unto us also when Thou sayest these strange words, "All things are possible to him that believeth"? Dost Thou, at whose feet all things were laid, place all things beneath our feet? Dost Thou, to whom all power is given in heaven and on earth, send Thy power to us, place Thy power into our keeping? So Thou dost speak in this Thy Word. Oh, that our faith were but as Thou wouldst have it be. We confess unto Thee that our hearts are still divided. Lord, pity us in our poor struggles to trust Thee as we should. So few things are possible to us now; and Thou wouldst have all things possible to us. Grant us increase in wisdom, in knowledge, in stature, in favor with God. Feed us daily with the bread of life, which can strengthen our souls. Exercise us in the arts of a faith which can not be denied. Purify our hearts of doubt. Turn our thoughts heavenward, away from our foes and our would-be friends which are of this world. Make us both bold enough and wise enough to overcome the assaults of Satan. Bend our wills toward Thee, making them conform to Thine. Fill us with a love of those things which Thou dost choose for us. Bless us with the experience that our faith is growing stronger and purer. Cleanse us of the dross which is yet mixed with our love of Thee. And thus, dear Lord, make more and more things possible to us through our faith in Thee. We ask it in submission to Thy will. *Amen.*

APRIL 27

Read Joel 2: 23-32

VERSE 26 — *Ye shall eat in plenty and be satisfied.*

GOD OF LOVE, bountiful and kind toward us, Thou wouldst have us be glad and rejoice in Thy goodness. Thy mercies are new every morning and fresh every evening. Thou satisfiest the longing soul and fillest the hungry soul with goodness. Why should we not be joyful in Thy continued and ever increasing bounty? Do Thou fill our souls with laughter, and turn our mourning into dancing. Sorrow may endure for a night, but joy cometh in the morning. Lift up our souls out of all our sadnesses. Make our countenances cheerful and bright with the oil of Thy gladness. Help us to show the children of this world that Thy service is only joy, that our homes have been made abiding-places of delight because we have Thee and Thy Son, Jesus Christ, with us. Truly, we do eat in plenty, and are satisfied. We thank Thee this day with deeply moved hearts for Thy best Gift, the Holy Spirit, proceeding from Thee, sent by the Son. Thou dost pour Him out upon us without measure. Through His indwelling Thou dost teach our sons and daughters to confess the name of our blessed Lord. In our old age He will yet be with us, granting us visions of the glory which shall one day be revealed in us. When the great and terrible day of Thy vengeance cometh, we shall be secure in the shadow of Thy presence. Forgive us our discontent when our earthly lot seemeth to vex the flesh. Silence the voice of our murmurings, and make our very lives a song to Thy praise, even as Thou dost love us in Jesus. *Amen.*

APRIL 28

Read First John 1: 1-10

Verse 3 — *Our fellowship is with the Father, and with His Son, Jesus Christ.*

LORD GOD, Thou didst, even before sin came into the world to bring unhappiness and death, say that it is not good for man to be alone. It is by the nature which Thou didst give us that we long for companionship. Most unhappy are we when we are separated from Thee. Yet, how often we turn away from Thee, forsake Thy house, neglect Thy Word, and thus fail to enjoy Thy fellowship. Why are we not more constant? Why do we not stay closer by Thee and by the cross of our Savior, Christ? We do not know, we can give no answer. Thou canst search our hearts. Thou dost know wherein our weaknesses consist. We plead our guilt, and ask Thee in Thy mercy to bestow upon us greater wisdom and steadfastness. How sweet the fellowship with Thee and with Thy Son! What hours of bliss, when we are close to Thee in living faith and abiding love! Thou art Light, and in Thee there is no darkness at all. The cleansing of our hearts and consciences cometh through Jesus' blood. Continue Thou Thy fellowship with us, although we often offend Thee; and do Thou enable us to exercise a nearer fellowship with Thee. In Thee may we likewise have brotherly fellowship with all Thy saints here upon earth. Thou art pleased when brothers dwell together in peace and unity. We need Thy Spirit, else will we not live in peace with one another. When our service of Thee here on earth doth end, grant us to have fellowship with Thee face to face forever, for Christ's sake. *Amen.*

APRIL 29

Read Matthew 7: 21-29

VERSE 21 — *Not every one that saith unto me, "Lord, Lord!" shall enter into the kingdom of heaven.*

LORD GOD, behold, we are of unclean lips, and we dwell in the midst of a people of unclean lips. With our lips we cry unto Thee, and meanwhile our hearts are far from Thee. With our lips we make bold confession, and meanwhile our souls are untouched by love for Thee. With our lips we proclaim Thy truth, and meanwhile in our lives Thy truth doth not guide us and lead our footsteps. We know we can not be of Thy kingdom unless our hearts are sincere. With the heart man believeth unto righteousness. Without faith it is impossible to please Thee. Deepen within us the life of the new spirit which Thou hast created there. Consecrate our inmost souls unto Thyself. Make the shallowness and thoughtlessness of merely outward confession an abomination in our sight. Cause us to abhor taking Thy name upon our lips only. Cry into our consciences that Thou wilt not hold him guiltless who taketh Thy name in vain. Only if we truly believe in Thee have we so builded that our house will stand. Let us not forget that storms and tempests and tides may dash against the houses in our hearts. Build us upon the rock, laying in our hearts deep foundations of conviction and trust. When the last great tempest of Thy judgment breaketh, and sun and moon and stars and earth all pass away, grant us the reward of those who have remained faithful unto the end. We ask it, holding fast our Savior's cross. *Amen.*

APRIL 30

Read Mark 10: 42-52

VERSE 44 — *Whosoever of you will be the chiefest shall be servant of all.*

JESUS, LOWLY MASTER, what a power doth pride have in these sinful natures of ours. Why should our spirits be proud, when we know we are mortal, when we must acknowledge that Thou alone art the Eternal and Changeless One? Why should we lift up our minds in pride, when we know our own wisdom is but folly in Thy sight? Why should we exalt ourselves above others of our fellow men, when we know Thou hast made of one blood all the nations of the earth? Doth our pride ever lead to happiness? Can we say unto our souls that pride doth guard them against evil and save them from death? Rather let us teach these haughty natures of ours that shame and confusion should be theirs, by reason of their unworthiness and sin. Thou hast given us an example of humility and lowliness, and Thou hast pleaded with us to follow Thine example. We need Thy Spirit, Lord, to follow Thee in service which seeketh not our own gain. Humble us, O Lord, humble us into the dust. Save us from the conceit of our own imaginations. If need be, send us distress and suffering, and loss and cross, to break our stubborn spirits. We can not have joy unless Thou banish our pride. Chasten us, although it cause us pain. Sweeten us by the bitterness of affliction, until we are transformed into Thy lowly image — only to learn that Thou hast thereby highly exalted us. *Amen.*

MAY 1

Read Psalm 23

VERSE 4 — *"Though I walk through the valley of the shadow of death, I will fear no evil."*

GRACIOUS SAVIOR, Jesus Christ, who dost never let us want; who dost make us lie down in green pastures, who dost lead us by the still waters; who dost restore our souls; who dost lead us in the paths of righteousness, as a shepherd leadeth his flock in safety and plenty: we sing Thy loving-kindness this day and evermore. Thou mightest have sought sheep in other pastures, but it was Thy good pleasure to seek and to save us. Never dost Thou weary in going after our souls. Again and again we have strayed, but Thou hast recalled us. Again and again we have erred into the power of the wolf, but Thou hast rescued us. Do not cease Thy watchful care over us, lest we be lost forever. We can not forget, dear Savior, how Thou didst lay down Thy life for us. Surely, Thou wilt freely give us all things. No good thing wilt Thou withhold from us. Do evil-minded men oppose? Thou preparest a table for us in the presence of our enemies. Do they bring shame and disgrace upon us? Thou anointest our heads with oil. Do they bring us into want? Thou makest our cup to run over. Are we made homeless and friendless? Surely, goodness and mercy shall follow us all the days of our lives, and we shall dwell in the house of the Lord. Doth death come to terrify us? Though we walk through the valley of its shadow, Thou art with us, Thy rod and Thy staff, they comfort us. Thanks be to Thee, Lord Jesus, for Thy redeeming, comforting love. *Amen.*

MAY 2

Read Numbers 13: 26-33

VERSE 30 — *"Let us go up at once and possess the land; for we are well able to overcome it."*

O GOD of might and sovereignty over all the powers of heaven and earth, when will we learn that we dishonor Thee as long as we are fearful and shrinking? Thou hast sent us into this world and Thou dost preserve our lives in order that we may honor Thee by our reliance upon Thy providence. So faithful and true Thou art that Thou hast left us no excuse for littleness of faith. How can we behold Thy love and Thy power in Him who became flesh for us, bearing the terrible burden of all the world's sin and guilt, and then still continue in our doubts and fears? Great mighty God, stir our hearts by the power of Jesus' cross to that strength and courage which alone befit the hearts of Thy people. Help us put Thine enemies and ours to shame by our confidence in Thee and Thy presence and Thy help. We will not make light of the tasks which lie before us. Every day bringeth us burdens and battles which, we know, will test us to the utmost. But every day likewise bringeth us prospects of victories which shall be ours if we but go up at Thy command and possess what Thou hast destined for us. Our eyes have often seen what power the Savior of men's souls can bring into men's hearts. The story of the conquests made by the Church of Christ is one of constant guidance by His hand. Be with us, that we faint not. Grant that we may press forward with renewed zeal. Give us abiding joy in Thy service, and save us from all unholy fear. We ask this in Jesus' name. *Amen.*

MAY 3

Read Numbers 14: 1-10

VERSE 9 — *"Only rebel not ye against the Lord, neither fear ye the people."*

LORD GOD, we can not wonder that these hearts of ours are slow to learn the lesson that Thou delightest in us; for our hearts are deceitful and desperately wicked. Our old nature is still inclined to love sin and to believe that in sin's service there are surer rewards than in Thy service. When we have been awakened to the wretchedness of sin, somehow, we fear Thy holy presence, and our hearts are slow to believe that Thou and we can have friendship with one another. Even after Thou hast won us to Thyself, rebellion ariseth in our old nature, and we go astray from Thee and Thy paths. Hold Thou before our eyes the blessed truths of the gospel of Jesus, and convince us that Thou delightest in us because we are washed by His blood. Surely, Thou couldst not have sent Him into our flesh, Thou couldst not have sacrificed Him on the cross, if it were not Thy sincere will to make us truly Thine. Impress this saving truth upon our hearts especially when we are in temptation, and when we are required to go the way of the cross in our following of the Savior. Make us understand that, even when it doth seem that Thou hast called us away from pleasure and ease and dost lead us into danger and hardships, Thou dost still delight in us, and wilt lead us through to a perfect understanding of Thy loving purposes. Oh, preserve us from rebellion against Thee, even as our dear Lord bore the cross without murmuring or disobedience. We ask it in His name. *Amen.*

MAY 4

Read Romans 11: 33-36

VERSE 33 — *How unsearchable are His judgments, and His ways past finding out.*

ALL-WISE GOD, Thou who needest not that any man should counsel Thee, Thou who seest and knowest all things, who art a Searcher of the inmost thoughts of our secret minds: we come before Thy throne to bless and worship Thee in Thy great and infinite being. It is not in our power to search out Thy judgments. Thy ways are past our finding out. Thy knowledge is too deep for us. Oh, let this truth work humility and submissiveness in us. Many there are whose proud minds are determined to comprehend and understand Thee by their own power, and whose purpose is, if Thou dost not come within the reach of their thoughts, not to acknowledge Thee as God and Lord. Keep us from such folly. May we not incline our ears to their teachings and may we be untouched by their unbelief. Give us the wisdom to confess that our God must be He who is above the range of human understanding. Make us satisfied with that which Thou hast revealed of Thyself. Thou hast made known to us all we need for our lives here in this world and for our lives in eternity. Thou hast brought Thyself very near to us in the humiliation of Thy dear Son. Even though the greatness of Thy love and mercy be unsearchable, we know and have its saving power, and we are content. Keep us with Thee, Lord God, and make us more and more Thine own in humble and childlike faith in Christ, in whose name we bring this our prayer before Thee. *Amen.*

MAY 5

Read Zephaniah 1: 14-18

VERSE 18 — *Neither their silver nor their gold shall be able to deliver them.*

HEAVENLY FATHER, wilt Thou try once more to teach us the lesson that earthly riches avail little in Thy sight, and that what we need most of all for happiness in our lives can not be bought with silver and gold? We know these precious metals are good gifts; and when we possess them we would sanctify them to the uses of Thy kingdom. They are Thy gifts, and Thou art pleased when we use them for Thine honor and our neighbors' welfare. But Thou wouldst have us always remember we must not make them our gods, and that there are other treasures far superior to them, which Thou wouldst give us abundantly. Save us from the lot of those who put their trust in money and who, because they have money, care not for Thee, or even openly scoff and defy Thee. Let us think often of our Lord Christ, who became poor for our sake, who had not where to lay His head, and who, when He died on the cross, left no earthly goods to those who were His own. Whatever good earthly treasures may accomplish, give us eyes to see that when the great day of Thy judgment cometh they will all pass away, and we can not stand before Thy throne except through the merits of Him who bought us not with gold or silver but with His own blood. It is His righteousness which we plead when we think of the great day of Thy revealed wrath. May we use our earthly means for the upbuilding of His kingdom, and, even if Thou dost richly endow us with worldly goods, remain ever His humble followers. *Amen.*

MAY 6

Read Numbers 14: 10-19

VERSE 19 — *"Pardon, I beseech Thee, the iniquity of this people."*

GRACIOUS FATHER in heaven, we know Thou art willing to pardon all the iniquities of which we are guilty. Our lives are filled with transgressions and wickedness, yet Thou dost in mercy for the sake of the merits of Jesus Christ look upon us as though we had not sinned. Thou dost, as the great Judge of all mankind, pronounce us free from guilt and punishment, because our Savior's atoning sacrifice availeth in Thy sight. We can never sufficiently thank Thee for Thy mercy. Not one sin could we ourselves remove from the record written against us. To all eternity we must be separated from Thee and the blessedness of fellowship with Thee if Thou hadst not had mercy upon us. We pray Thee, have mercy on other souls, which until now have resisted the Holy Spirit's invitation. Our hearts are filled with sadness at the thought that there are many who do not accept Thy grace. Make us willing to bear any burden and to offer any sacrifice which may be needed to take Thy saving gospel to the souls of others. Make us soul-winners, Lord, our God. Stir up in us zeal for the conversion of our fellow men, whether they be far off in lands called heathen, or whether they be near at hand in our own community. We are our brothers' keepers, by the commission of our Lord and Savior. Grant us willingness to make His commission our highest concern in our lives. Make us like Him, who suffered and died for us. *Amen.*

MAY 7

Read Jude 1-7

VERSE 3 — *Earnestly contend for the faith which was once delivered unto the saints.*

O FAITHFUL GOD, who hast given the world Thine eternal truth in the holy revelation of Thy Word, what shame for men not to receive what Thou hast in great mercy vouchsafed to them. They yearn for freedom and they search and struggle for its benefits, yet they ignore the Savior's words, "Ye shall know the truth, and the truth shall make you free." Not satisfied with neglecting Thy Word, they make war against it, seeking to banish it from our minds; and, failing in this, seeking to pervert its sense and to rob it of its authority. Help us to realize what priceless treasure Thou didst deliver into our keeping when Thou didst have holy men who were moved by Thy Holy Spirit write the inspired Scriptures. Thou dost ask us to contend, and to contend earnestly, for the faith which hath once for all time been delivered unto the saints. Make us bold in our fight for this faith. Keep us untouched by the false teachings of this present day. Deepen our convictions of the truths of the Word, especially the gracious truths of the virgin birth, the life, the suffering, the death, the resurrection, of our Lord. Let us continue to see in Him the eternal Son of the everlasting God. Help us to battle against our own inward lethargy and carelessness. Glorify the faith in our eyes, and influence us so that we may always consider the highest purpose of our lives to be the upholding of the truth in Jesus. Hear us for His name's sake. *Amen.*

MAY 8

Read John 6: 37-44

VERSE 37 — *Him that cometh to me I will in no wise cast out.*

LORD JESUS, Friend of all sinners, filled with pity for all who are under the curse of the law, having compassion on us because we are as sheep not having a shepherd: we hear Thy loving invitation as it still goeth forth to the ends of the earth. As Thou didst speak by the mouth of the prophet of old, so dost Thou still, through Thy Word, cry out to the ends of the earth, "Turn ye, turn ye, from your evil ways; for why will ye die, O House of Israel?" Thou knowest, dear Lord, that we can not of our own will or strength turn from the evil and come to Thee. But Thou dost grant us strength to come, and Thou hast promised Thou wilt not cast us out if we come to Thee. Thus hast Thou spoken to us all. If we be the chief of sinners, Thou wilt not cast us out if we come to Thee. Though we have rebelled against Thee, Thou wilt not cast us out. Though we have remained away from Thee for many years, Thou wilt not cast us out. Though our sins be most grievous in the sight of God and man, Thou wilt not cast us out. Though our friends have cast us off, though we have become an offscouring among men, Thou wilt receive us — if we but heed Thy pleading voice and turn to Thee through Thy grace. And when Thou hast received us, eternal death will have no dominion over us, but Thou wilt raise us up to everlasting life at the last day. Thanks, eternal thanks, be given Thee. Lord Jesus, we come at Thy Word. Receive us, as Thou hast promised. *Amen.*

MAY 9

Read Acts 1: 1-11

VERSE 11 — *This same Jesus, which is taken up from you into heaven, shall so come in like manner.*

LORD CHRIST, Thou art all glorious. Thou didst bear the cross, Thou didst endure the shame, Thou didst taste of death, Thou wast borne to the grave. But Thy humiliation ended, and Thou didst come forth in might and splendor, and livest and reignest to all eternity. No longer art Thou with us in the visible flesh. It was best that Thou shouldst remove Thy visible form from earth, in order that we might believe in Thee in spirit and in truth. But Thou wilt come again, in the clouds of heaven, and all flesh will behold Thee when Thou dost come. We wait the day, dear Lord, and look forward to its dawning with faith and hope. But Thou hast given us a work to do while we await Thy return. We know not when Thou wilt appear. It is not for us to know times and seasons. Thou hast kept these in Thine own wise counsel. But, although Thou hast not given us wisdom to pierce the veil of the future, Thou hast given us Thy Holy Spirit and power to do the tasks of our calling as Thy followers. With our eyes fixed on that glorious day when we shall see Thee face to face, we yet turn eyes to the needy suffering fellow men who are with us here on earth. Lord, give us great grace and kindness, to serve them as Thou Thyself wouldst minister to them. Above all else, help us to turn many to Thee, and to fill their hearts with longings for Thy coming. Hear our prayer in mercy. *Amen.*

MAY 10

Read Isaiah 1: 2-9

VERSE 3 — *The ox knoweth his owner, and the ass his master's crib; but Israel doth not know, my people doth not consider.*

O GOD of faithfulness and truth, what fickle minds are ours, in spite of Thine unmerited continued goodness toward us. Thou hast brought us up as children of Thy favored household; yet how often we rebel against Thee and provoke Thee to anger by our disobedience, our lack of love and devotion, our inclination to serve the world and the flesh. Often the poor brute beast doth put us to shame. It knoweth its owner, it findeth its master's crib; but we fail to know Thee and to consider Thy goodness. We ask Thee to bear with us once again. Thou mightest cut us off this very day, this very hour. Thou mightest justly bring swift destruction on us for our unfaithfulness. But Thou hast given us this day, and hast shown us that our time of grace and opportunity is extended. May we no longer trifle. Awaken us to a sense of the earnestness and the responsibility of life. Work in us the conviction that we are Thine, sent into this world not to do our own pleasure but to fulfil Thy will. Let us discover in the gift of each added day of our lives a new call to repentance and faith. Show us the ugliness of unthankfulness. Remind us that all we have is Thine, that we are only stewards of Thy good things. Lead our minds forward to the day of accounting, and make us wise beforehand. Impress upon those of us who are still in youthful years that all of our lives belongeth to Thee. Have mercy upon us, for our Savior's sake. *Amen.*

MAY 11

Read Matthew 10: 28-39

VERSE 37 — *He that loveth father or mother more than me is not worthy of me.*

LORD JESUS, our Redeemer and our God, how good Thou art to us and to all Thy creatures besides. Even the sparrows upon the housetops and in the door-yards enjoy Thy love and are kept under Thy watchful eye. In Thy care of them Thou dost remind us of Thy boundless love and utter tenderness toward us. Not even the hairs of our heads are forgotten in Thy providence. Surely, with this infinite love bestowed upon us by Thee, we can not distrust Thy goodness on any day, in any way. Now Thou dost ask us to take a cross upon ourselves and bear it for Thee. Thou dost bid us confess our faith in Thee before men, no matter in what company, no matter in what circumstance. Thou dost direct us to be so bold that we will not fear men who have power to take our very lives. Thou dost remind us that they can not harm our souls. Thou dost require that we hold dearer the ties which bind us to Thee than the ties which bind us to father or mother or son or daughter. Thou dost ask us to love our lives less than we love Thy service. Master, enlighten us so that it may ever be plain to us that Thou dost not require too much of us. Magnify Thy love and Thy goodness to our feeble eyesight. Show us how true and faithful Thou hast ever been. Grant that we may rather die than be ashamed of Thee before men. Be with us this day, encouraging us to confess Thee in our lives, we beseech Thee, for Thy love's sake. *Amen.*

MAY 12

Read Romans 4: 20-25

Verse 20 — *Abraham staggered not at the promise of God through unbelief.*

DEAR HEAVENLY FATHER, make us understand that our faith is the victory which overcometh the world, but that unbelief is our weakness and will prove our destruction. Let Thy grace grow mighty within us, to the increase of our faith and to the confusion of the doubts and fears which so easily arise when the way is hard and the path is dark. How mighty Thou didst become in the souls of the heroes of old, who, although burdened, as it seemed, almost beyond endurance, yet did not stagger beneath the loads laid upon them. We know how they won the victory. It was through faith, the faith worked in them by Thy Spirit. Long years before the coming of our Savior, the patriarchs fought and won their battles by faith in Thee and in the promises of His coming. And this their faith Thou didst impute to them for righteousness. With them for our examples, we press toward the mark for the prize of our high calling in Christ Jesus. He was delivered for our offenses, but was raised again for our justification. Thou hast brought us to a living faith in Him. Forbid, O our Father, that any spirit of unbelief should enter our hearts, to make us stagger and fall. Thy promises for our final deliverance are overwhelmingly great, and we know we do not deserve them. Satan would have us fear Thou wilt not do for us as Thou hast said. We cling only to the Savior, asking Thee to impute His righteousness to us, and to keep us firm in His Word and faith unto our end. *Amen.*

MAY 13

Read Romans 12: 9-21

VERSE 21 — *Be not overcome of evil, but overcome evil with good.*

RIGHTEOUS GOD, Thou hast in Christ not only redeemed us from the curse of the law, but Thou hast given us strength to fulfil Thy holy law. His blood not only cleanseth us from the guilt of sin, but it giveth us power to do the good and to leave the evil undone. We would live near to Him, and in His strength conquer every evil desire and every wicked work. The longer we company with Him, the clearer do we see not only the hideousness of sin, but also its terrible power. We feel its power within us still, for we have not yet perfectly drowned out the old man with all sins and evil lusts. Daily we must do battle against the evil within and without us. Give us constantly a supply of grace from Thy Holy Spirit, and make us more like our Savior. Clearly as we see the power of sin, let us understand that the power of our Redeemer is greater, and that He, as the Stronger Man armed, can enter into the fortress of the strong man and despoil him of his goods. Then, as Thou dost increase in us the power to overcome evil and to do good, grant that we may not choose for ourselves only one or only a few virtues, but make us willing to grace our lives with every kind of good. As Thou dost fill us with a horror of all manner of wickedness, attract us to all manner of good works. To this end, make our whole nature pure and peaceable, loving and forgiving, honest and industrious, sympathetic and happy. Hear us, for Jesus' sake. *Amen.*

MAY 14

Read Psalm 37: 16-25

VERSE 23 — *The steps of a good man are ordered by the Lord.*

DEAR FATHER in heaven, how unwise it is for us to think of our lives as being unjustly planned and directed. How wrong of us to envy others, of whose lot in life we judge it is pleasanter than ours. How short-sighted we are, not to see beyond the nearer things into the great purposes which Thou hast in view for us. Thou dost order the steps of every good man. Thou dost not compel us, for Thou wouldst have us, in the strength of Christ, to choose the good course ourselves; yet Thou dost bring even Thine omnipotent power into action to order the ways of the good man. So dear are we to Thee that Thou dealest with each one of us singly. Every one of us is Thy child, by faith in Jesus Christ, and with Thee there is no respect of persons. Remove the dimness from our eyes, and let us see Thy purposes. Show us that few earthly possessions, held in trust in Thy fear, bring us more joy than great wealth held without Thy favor. Cheer us with the message that, even though we stumble and fall because our way of life is hard and rough, we need not feel cast down, because Thou wilt raise us up again. Let us never forget the way of sorrows our Master went, and how He despised the shame and the cross because He believed that joy awaited Him beyond the shadows. Thou didst not forsake Him except to make His joy complete; and Thou wast found by Him after the darkness had passed. Thou wilt grant us this same blessed experience, because Thou lovest us for His sake. *Amen.*

MAY 15

Read Acts 2: 1-13

VERSE 4 — *They were all filled with the Holy Ghost.*

O HOLY SPIRIT, Thou who wast in eternity with the Father and the Son, Thou through whose breath we were created, Thou whom our Savior called the Comforter: spread Thy sheltering wings over us and draw us more closely into the peaceful fellowship of Christ, where there is forgiveness, and joy, and rest. We crave to be Thy temples, O Spirit of God, hallowed by Thy presence, made glorious and radiant by the fire which Thou canst kindle in us. We desire to be confessors and witnesses of Christ crucified and risen again, made eloquent by the courage and wisdom which Thou canst instil. Give us a sense of our own unworthiness and weakness, but with it the confidence of unconquerable strength. Thou alone canst so work within us that we may have both the humility and the boldness of faith. Come to us through the good news of the gospel of our Lord. Find Thy way deep down into our inmost natures, and establish Thou Thy dwelling there, nevermore to be driven forth because we have grieved Thee. Forbid that we should ever desecrate the temple which Thou hast built in our hearts. Forbid that we should ever quench the fire which Thou hast caused to flame in our souls. Purify us, enlarge us, enlighten our eyes, strengthen the weak knees and the drooping hands, and be so mighty in us that the children of this world must look upon us in wonderment at that which Thou hast made us to be. We ask it all in the name of Jesus, our Lord, whose truth Thou dost delight to bear to us. *Amen.*

MAY 16

Read Romans 6: 13-23

VERSE 13 — *Yield yourselves unto God, as those that are alive from the dead.*

HOLY GOD, once again we dare to approach Thee, although we know Thou dost hate sin with jealous hatred and that we have often erred and strayed from Thy ways, like sheep which are lost because they have turned away from the care of their shepherd and have loved to choose their own ways. We feel the power of death in our members. The pall of death is over all, hiding from us many things which are pleasant, making blacker and uglier the things which terrify us. And Thou hast taught us that death is the wage of sin. We know, O God, that Thou speakest truly and faithfully; and oh, the relief which cometh to us because Thou dost likewise say eternal life is Thy gift. We need not earn it or try to merit it. Life is Thy gift, brought to us because Another hath earned it for us — no other than Thy beloved Son, in whom Thou wast well pleased not only because He was in Thy bosom from eternity, but because He came so willingly to do Thy pleasure. Through Him life is Thy gift to us. Because of Thy yearning compassion we are alive from the dead. O God, accept our pledge this day. Sin shall have no more dominion over us, by Thy grace and Jesus' fellowship. We yield ourselves to Thee and to Thy Holy Spirit. The most crafty of our former sins shall have no more dominion over us. Those which assail us at our weakest points shall have no more dominion over us — for Jesus is the Captain of our salvation, and the victory is His. *Amen.*

MAY 17

Read First Corinthians 2: 9-16

VERSE 14 — *The natural man receiveth not the things of the Spirit of God.*

FATHER IN HEAVEN, shall we forget, now that Thou hast made us children of Thy household — shall we forget that we were born in sin, that we were dead in trespasses; that whatsoever is born of the flesh is flesh; that the natural man receiveth not the things of Thy Spirit? How easy it is for us to forget. Ah, it is the old root of pride in us which doth cause us to lift up our heads, as though we of our own power and choice had forsaken our sinfulness and had come to Thee. Pardon us despite our pride. Root its remnants out of our natures. Keep us very humble as we continue to enjoy the marvelous gifts of Thy Holy Spirit. So wonderful is that which Thou hast done for us that no eye hath ever seen and no ear hath ever heard its like, nor hath it ever come into the mind of man to think thereof. So safely wouldst Thou guard us against the wiles of the natural man That Thou hast given us the mind of Christ. Nothing hast Thou left undone which is needful for the establishment of Thy kingdom. Thy Holy Spirit hath spoken words of heavenly revelation, to convince our minds of Thy truth and to make us strong enough to stand. Oh, draw us daily to the fountain of divine truth, Thy holy Word, from which Thy Spirit floweth out into our hearts to bless us abundantly. Make us devout hearers of Thy Word. Remind us that from its truth we gather what we need to make and keep us Thine and to heal us of the blindness which was ours by nature. We ask this in Jesus' name. *Amen.*

MAY 18

Read Matthew 11: 25-30

VERSE 30 — *My yoke is easy and my burden is light.*

BLESSED LORD JESUS, Thy pleading voice falleth on our ears, bidding us come away from the weariness and the disappointments and the vanity of all earthly things, to find true rest and peace with Thee. Who like Thyself doth understand our infirmities? Wast Thou not in all points tempted as we are? Didst Thou not take upon Thyself all our burdens and sicknesses? Didst Thou not experience our toils and distractions? Verily, there is none of our distresses unknown to Thee. Thou art the Lamb of God, bearing our load, with all its pain and misery. We can not wonder that there is understanding in Thy voice as Thou dost bid us come to Thee, weary and heavy laden. We do not wonder that there is conviction in Thy voice as Thou dost promise us rest. Take us captive, O Master, in Thy yoke. Thou wouldst be our yoke-fellow, bearing the greater part of the load for us, cheering us by Thy companionship, making us brave again when trials have dismayed us. Truly, Thy burden is light, because Thou dost bear it for us and dost give us Thy strength. Have we sometimes grieved Thee by turning deaf ears to Thy pleadings? Have we sometimes joined ourselves to the world's wise and prudent ones, who will not understand their need of Thee? Call us to Thee again, patient Lord, meek and lowly, and we will by and by delight so greatly in the lightness of Thy burden that we will never stray from Thee again. Hear us in love and mercy. *Amen.*

MAY 19

Read Numbers 27: 12-22

Verse 13 — *Thou also shalt be gathered unto thy people.*

ETERNAL GOD, who art from everlasting to everlasting, who wast before the worlds, who didst reign before the mountains were formed, who art Life, who hast life, who givest life: grant us the wisdom to believe and the courage to consider that we are mortal; that we are but strangers and pilgrims here on earth; that we have no continuing city here below; that we are as a breath of air; that we pass away and the place which knew us knoweth us no more. As we contemplate our own weakness and mortality, bestow upon us the peace which passeth all understanding by helping us to realize that Thou art ours and we are Thine, and that Thine everlasting arms will be beneath us when we are trembling at the approach of our death. Yet, O God, why should we tremble at death's approach? Thou hast redeemed us, O Lord God of truth, with an eternal redemption. No harm can come nigh our dwellings even when death cometh. Thy Son hath conquered death for us. When we close our eyes upon the scenes of this earth, we shall open them in Thy presence, gathered unto our people, the saints who have gone before us. Oh, make us unafraid of the thought of death. Let the voice of our Savior assure us, saying, "I am the Resurrection and the Life: he that believeth in me, though he were dead, yet shall he live; and whosoever liveth and believeth in me shall never die." Grant us His living presence as we go to meet our last hour. We ask it in His name. *Amen.*

MAY 20

Read Isaiah 10: 12-19

VERSE 15 — *Shall the ax boast itself against him that heweth therewith?*

ALMIGHTY GOD, Thou art the Potter, we are the clay. Thou canst do with us as it pleaseth Thee. Who are we, that we should imagine a vain thing against Thy great might? What are we that we should think of withstanding Thee? We are but as the dust of the ground. Before Thy sublime majesty we are but as vanity. Moreover, we have sinned against Thee. Yet Thou dost not, in the fierceness of anger, lay Thy heavy hand upon as we have deserved. Thou lovest us as a father, and dealest with us in tenderness and loving-kindness. Only with the froward dost Thou show Thyself froward. We know that in Thy might Thou canst and wilt humble all our enemies and all the foes of the Cross of Jesus. None can withstand the avenging wrath of Thy justice. Comfort us with the assurance that those who now oppose us in our faith can never prevail. Convince us that truth, crushed to earth, shall rise again because Thy eternal years are hers. Let us not waver in our assurance that all things must work together for our good. As for our enemies and those who hate the Cross of our Savior, have mercy on them. Thou hast often had patience with the rebellious sons of men. Spare them, that mayhap they may see the folly of their ways and kiss the Son before His anger consume them. Make us Thine instruments in overcoming the power of the evil one, and let us never again be found among those who rebel against Thee. Hear us, for the sake of Him who overcame for us. *Amen.*

MAY 21

Read Acts 2: 37-47

VERSE 38 — *Repent, and be baptized, every one of you in the name of Jesus Christ.*

HOLY SPIRIT, come to us and work true repentance in our hearts. Cast down the pride which maketh us unwilling to bow our knees in contrition and faith before the Cross of Jesus, our only Lord and Savior. Remove far from us all thoughts of self-sufficiency and haughtiness. Whatever we may need to humble us, let that be our portion. Do not spare us. Chasten us in love, yet in earnestness. We know we can not belong to Christ unless we repent. We know we will not truly repent unless Thou workest in us, crushing us with the hammer of the law, then healing us with the balm of the gospel. O Spirit of wisdom and truth, Thou dost understand us far better than do we ourselves. Thou knowest the sources of our stubbornness. Thou knowest the needs of our hard hearts. Bring vividly before us the righteousness and justice of our God, then let us see the virtue and the grace of Jesus' blood. It is written that the promise is unto us and to our children and to all who are afar off. Our hearts cling to this promise. Thou wilt break down effectually our proud resistance. The warmth of Thy mercy will melt the coldness in our souls. Complete Thy divine work in our behalf, and grant that there may be worked in us that repentance which is never repented of, a repentance of no regrets and no looking backward to the service of sin. Do this for our Savior's sake. *Amen.*

MAY 22

Read First Corinthians 3:1-11

VERSE 11 — *Other foundation can no man lay than that is laid, which is Jesus Christ.*

LORD CHRIST, amid the changing things and times of this earthly existence, amid the crumbling ruins of kingdoms and empires, amid a people who come and go like shadows fleeting over the plain, we feel the need of firm foundations under us. The storms of sin and its manifold curse, the tempests of trouble and temptation, would sweep us to swift destruction, had we no rock on which to stand. Whither shall we flee for refuge and abiding safety? Ah, there is a sure Foundation, that can never be moved, not even by the last great consummation. It is Thou Thyself, Lord Christ, the true and tried Foundation, laid by the hand of God. Other foundation can no man lay which will abide. Many of earth's builders have laid foundations, but they have wretchedly crumbled. Thou art the only Rock. We build on Thee, and on Thee alone. Thou hast never failed us. Now, Lord, grant that we may not build on Thee otherwise than Thou dost desire. The carnal mind often maketh itself manifest in us, and to be carnally minded is enmity against Thee. As we labor together with God, building up Thy kingdom on Thee as the Foundation, preserve us from error and false doctrine, and from strife and dissension among ourselves. Thou must be the Head of Thy Church, even as Thou art its Foundation. Thou must be All-in-all to us, else we shall fail. Look upon us in mercy, and further the work of our hands, for the sake of Thine infinite grace. *Amen.*

MAY 23

Read Deuteronomy 31: 1-8

VERSE 6 — *He will not fail thee nor forsake thee.*

MERCIFUL HEAVENLY FATHER, how often we have failed Thee and forsaken Thee. How little is required to make us weary of Thy service, to make us unwilling to bring Thee the sacrifices which alone can please Thee. How often the world allureth us into its pleasures, sinful pleasures, which are of the flesh and its lusts. How easily we listen to the voices of ungodly companions. And how different art Thou! Thou wilt never leave us, nor fail us, nor forsake us. As Thou wast with the men of old, guiding them through long wilderness ways, companying with them from beginning to end of life, blessing them in the hour of death, and placing in their stead others to carry on Thy work of love, so Thou art still with Thy people, going with them on every way on which Thou dost send them. As Thou didst overwhelm their enemies, even the most scornful and powerful of them, Thou dost still overwhelm those who rise up against Thy people. Thy chosen ones are dear to Thee, as the apple of the eye. But always Thou hast bidden them to be strong and of good courage. It is herein that we fail. Speak Thou to these curious hearts of ours and teach them to be still in Thine almighty presence. Guard Thy Church to-day. Grant that it may not lack in brave workmen who will build the walls, though they must needs hold the sword in one hand as they build. We ask this all in His name who is the Church's one Foundation, Jesus Christ, blessed forever. *Amen.*

MAY 24

Read Luke 12: 29-40

VERSE 32 — *It is your Father's good pleasure to give you the Kingdom.*

O GOD, great Ruler of the universe, King of Kings, Lord of Lords, Captain of the hosts of heaven, seated on the throne of light, eternal in the heavens: can it be that it is Thy good pleasure to give to us poor creatures the Kingdom? So Thou hast said in Thy Word, the Word which liveth and abideth forever, the Word of which not one jot or one tittle shall ever fail. Thou desirest to give us the Kingdom. Thou desirest to make us sons and daughters of the King. Thou desirest thus, purely out of Thy good pleasure, freely giving us all, not asking payment of us in return. Truly, O our God, we should not be tardy in rendering Thee the gifts of faith and unshaken confidence. Thou wouldst not have us be of doubtful mind, for doubt in our minds doth always manifest our inward denial of the truth of Thy Word and promises. It is true, we are but a little flock. Many are called, but few are chosen. Many there are who go in at the broad gate, few who find the strait gate and the narrow way. But what of that, when Thou art with us, and when Thou hast promised to give us the Kingdom? Thou knowest, before we come to complain to Thee, how few we are and how strong our enemy. Thou knowest all things, Thou knowest all our needs, Thou knowest our fears; and, because Thou knowest, we will no longer fear, but trust and obey. We gird up our loins, Lord, and our lamps are burning. We are ready. Bless us and enrich us more and more, through Christ, our Lord. *Amen.*

MAY 25

Read Acts 3: 1-11

VERSE 6 — *"In the name of Jesus Christ of Nazareth, rise up and walk."*

JESUS, how mighty is Thy great name. Thou didst send out poor weak men into the world, burdening them with the great commission to preach Thy gospel to every nation; and they went forth with no power of their own, relying only upon the might of Thy name. Thy name had been dragged down into the dust. It had been nailed in mockery above Thy head as Thou didst hang upon the cross, a condemned malefactor. The mighty ones of Thine own nation had railed and scoffed at Thee. Yet in this despised name Thou didst send Thy followers out into the wide, wicked world. Wherever they went, the power of Thy name was made manifest. Through it they healed the sick and deformed, cheered the broken-hearted, and, best of all, brought forgiveness and heart-happiness to poor erring mortals everywhere. Jew and Gentile, male and female, bond and free, they all were raised up by the power of Thy wondrous name. Oh, make us confident that this power is with us to-day. Make the world see that only in Thy name is found the strength to right all wrongs and to heal all hearts. Increase our boldness in proclaiming and confessing Thy name, though our enemies become more and bolder. Let the power of Thy name console us in all our troubles, and let it sustain us in the hour of trial. Let it hold us by the hand as we go down into the dark valley of the shadow of death, for Thy mercy's sake. *Amen.*

MAY 26

Read Joshua 1: 1-9

VERSE 5 — *There shall not any man be able to stand before thee.*

LORD GOD, when we are with Thee no man can withstand us. The faith which we hold and the life which we lead are not pleasing to the worldly-minded. They will not confess that Jesus is their only Hope, they will not acknowledge Him as their Lord and Master, for whose service their lives have been given to them. As we continue our trust in His merits, as we grow in grace and holiness of life, we are a rebuke to them, and a thorn in their flesh. We thank Thee for Thine assurance that not one of them shall be able to stand before us. Protect us, now, from growing over-confident, from relying upon our wisdom and power. We can not trust ourselves away from Thee, not for one hour, lest we fall into the error of building upon our own wisdom and strength. We know Thou wilt be with us, to uphold and to bless, only as long as we are true to Thy Word. It is through this Word alone Thou dost bring life and might and courage to us. Let us never fail to draw from its exhaustless treasures all we may need for the toil and battle of our lives. Impress upon us again the stern truth that Thou art a very jealous God. Impart to us an earnest longing for the living truth of Thy Word. Show us that Christ is He to whom every path in Thy Word leadeth, and charm us with the delight of coming to Him for every blessing. Be merciful to us, for His sake. *Amen.*

MAY 27

Read First Corinthians 3: 16-23

VERSE 16 — *Ye are the temple of God, and the Spirit of God dwelleth in you.*

GOD of all glory, what condescension on Thy part, to come to us and make our imperfect hearts Thy holy temple. We can not understand how Thou canst dwell within us. Yet Thou Thyself hast said that the Holy Spirit maketh our hearts His home, His abiding-place, His temple. We tremble at the message Thou hast brought us in these words. We know it is only in infinite love that Thou canst so condescend to us. We know Thou couldst not dwell in us, O Holy Spirit, if the Son had not redeemed us unto God by His blood. We know that only in Him are we made accepted. May His grace be mighty in our weakness, so that we may never defile our hearts, which are Thy temple. Thou wilt destroy him that defileth Thy temple, and justly. Thou only canst defend us against the evil in ourselves. Thou only canst keep us from working sacrilege in the holy places of our redeemed and regenerated souls. Save us from the folly which the world calleth wisdom, endue us with the wisdom which the world calleth foolishness. Show us ever again the ignorance of sinfulness, its hurtfulness, its doom. We are of Christ, and Christ is of God — then let us have the mind which was His, which was always to do the will of the Father. Whatsoever things are lovely and of good repute grant us in rich abundance. We ask it, not because we believe we have merited anything from Thee, but solely for Jesus' sake. *Amen.*

MAY 28

Read Revelation 3: 14-22

VERSE 18 — *I counsel thee to buy of me gold tried in the fire.*

GOD OF WISDOM and all knowledge, who seest and knowest all that was, that is, that shall be; who triest the hearts and reins of men; who discoverest the secrets of all hearts: create in us the desire for true wisdom, and teach us we must come to Thee if we care to have it, taking our own reason captive, because it hath been led into darkness by sin. Thou dost counsel us to distrust all other helpers and to trust wholly in Thee. Thou dost reveal unto us that Thou hast gold tried in the fire. We come to Thee, O Lord, and beg of Thee a double portion of Thy gifts. Enrich us with the gold of Jesus' perfect atonement. Gladden us with the gold of the forgiveness of all our sins. Brighten our lives with the gold of virtue and true holiness, which is ours by the cleansing blood of the Savior. Teach us that Thy chastenings are also of gold, sent to us to make us partakers of blessings which could not otherwise be ours. Deliver us from the unhappiness of divided minds. Let our decision for Thee be firm and unquestioning. When Thou standest without and knockest, may we be instantly heedful of Thy nearness. Come Thou unto us and sup with us, having with us that intimate communion which only mutually loving hearts can enjoy. Thou art Love itself, and Thy love constraineth us to love Thee in return. Flood our lives with the light of Thy dear love, and be with us at the end, for Thy mercy's sake. *Amen.*

MAY 29

Read Isaiah 26: 1-9

VERSE 3 — *Thou wilt keep him in perfect peace whose mind is stayed on Thee.*

FATHER IN HEAVEN, Thou art a God of peace, and canst give the blessedness of peace. It is by sin that war and the horrors of war, bloodshed and destruction, have come into the world, which Thou hadst given us as an abode where there was only rest and peace. And, as sin hath filled the world with its curse, so it hath filled our hearts with unendurable distress. If there were no deliverance from the unrest of sin, we should perish in despair. But Thou hast looked down upon us in pity, and hast made a path of peace for us. It is stained with the tears and blood of Him who walked it to its end. It leadeth to a dreadful cross on bleak Calvary. But it is the way of peace, and there is not one suffering soul which can not find peace, perfect peace, at the end of the way which Jesus trod. Father, lead us to Him. Let our minds be stayed on Him. Thou wilt keep him in perfect peace whose mind is stayed on Jesus. We know Thou speakest truth, for our own souls bear witness to the possession of perfect peace, which they have found in His wounds and blood and death. Have mercy upon this distressed world of ours. Help men and nations to see that peace can come only through faith in Him who is the Propitiation for the world's sins. Let them learn that conscience will torture unto eternal despair unless peace is found in forgiveness and pardon. Oh, bring this world to the feet of Christ, to whom it doth belong. *Amen.*

MAY 30 (Memorial Day)

Read First Thessalonians 4: 13-18

VERSE 14 — *Them also which sleep in Jesus will God bring with Him.*

SAVIOR, how often we try to look into the land beyond. We know it lieth there, for Thou Thyself hast told us, and Thou Thyself didst with Thy body go thither when Thy mission in the visible flesh had been fulfilled. Yet, sometimes we wonder; for loved ones have left us, and our love for them hath not ceased. We would fain have assurance that it is well with them. Thanks be to Thee, for Thou hast not left us without hope. Thou dost bid us not to sorrow for them who have died in the faith in Thee. Their passing is not death. They are but asleep, and they sleep in Thee; and Thou hast said God will bring them with Thee. Where Thou art Thou wouldst have Thy servants be. As Thou didst die, but didst rise again, and as Thou hast passed into eternal glory with the body of Thy sufferings, so those who sleep in Thee shall one day arise in their own bodies and shall ever be with Thee. We need have no anxious fears for them. The day cometh when Thou wilt again appear to the sight of mortal men. Thou wilt not come to suffer and die, but with the shout of the deliverer and with the glory of the heavenly hosts. We shall be caught up in the clouds to meet Thee in the air. But they who have died will not be forgotten. Raised from their places of repose, Thou wilt gather them all to Thee, and together they and we, who have been Thine, shall live with Thee, body and soul, forever. Lord, strengthen our hope and faith, for Thy name's sake. *Amen.*

MAY 31

Read Second Corinthians 4: 11-18

VERSE 18 — *We look not at the things which are seen, but at the things which are not seen.*

GOD, OUR CREATOR, when Thou didst give us eyes that we might be seeing, they were not blinded by sin, and evil desire did not control them; but now they, with our whole nature otherwise, are under the blight which sin hath worked. Thou wouldst have us believe the things which we do not see. Thou wouldst have us possess a faith which is the substance of things hoped for, the evidence of things not seen. Thou wouldst have us prize the unseen and eternal things above those which our bodily eyes behold. Thou wouldst have our faith be so sure that we boldly speak of the things which are revealed to us, though they are hidden from our bodily sight; and Thou wouldst have us turn our eyes away from the ills and evils which inflict themselves upon our mortal bodies, and see the eternal weight of glory which is worked for us by the light affliction of these days. Impart Thy Spirit to us, and may He direct our eyes aright. Surely, we must faint by the way if we steadfastly behold the things which are seen; but, if we will look upon the eternal things, our inward man will be renewed day by day, even though the outward man perish. Lord, that we might receive our sight! Thus a blind man prayed, thus we lift our cry to Thee. Make the unseen things beautiful to our eyes of faith, and keep our glances steadfastly set upon them, until we have passed into that eternal glory which is Thine forever. Hear us, for Christ's sake. *Amen.*

JUNE 1

Read Joshua 4: 1-9

VERSE 7 — *These stones shall be for a memorial unto the children of Israel forever.*

MERCIFUL GOD, gracious heavenly Father, numberless are the blessings which we receive at Thy hands. Not a day of our lives doth pass without our having received from Thee untold benefits. We ourselves, our household, our community, our land, our world — all are in Thy keeping, and are fed from Thy liberal hand, guided by Thy favor, blessed with Thy providence. Yet — how forgetful we are of Thy goodness. Sometimes we forget not only Thy kind mercies, but even Thee Thyself. Ungratefulness is oftener found among us than thankfulness. How Thy heart must hunger for the thanks and praise which belong unto Thee. How hurtful it is to our own souls to be so forgetful of Thee. Let us mark our ways through life with memorials of Thy love. When we are inclined to overlook what we should remember, do Thou come and revive our memories. But, Father, Thou hast already done thus. Into the midst of humanity's way Thou hast set the Cross of Jesus. There it stands, towering over the wrecks of all the memorials which proud men have built for themselves, ever anew to remind the world that Thou art gracious and of fatherly compassion. Direct our eyes to Jesus' Cross when we have again forgotten our duty to Thee, and let us find in it not only remembrance, but strength to go our way and to give Thee thanks with more than the service of our lips. Grant us this, for His dear name's sake. *Amen.*

JUNE 2

Read Revelation 4: 8-14

VERSE 13 — *Blessing and honor and glory and power be unto Him that sitteth upon the throne.*

SAVIOR, Thou who didst become a spectacle of pitiful misery as Thou didst hang upon the cross of Golgotha, Thou art now enthroned forever, high above all the kingdoms and principalities and powers. Angels and all the heavenly host bow before Thee, waiting for Thy commands. The day will come when all knees are bowed before Thee, some in love and adoration, some in terror and consternation. On that day grant unto us to be among those countless kindreds and tongues and peoples and nations who stand round about Thy throne, singing aloud Thy praises. Thou hast redeemed us unto God, and the price of our ransom was Thy blood. Blessing and honor and glory and power be unto Thee. Yet, we would not look with idle longing and impatient yearning toward Thy great day. Here in this life, now in this present, we would magnify Thy name and extol Thy power and love. Be thou enthroned in our hearts, upon a throne which is high and lifted up, and make us Thy willing slaves. Oh, fill our hours with the service which is pleasing to Thee. Let our voices here on earth be like the voices of angels whom Thou hast sent to bring the message of peace and salvation to the ears of men. Let no day pass on which we have not thought of Thy precious blood and have not given Thee honor. Unite us as Thy people to hold Thy Cross before the dying eyes of a world lost in sin. Bless all that is done to spread Thy gospel in heathen lands. Help us save those of every kindred and nation, for Thy love's sake. *Amen.*

JUNE 3

Read Acts 4: 1-12

VERSE 12 — *There is none other name under heaven given among men, whereby we must be saved.*

JESUS, Thy name is indeed a blessed name. Jesus — so did the angel give command that Thou shouldst be called, before Thou wast born in Bethlehem. It did not matter that Thy coming was lowly, that Thou wast not heralded in the halls of learning and before the seats of the mighty. Thou wast nevertheless He who would save His people from their sins. Thou hast done more for men than any earthly conqueror. Thy name hath brought blessings into the farthest corners of the world, into the most hidden recesses of obdurate human hearts. In spite of dungeon, flame, and sword, in spite of the hatred and cruel opposition of wicked men, in spite of the claims of other so-called saviors, Thy name hath gone on its way, bearing blessings wherever it went, healing, comforting, rescuing. The builders rejected Thee, but Thou didst become the Head of the corner. There is no other name given among us by which we can be saved. Thou art the Way: to Thee alone from sin and death we flee; and he who would the Father seek must seek Him, Lord, by Thee. Preserve us amid the wiles of those who in our own day seek to lead us astray after other helpers. Pity those who to-day have wandered from Thy fold, and bring them back to Thyself, their only Hope. Teach us to safeguard others in their allegiance to Thee, the only Savior of souls. We ask it all because Thou hast bidden us to come and accept Thy grace. *Amen.*

JUNE 4

Read Psalm 48:1-14

VERSE 2 — *Beautiful for situation, the joy of the whole earth, is Mount Zion.*

LORD, Thou art great, and greatly to be praised. Thou art, as it were, exalted high upon a mountain of holiness, above our understanding, above the highest flights of our little minds. We look up to Thee in reverence and childlike fear and deep adoration. But best of all we know Thee as Thou art with us in the Church which Thou hast founded through the blood of Thy Son, our Savior, Jesus Christ. Beautiful for situation, the joy of all the earth, is Thy Church, Thy holy Zion. Thou art known in her palaces. Thou art known there as the God of love and mercy and truth. Thou art known there as the Father of our Lord. Thou art known there as the great Deliverer from sin and death and damnation eternal. Thou hast founded Thy Church so secure that the gates of hell can not ever prevail against her. We walk about Zion, we mark well her bulwarks, and we rejoice in Thy goodness, that Thou hast made the Church our dwelling-place. May we never leave her sheltering walls. May we ever help build her pinnacles. May we ourselves be made by Thy grace living stones in the building which Thou dost erect. May we never prove traitors to Thy Church's cause. Give us the spirit of sacrifice, moving us to do as much as lieth in our power for the glory of Thy Church. Above all, give us wisdom to remember that her chief beauty is Jesus, crucified once for all for the redemption of souls. Hear us, O Lord who art great, and be Thou ever greatly praised, in Jesus' name. *Amen.*

JUNE 5

Read Second Corinthians 5: 7-17

VERSE 10 — *We must all appear before the judgment seat of Christ.*

O CHRIST, who art lovely and comely, who didst come into our world not to condemn and destroy, but to save to the uttermost: we know Thou wilt one day judge all the earth, the quick and the dead. We must all appear before Thy judgment seat, to receive the things which have been done in our bodies, whether they be good or bad. We know what alone will avail us at Thy judgment. Thou who wilt be our Judge art yet our Savior and our Advocate. When Thou didst die, Thou didst die for all; and, in the court of God, if Thou didst die for all, then were all dead. We will not fear as we go to meet the day of our God's righteous wrath. We know He can not condemn us, because we are Thine. In us He seeth Thee, and in Thee He seeth perfect righteousness. Keep us firm in this joyful assurance until our end. But have us bear in mind that every day of our lives is a day of judgment. Thou, God, seest us. Thou beholdest our deeds, Thou dost listen to our words, Thou dost understand our thoughts. Knowing this, may we always be afraid of Thy displeasure. Constrain us powerfully by Thy love, O Christ, to walk as behooveth Thy followers. Relieve us of the fear which maketh us anxious and leadeth us into folly. Let us ever walk by faith, and not by sight, living not unto ourselves but unto Thee, proving that we are indeed new creatures, born not of the will of the flesh but of the will of God. Receive our prayer in mercy. *Amen.*

JUNE 6

Read Matthew 13: 3-10

VERSE 3 — *Behold, a sower went forth to sow.*

DEAR FATHER, Thou heavenly Sower of good seed, to Thee belongeth both the field and the seed, and to Thee one day will belong the harvest of golden grain. What infinite pains Thou hast taken to make our hearts bring forth the yield which will be fit for the heavenly garners. What tender patience Thou dost ever exercise with the struggling plants as they strive upward in our hearts. Thou didst not spare Thine only-begotten Son, for only through His sufferings and death couldst Thou restore the soil of our hearts to goodness. Yet, with all Thy love and care, how poor the harvest is. Grant us to see the dangers which threaten the rising plant of faith and good works in our hearts. Hinder the devil from hardening us; for hardened hearts do not receive Thy Word. Hinder the world from making us shallow-minded; for shallow souls do not retain Thy Word. Hinder life's cares as well as life's pleasures from becoming strong in us; for they will choke the plants which Thou hast planted. By the sharp plow-share of Thy law and by the glorious gospel of Christ prepare our hearts for a bounteous harvest. Watch over us, for we can do nothing of ourselves. Our hearts are Thine, the Word is Thine. Make sure the harvest in us, and grant that it may be a hundredfold. To this end, foster in us a love for Thy Word and a diligent use of Thy holy Sacrament. We ask it for Christ's sake. *Amen.*

JUNE 7

Read Jeremiah 6: 13-20

VERSE 16 — *Stand ye in the ways, and see, and ask for the old paths.*

JESUS CHRIST, the same yesterday and today and forever, unchanging und unchangeable from all eternity, firm and fearless when Thou didst go the way of sorrows for us: look upon us in tender pity as we day by day give evidence that we are wavering and changeable. Thou wouldst have us stand in the ways in which Thou hast directed us; Thou wouldst have us see the beauty and the safety of constancy in our faith; Thou wouldst have us, in every perplexity, ask for the old paths. But there are so many forces at work to attract us into ways not of Thy choosing, ways which lead away from Thee, ways which are unsafe and end in destruction. The thought of worldly gain often misleadeth us. The voices of false teachers, who promise us peace where there is no peace and can never be any peace, allure us from the tried ways of loyalty to Thee. Our own wayward wills insist upon serving Thee in ways which are displeasing to Thee. Point us ever and again to the true way. Make this way plain to us, as we meditate on Thy holy Word. The sacrifices of God are a broken and a contrite heart, never a heart that lifteth itself up in its own wisdom. Keep our feet on the way of truth. Thou hast never led a soul astray that went upon the path which Thou hast marked with Thy shed blood. No other path hath ever led a soul to lasting peace. Make us wise, O heavenly Master, and let no foe rob us of the wisdom Thou hast given us. Do this because Thou lovest us. *Amen.*

JUNE 8

Read Acts 4: 13-20

VERSE 20 — *We can not but speak the things which we have seen and heard.*

LORD, MERCIFUL GOD, we thank Thee that in times past Thou didst raise up men who were bold to confess Thy name and to proclaim Thy truth. We thank Thee that Thy Holy Spirit so moved in them that they could not keep silence, even when they were threatened with death by the powers in authority. We thank Thee, Lord Jesus, that Thou didst choose men to company with Thee as Thou didst go in and out day after day, that Thou didst win their hearts, that Thou didst take possession of them wholly. We thank Thee, O Holy Spirit, that Thou didst come upon these men and didst make them wise and constant, and didst make them understand that we must obey God rather than men. It is through their testimony Thou hast enlightened us and drawn us into living communion with the Savior. Behold, in our own day Thou dost have need of souls who can not but speak the things which they have seen and heard. We have seen Thy goodness, we have heard the story of Thy redeeming love. Send us out into this needy world, endued with courage from on high. Thou mayest not give us power to work miracles, Thou mayest not reveal Thyself to us in heavenly visions; but Thou hast convinced our hearts of Thine infinite love, and this doth suffice us. We would be strong in our faith, dear Lord, and we would serve Thee earnestly. Grant that we may not dishonor Thee by cowardice, by silence when we should speak, by concealment when we should stand forth openly. We ask it for Thy great mercy's sake. *Amen.*

JUNE 9

Read Galatians 3: 21-29

VERSE 29 — *Heirs according to the promise.*

DEAR LORD CHRIST, we have been baptized into Thee. According to the word spoken by Thy chosen messenger we have put Thee upon ourselves, being clothed with Thee as with a beauteous garment, being protected by Thee as by protecting armor, being made glorious by Thee as by the living light of the heavenly sun. We know that we were not ever thus, for we were born in sin and were all children of wrath, having merited nothing except the punishment of avenging justice. But in Thy Father's mercy, while we were yet under sin, the plan of our redemption was concluded, and Thou wast sent to be our Deliverer and Mediator. Thy holy law hath shown us our sinfulness and our hopelessness, and it hath convinced us of our need of Thee. Thy sweet gospel hath poured oil and wine into the wounds dealt to us by the law, and we are Thine, translated into a new life, which hath come not through the law itself but through Thee, the law being our schoolmaster, to lead us to Thee. In Thee we are heirs of the very throne of God, destined to share in every good gift which He can bestow upon us in this life and in the life to come. Lord, let us always treasure Thee and wear Thy righteousness as our best loved garment, and may we not forget that we who have been baptized into Thee and have thus put Thee on are one in Thee. Grant us unity and peaceableness, and faith unto the end, for Thy love's sake. *Amen.*

JUNE 10

Read First Peter 5: 1-10

VERSE 6 — *Humble yourselves therefore under the mighty hand of God.*

MIGHTY GOD, we come to Thee to-day to humble ourselves under Thy hand in childlike awe and worship. We do not fear Thee as a slave feareth a hard master, yet we are Thy bond-servants, owing allegiance to no other, and wholly submissive to Thee. We know that as Thy subjects we shall receive only blessings from Thee. Thou art so great and we are so poor and frail that we can not but place ourselves willingly and trustfully into Thy mighty hands, knowing that thus all will be well with us. We have many cares, but we cast them all upon Thee. Thou pitiest us as a father pitieth his children, and Thou dost make all things work together for our good. Give us at all times minds which remain free from pride and self-righteousness. Thou resistest the proud, but givest grace to the humble. We would be humble, Lord. To this end grant us soberness and vigilance, lest the giddiness of the world and the wiles of the devil overtake us. With all Thy goodness, we are still far from perfectness. All our dependence is placed on Thee. Do Thou, by whatever means may seem best to Thee, control and lead us so that we may be established, strengthened, settled, perfected. As we are subject to Thee, teach us likewise the blessedness of subjection to one another in Thy kingdom. Move us to show consideration and kindness, sympathy and tolerance, to our fellow believers, when they err from Thee and when they offend us. We ask it in our Savior's name. *Amen.*

JUNE 11

Read Joshua 24: 14-22

VERSE 15 — *"As for me and my house, we will serve the Lord."*

ETERNAL GOD, who dwellest in heaven, Father, Son, and Holy Spirit, in blessed communion and unbroken fellowship: Thou dost set the solitary in families. Of the many blessings which Thou hast established for our happiness, among the chief is the household, the home, where in godly fear and favor we dwell together as members of one family. What desolateness is theirs who are homeless. What blessedness is theirs who have the shelter of a home in which Thou art God and Savior. How highly favored the land in which are many godly households. Verily, Thou dost make our homes the foundations of our nation's security. But ah, in how many of these homes false gods are still worshiped. We pray Thee to-day to make our own home and the homes of our fellow men truly godly. Lord Jesus, how Thou didst love to enter households and enjoy their hospitality and fill them with Thy benign presence. How salutary to have Thee grace the board and break the bread. Abide Thou with us, and bring with Thee the Holy Spirit, whom Thou hast promised to us. Make us a household united in the fear of the one true God. Break in pieces and cast out the idols which may still be concealed in our homes. Sanctify the ties which bind us together as husband and wife, as parents and children, as brothers and sisters. Make it our highest concern to render daily acceptable service to God. Thou canst do all things, Lord Jesus. Hear us in mercy. *Amen.*

JUNE 12

Read Galatians 4: 1-11

VERSE 6 — *God hath sent forth the Spirit of His Son into your hearts.*

HEAVENLY FATHER, we plead with Thee to hasten in us the work of Thy Holy Spirit. We are so slow to grow in grace, we are so unthankful for our countless blessings, we are so weak in our faith. Thou hast sent forth the Spirit of Thy Son into our hearts. Oh, make Him mightier there. Break down our stubborn wills, root out the old nature which doth still cling to the things which please the flesh, and let the Spirit of Jesus Christ possess us mightily. Thou art our Father, we are Thy children, bought with His blood. Yet too often we do not approach Thee familiarly, as little children would accost their beloved father. Too seldom our lips and hearts say to Thee, "Abba." Still do we turn to the weak and beggarly elements, the things which were but a shadow of the body which was to come. Too often doth it seem that the preaching of Thy Word to us is vain. Make us more earnest and zealous in our spiritual life. Prosper the work of all those whom Thou hast commissioned and sent to preach the saving gospel of the Cross. Bless what we are endeavoring to do to Thy glory in our schools and other institutions. Safeguard us in all our service against deadness and unspirituality. Endue our faith with true life, and fill our life with divine energy. So influence us that others may see in us living imitations of Thy Son, letting our light shine so inviting that they may glorify Thee when they behold us. Grant this, because we are Thine through Christ. *Amen.*

JUNE 13

Read John 8: 23-32

VERSE 32 — *Ye shall know the truth, and the truth shall make you free.*

BLESSED JESUS, Thou art indeed from above. No man can understand Thy person and Thy work except by heeding the mysterious revelation that before Abraham was Thou wast, very God of very God, begotten, not created, begotten of the Father from eternity. Verily, no man can do the works Thou didst perform, nor speak the words Thou didst utter, nor exercise the power Thou didst manifest, except he were the eternal God Himself. Thou art from above; and Thou hast brought to us, who are from beneath, the truth which can and will make us free, if we will but believe that Thou art He. He that sent Thee, the everlasting Father, is true; and His Word and Thine is truth. Yet Thou didst come unto Thine own, and Thine own rejected Thee. They did lift Thee up, Thou guiltless Son of Man, upon the guilty cross. But even thus, nailed to its cruel beams, in the power of Thy fierce enemies, Thou canst make men free, canst give to them the liberty which is freedom in deed and in truth. We bless Thy name, dear Lord, because Thou hast given us the glorious liberty of the children of God. We shall not die in our sins, because Thou hast delivered us. No man can pluck us out of Thy hand, for Thou hast redeemed us with an eternal salvation. Endless praise be Thine, O Lord, Thou valiant Liberator of those who were bound. Now continue to us our liberty, and preserve for us the saving truth, for Thy great name's sake. *Amen.*

JUNE 14 (Flag Day)

Read Exodus 14: 23-31

VERSE 30 — *Thus the Lord saved Israel that day.*

ALMIGHTY MAKER of heaven and earth, omnipotent Ruler of wind and wave, Thou who dost turn the hearts of kings, Thou who sittest in the heavens and dost laugh all Thine enemies to scorn: we sing Thy praise this day for the goodness which Thou hast shown our land in bestowing upon it victory over every foreign foe. In Thy name we have set up our banners, and Thou shalt be our Refuge, our high Tower, our Rock of defense, henceforth, as long as the world may stand. We thank Thee for the liberties which we enjoy in this land, for law and order, for protection and provision. We thank Thee for peace and prosperity, for abundance and security. We know that our armies and navies, our law-makers and executives, would avail us nothing except for Thy favor. We confess, O God, that our land is still full of sin and wickedness, in low and in high places. We are not a nation which hath learned that sin is a reproach. There is violence and extortion, greed and dishonesty, lust and intemperance, among us. Upon these and all other sins Thy hand must lie heavy. Be merciful to our country. Thy Son, Jesus, is the only Hope of the world's nations. He is the Light of the world. Bring more and more of those who dwell beneath our flag into subjection to His redeeming gospel. Make us, in as far as this can be, a Christian nation; and make us who belong to Christ shining examples of true patriotism and citizenship. Do this, for we ask it in Him. *Amen.*

JUNE 15

Read Judges 6: 11-16

VERSE 13 — *If the Lord be with us, why then is all this befallen us?*

GRACIOUS GOD, although we know of Thy unchanging mercy and loving-kindness, our minds are often perplexed because of Thine incomprehensible providence. If Thou art indeed with us, as Thou hast said and promised, why then is all this befallen us? Why doth sickness afflict us? Why doth death come and take from us our best beloved? Why are we plagued with poverty, with opposition, with enmities, with danger to life and possessions? Why doth the evil flourish and the good languish? Why is prosperity granted to others, while adversity is our portion? Why is the wicked man successful, even though he live in idleness, while we, with industry and toil, accomplish so little, or fail? Dost Thou wonder that we ofttimes fear Thou hast forsaken us? But, O gracious God, forgive us the thought. It is our weakness of faith which hath spoken. If Thou wilt but give proof of Thy presence, we will rest content, and trust Thee once again, and pledge Thee a better faith. Unnumbered deliverances hast Thou granted to those who trust Thee. Thou wilt, in Thine own good season, clear away all our clouds, banish all our doubts, solve all our perplexities. Do not try us above that we are able to bear. Send us Thy help in good season, lest our hearts grow faint and we fall by the way. Sustain us by Thy Spirit, and revive us. Use us, in Thy strength, to overcome our own troubles. We pray this all in His name who hath redeemed us from sin and death. *Amen.*

JUNE 16

Read Matthew 13: 31-35

VERSE 33 — *The kingdom of heaven is like unto leaven.*

ALL-WISE GOD, how well Thou hast done all things. There is no darkness to make Thy footsteps uncertain. The night and the light are both alike unto Thee. We adore Thy wisdom as Thou hast shown it in the building of Thy kingdom of grace among us. None but Thyself could have planted this kingdom in the midst of the ungodly generations of this earth and have made it prosper as Thy Church hath prospered unto this day. Like the grain of mustard seed, it hath grown from insignificantly small beginnings to the mighty tree which it hath come to be at this day. Like leaven placed into many measures of meal, it hath leavened all the life of this world. Even they who will not enter Thy kingdom, but stand without and war against it, possess a multitude of benefits which would not be theirs but for the growth of Thy kingdom among us. Yea, Thou art all-wise, and Thou doest all things well. It is Thy work, the establishing of the Christian Church, the spreading of Jesus' life-giving gospel. Accept our heartfelt thanks for making us parts of this kingdom. Now do Thou in our own hearts cause the seed of the Kingdom to grow and flourish, cause the leaven of the Kingdom to convert our natures. Guard us against the spirit of our times, which seeketh to take from our Savior His glory as the only Redeemer from sin. Ground us more and more deeply in Him, and make us a leaven, working in the lump of worldliness for its conversion. Hear us for His sake. *Amen.*

JUNE 17

Read Acts 5: 24-33

VERSE 29 — *We ought to obey God rather than men.*

O CHRIST, Thou who Thyself wast fearless, and who didst make Thy followers in early times unafraid in every danger: we pray Thee to grant us the spirit of true soldiers of the Cross. Thou wast the Lion of Judah, yet not in fierceness, but rather in kingly courage to bear every suffering and pain which came upon Thee because Thou hadst come to destroy the works of the devil. When they took Thee, to slay Thee and hang Thee upon the cursed tree, Thou didst not falter. Thou hadst come to fulfil all righteousness, and Thou didst remain steadfast unto the end. Now Thou art exalted, a Prince and a Savior. Them who put their trust in Thee Thou dost make valiant and unconquerable, nay, more than conquerors. Men would have us prove false to Thee. They entice us to betray Thee, and to deny our faith. They threaten us with earthly loss and failure if we stand unmoved in our faithfulness to Thee. They belittle our convictions, laughing us to scorn, mocking us with derision, even as they reviled Thee, even as they jeered those whom Thou didst send. Do Thou write deep into our hearts and consciences the truth that we ought to obey God rather than men, no matter what positions of power these men may occupy. The love of many hath grown cold. Grant that ours may burn the warmer. Create in us perfect fearlessness of what men may think or say, and let our only thought be to remain true to Thee. *Amen.*

JUNE 18

Read Philippians 2: 1-11

VERSE 2 — *Fulfil ye my joy, that ye be likeminded.*

LORD JESUS, Thou didst say that Thou alone art our Master, and that all we who follow Thee are brothers. Thou hast taught us that every one who doth labor in the vineyard shall receive alike, every man a penny. Yet into the circle of Thy first followers the spirit of rivalry and jealousy entered; and into Thy Church to this day the evil spirit doth intrude, weakening Thy kingdom and working harm to immortal souls. Thou who wast so meek and lowly, drive far away from us the spirit of strife and vainglory. Thou who didst humble Thyself to do the meanest duties for Thy disciples, put into our minds the unselfish spirit which doth esteem others better than ourselves. Thou who didst take upon Thyself poverty and hardship for our sakes, move us not to think first and always of our own possessions, but to look upon the things of others, to help them to improve and protect their property and business, and to be of service to them in keeping it. We need Thy effectual redemption to lift us into the higher life in which we will be a joy to Thee and the Father in heaven. Give Thy Church noble-hearted leaders, who do not make an occasion for self-interest of their stations in Thy kingdom. Let this mind be in us all which was in Thee, when Thou didst humble Thyself to the obedience of bearing the cross and dying on it. Point us to the glory into which Thou hast been exalted, and make us ever more like Thee, for Thy great mercy's sake. *Amen.*

JUNE 19

Read Revelation 7: 9-17

VERSE 17 — *God shall wipe away all tears from their eyes.*

MERCIFUL GOD, how often tears come to our eyes as we go the weary way of life. Verily, this earth is a vale of tears, and their fountains are never exhausted — tears of pain, tears of sorrow, tears of disappointment, tears of anger, tears of loneliness, tears of bereavement, tears of home-sickness. We eat our bread with tears, we water our pillows with their floods. And now Thou dost ask us to believe Thou wilt one day wipe them all away from our eyes, and wilt dry up their fountains, and that tears will nevermore blind our sight and scald our cheeks. Thou dost point us to a land where the dwellers wear white robes, and where the palms of victory are in every hand. Thou dost say fountains of living waters flow there. And, lo, it is the land where Thou art enthroned, surrounded by a great multitude, whose garments have been washed in Thy blood and who have come out of great tribulations in this life. O our God, give us faith and courage to dare lift up our eyes and have a vision of the blissful life which Thou hast in store for us beyond the grave. Sweeten our days of adversity with thoughts of the joy unspeakable which awaiteth us there. Take the bitterness from our tears by the hope that they are all precious in Thy sight, and that Thou wilt give us laughter in their stead. But above all else, teach us that only through the blood of the Lamb that died on Calvary can we ever enter where unending perfect happiness is found. We ask it in His name. *Amen.*

Read Psalm 50: 1-15

VERSE 15 — *Call upon me in the day of trouble, I will deliver thee.*

LORD, Thou dost ask us to call upon Thee in the day of trouble. Thou seest and knowest that all our days are days of trouble. As by one man's sin death hath entered the world, so death hath come unto us all, for that we all have sinned; and when death came upon this world, and the curse, the days of our lives were turned to darkness and sorrow. When Thou dost ask us to call upon Thee in the day of trouble, Thou dost bid us come to Thee every day, with all our burdens, all our cares, all our sorrows, everything that doth vex and perplex us. Happy we, that Thou dost promise to deliver us. We know Thou wilt keep Thy promise, for Thou art the God of truth and uprightness. Thou art also the God of resources which are infinitely abundant. Thou needest not to come to us in hunger or in any want. Every beast of the forest is Thine, and the cattle upon a thousand hills. Nor dost Thou need our offerings upon Thine altars; for the world is Thine, and the fulness thereof. Yet will we gladly offer Thee our thanksgiving and pay our vows, not because Thou hast need of them, but because our hearts move us to show Thee our gratefulness for Thy great goodness. Forsake us not in any trouble, mighty God. Especially do we pray Thee to free our souls from the guilt and the power of sin. Shine upon us out of Thy Zion with the comfort of Jesus' gospel, unto the eternal salvation of our souls, through His merits. *Amen.*

JUNE 21

Read Colossians 3: 1-11

VERSE 3 — *Your life is hid with Christ in God.*

DEAR SAVIOR, Thou who art exalted to the right hand of Thy Father's majesty on high: Thou dost direct our thoughts away from the life which is now toward the life which is to be. Thou dost bid us seek those things which are above. Thou dost instruct us to mortify our members, to deaden in ourselves the inclinations of the flesh, and to hide our lives with Thee in God. Thou wouldst be all in all to us, and Thou wouldst be in us all. Draw us more and more fully away from the anxieties of this earthly life and from the delights of our sensual nature into the mind which doth betoken that we are Thine and that Thou art in us. Let our lives be safely hid in God, who is Thy Father and ours: hid so secure that the enemy can not trouble us; hid so deep that the sufferings of this present time can not frighten us; hid so blessed that the lure of the world's pleasures can not attract us. Be Thou our Strength as we try to mortify the lust of the flesh and the lust of the eye and the pride of life. Communicate Thy spirit so fully to us that our composed minds may be cities of refuge into which our distressed fellow men may flee, to find Thee there in Thy beauty and glory. Apply Thy saving blood to our hearts and minds and consciences, and let us experience the sweetness of communion with God through Thee here upon earth; and at last, after this world's toils and pains, find with Thee above the unseen things which we have sought by Thy grace. *Amen.*

JUNE 22

Read Second Thessalonians 3: 6-16

VERSE 13 — *Be not weary in well doing.*

JESUS, MASTER, to whom we belong, and to whom we have vowed that we will follow Thee unto the end; the way is long, the heat of the day is grievous, the wilderness is lonely, the burden is heavy upon our shoulders; and we know unseen dangers lie in wait for us at every turn. Dost Thou wonder that we grow weary and faint-hearted? Ah, if we would but avail ourselves of Thy strength, it would be otherwise. It is not because of Thy neglect of us that we grow weary in well doing: it is only because of our unfaith and unwisdom. The world so sorely needeth us. Thy kingdom crieth aloud for laborers in its vineyards, for watchmen on its walls, for valiant men in its armies; and from us comes the answer of weariness and exhaustion. Jesus, breathe upon us with the Spirit whom Thou canst send, and make us active in Thy service. Too long have we, ofttimes for no better reason than that we choose to enjoy leisure, laid Thy work aside and taken our ease. Rouse us in mind and in conscience to the need of our service. Call to our minds the unwearied journey to the cross, where Thou didst sacrifice Thyself that we might have forgiveness and life. Shame us into truer labor for Thee. Chasten us on account of our self-seeking. Draw us by Thy love into sacrifices which do not tire, and into self-effacement which sets its face firmly against defeat. Bear with us, until Thou canst fashion us perfectly after Thine own likeness, for the sake of Thy gentle long-suffering. *Amen.*

JUNE 23

Read Hosea 8: 1-8

VERSE 7 — *They have sown the wind, and they shall reap the whirlwind.*

HOLY GOD, who art altogether righteous and without sin, who didst form man out of the dust and didst breathe into him and thus make him a living soul, and who didst bestow upon him the image of Thine own true purity and holiness: Thou, far better than we, knowest the nature of man and the nature of sin. We trifle with evil as though it were harmless. We forget that every sin is rebellion against Thy holy law, and that the wage of sin is death; **death in the body, death for the soul, death eternal.** Arouse us to a keener sense of the seriousness and consequences of transgressing Thy commands. Canst Thou not teach us, as we view the awful price our Savior paid to atone for our sins, that their wickedness is of the deepest dye? Canst Thou not convince us, as we behold Him forsaken by Thee, His eternal Father, on account of our sins which He had taken upon Himself, that sin can hope for no toleration from Thee? On all sides men are striving to make light of sin; to call it by names which make it seem less abominable; to make us less afraid of its wage. Do Thou oppose their endeavors. Show us sin in all its subtlety. Impress upon us the fact that it groweth from small beginnings into growths which can not be uprooted. Warn us against sowing the wind, lest we reap the whirlwind. Make plain to us that Thou dost visit the iniquity of the fathers with such severe punishments that their children's children feel Thy heavy hand as it was laid upon their fathers. But have us bear in mind that, although Thou hatest sin, Thou lovest the soul of the sinner, and wilt save it through faith in Jesus. *Amen.*

JUNE 24

Read First Samuel 2: 27-35

VERSE 30 — *Them that honor me I will honor.*

GOD OF GLORY and majesty, why will mortal man be blind enough to trifle with Thee? Is it not enough that Thou art gracious and full of compassion, forgiving iniquity and transgression and sin? Is it not enough that Thy Son bled away His life for the redemption of sinners? Why must mortal man, presuming upon Thine indulgence, made foolish by the weakness of the flesh, yet tempt Thee and make light of iniquity and guilt? Though Thou art the God of love, Thou hast not withheld from us the truth that Thou art angry with the wicked every day; and that with Thee there is no respect of persons; and that, even though they who transgress are of those whom Thou hast highly favored and accepted, their sin will find them out and will not be left unpunished. Make us watchful of those false teachers who would have us believe Thou canst not punish because Thou art loving and kind. Thy holy Word hath shown us many an example of Thy stern dealing with men whom Thou hadst favored and honored. Only them that honor Thee wilt Thou honor. Thou carest not for the person of any man, however high he hath been exalted. No man can plead his former service of Thee as good reason why he may permit himself to disregard Thy will in any matter. Thou wilt require it at his hand. When we have done our utmost for Thee, we are still only unprofitable servants. Defend us against all the wiles of the flesh and the tempter. Make us ever vigilant in our faith in Christ Jesus, our only Savior. *Amen.*

JUNE 25

Read First Timothy 2: 1-10

VERSE 5 — *One God, and one Mediator between God and men.*

LORD JESUS, Thou didst teach men always to pray and never to grow faint. Thou didst instruct them to ask, to seek, to knock at the door of the Father's store-houses. Thou didst teach Thy followers the words of a matchless prayer. Thou didst promise that where two or three are gathered in Thy name, there Thou wouldst be in the midst of them. Thou didst assure them that, if they would but ask according to Thy will, in Thy name, their prayer would not remain unanswered. We trust Thee, accepting Thy command and Thy promise concerning prayer, knowing Thou art the one Mediator between God and us, and that, by reason of Thy most holy and precious sacrifice, Thy mediation is acceptable unto the Father. We know that He, too, doth bid us pray. We know that Thou, O Holy Spirit, art poured into our hearts to make us prayerful. We lift up our hands to Thee. Put us on guard, lest our hands of prayer be not holy. Cleanse our hearts of wrath and doubting when we approach Thee with our petitions. Widen our vision and our charity, in order that we may include all men in our supplications, friend and foe, ruler and subject, kinsfolk and stranger, those near and those far away. Thou wouldst have all men to be saved, and Thou wouldst have us intercede for all. Make us more devoutly prayerful, O Spirit of God, through Him who is our Mediator and Intercessor with Thee, Jesus, our Lord. *Amen.*

JUNE 26

Read Luke 12: 49-57

VERSE 49 — *I am come to send fire on the earth.*

HOLY SPIRIT, Thou didst come down in flames of fire and on the day of Pentecost didst impart Thyself to each one of the followers of the Lord. It was He who had said that He was come upon earth to send fire. It was He who had promised His disciples they should be baptized with Thee and with fire. Come to our darkened hearts with that divine fire, and let us be bathed in its warm light and filled with its bright glow. Make us more fervent in the life which is in Christ Jesus, our Lord. Let the radiance of our joy in His redemption shine forth all round about us. The world lieth in deadness and coldness. It loveth the fitful flames of all manner of strange unholy fires. Men do not love Thy fire, nor do they love us for bringing its warmth among them. We disturb their peace with its brightness, and they are minded to destroy our welfare because we bear Thy holy fire unto them. Our very households are divided, father against son, mother against daughter, because we have received our Lord's heavenly fire into our hearts. May this not offend us or cause us to withhold our service, even as the terrible baptism which He was compelled to endure did not affright our blessed Master. Help us fill every land from shore to shore with the glorious light of the gospel. Kindle many hearts into new life, and restore the zeal of early Christendom to our times. We know we are asking much of Thee, but Thou wilt vouchsafe it unto us for Christ's sake. *Amen.*

JUNE 27

Read First Samuel 3: 2-13

VERSE 9 — *"Speak, Lord, for Thy servant heareth."*

JESUS, OUR MASTER, what condescension Thou hast shown in receiving us mortal men into Thy health-giving service. Thou art Thyself almighty. All power is given unto Thee in heaven and on earth. By Thee were all things made, and without Thee was not anything made that was made. By Thee all things consist. Thou upholdest all things by the word of Thy power. Yet Thou dost ask us, in our weakness and imperfectness, to enter Thy service and to aid Thee in the greatest work to be done on earth, the work for which Thou didst lay down Thy very life. We will be Thine obedient servants, Lord. Show us Thy ways, teach us Thy paths. What wouldest Thou have us do? Speak, Lord, for Thy servants hear. Like Thy servant of old, we know we must dwell close to Thy holy place to be Thy faithful helpers. Apart from Thy Word, apart from Thy Church, there is no promise that we may please Thee. Consecrate us and all we are and have. Deepen our convictions of the truth of Thy Word, and increase our zeal to fulfil Thy good pleasure. Let us be like loyal servants who constantly look upon their master to know his every wish. Put down within us all thought of choosing our own work or our own means to do Thy work. Let no sacrifice seem too great to us for Thee, as Thou didst consider no sacrifice too great to bring for us; and, as Thou wast obedient unto death, give us the spirit of perfect obedience, for Thy great love's sake. *Amen.*

JUNE 28

Read Jeremiah 16: 5-11

VERSE 9 — *The heart is deceitful above all things and desperately wicked.*

SPIRIT OF GOD, who dost stir within us to form again the image of righteousness and holiness and happiness with which we were created, what uncertain hearts these hearts of ours are. How often they deceive us. Again and again we have thought we had won the final victory over the evil nature in us, only to discover that we had again been deceived. Thou art the Searcher of hearts. Search deep down into our inmost natures, and lay in us a firm foundation of trust in Jesus, our God and Savior. Help us to see the folly of trusting men, though they be princes and kings, though they have wealth and wisdom. Show us also the folly of building our houses by unrighteousness. Open our eyes to the lasting blessedness which comes with perfect trust in our God and His Christ. Make us like the spreading tree, its roots sunk deep into the cool ground, its sustenance made sure by the streams of living water. Let the roots of our faith sink themselves into the Rock of Ages, cleft for us; and let them draw daily nourishment from Jesus' blood, from His Word, from His most holy Sacrament. We are always unhappy when our hearts are wavering. Abiding peace and joy come to us when our hearts are fixed. We commit them to Thy keeping, leaving it all to Thee how Thou wilt deal with them, what Thou wilt require of us. Holy Spirit, attend us like the cloudy pillar and the pillar of fire, to save us from the misery of our deceitful selves. We ask it, trusting in Jesus' Cross. *Amen.*

JUNE 29

Read Acts 8: 26-37

VERSE 30 — *Understandest thou what thou readest?*

O LORD, who didst teach as one having authority, and not as human teachers who are without the Spirit of God: as we come to the rich treasure-house of Thy marvelous Word we are overwhelmed by the knowledge that our natural man can not receive its deep mysteries. Even its plain sayings will be wrongly interpreted if we are not on guard against the deceptions of the blinded eyes of our own human reason. It was man's erring reason which led mankind into sin and wretchedness. It was man's erring pride which nailed Thee on the cross. It is man's hardness of heart which doth make him deny that Thou couldst and didst come forth from the tomb, with Thy body clothed in immortal glory. We will not understand what Thy holy Word would teach us if Thou art not with our minds, to lay Thy compelling hand upon them and make them read with eyes of faith. Create in us devout reverence for Thy Word. Let us approach it with full willingness to let Thee speak, and to let Thee be Thine own Interpreter. Ward off from us all thought of sitting in judgment upon Thee. Rid us of the folly of measuring Thee and Thy ways and works by the standards of our human understanding and experience. Let us not wonder when we find Thou art above the powers of nature, Thou their Giver and Governor. Help us find in the sacred record, as the foremost in its revelations, that Thou lovest us and hast no desire for our destruction, but wouldst eternally save us all. We ask it in His name who is the Heart of all Scripture. *Amen.*

JUNE 30

Read Second Timothy 2: 1-10

VERSE 3 — *Endure hardness, as a good soldier of Jesus Christ.*

CHRIST, the Captain of our salvation, Thou great Hero in the strife which Thou didst wage with the powers of darkness, wrestling with them for the rescue of our souls from their firm grasp: we thank Thee for Thy victory. Thou hast truly triumphed, and hast proved Thyself the Lord over death and hell, the Redeemer of souls, the Price that God must accept as a ransom for us all. It was a mighty battle Thou didst wage, it was an awful task Thou didst perform; but Thou didst manfully endure it to the bitter end. Now dost Thou send out Thy trumpet call to us, that we, whom Thou hast saved, go forth to battle in Thy cause. Thou wouldst have us be good soldiers; but we can not serve Thee well unless we are willing to endure hardness, after Thine example. Lord Christ, may we not commit the error of giving Thee but a portion of ourselves, entangling ourselves in earthly concerns otherwise. Take us wholly into Thy command: so wholly that no suffering may deter us and no craftiness may move us to strive unlawfully, against Thy will. Draw us so close to Thee that our surrender to Thee may be complete. Give us visions of the glorious crown which is to be ours when the victory hath come; but let us rather see in Thee Thyself our highest reward, and find in Thy pleasure our highest joy. Bless us in this our prayer, and grant these things likewise unto our comrades in arms, for Thy glorious name's sake. *Amen.*

JULY 1

Read Matthew 18: 23-35

VERSE 33 — *Shouldst thou not also have had compassion?*

O GRACIOUS and most merciful God, how compassionate Thou wast when Thou didst send Thy Son into our flesh, that He, having taken to Himself our human nature, might in truth become the Redeemer of our souls. What compassion Thou hast shown by coming into our hearts and working in us that faith which maketh us partakers of the righteousness of Christ. What mercy Thou hast shown us in keeping us in Thy grace, even though every day we prove unworthy of Thy great goodness. Should not Thy loving-kindness work in us a spirit of reconciliation and forbearance with those who wrong us? Yet how slow we are to cultivate the godly virtue of mercy toward others. Daily we pray Thee to forgive us our trespasses as we forgive those who trespass against us. We read in Thy Word that Thou canst not forgive us if we refuse to forgive those who sin against us. But our old spirit of vengefulness will not die. Bear with us yet a while, and permit Thy transforming power to have its perfect way in us, until we can look upon the wrongs which others do to us and not have our hearts heated to the thirst for revenge. Let us dwell often and deeply on the sweet grace of our Savior, and may it so renew our hearts that we may be able to suffer even the most cruel wrongs in the spirit which was His when He was led to the cross. Heal us of the fevers of hot-tempered anger, and likewise of the chill of cold-blooded revenge. We ask it for His sake. *Amen*

Read Acts 9: 1-12

Verse 5 — *I am Jesus, whom thou persecutest.*

DEAR LORD, can it be that Thou art still persecuted? Can it be that, after all Thy love and devotion, after all Thy sacrifice and intercession for men, they still misunderstand Thee, still rebel against Thee, still strive to banish Thee? Alas, it is but too often true. The natural man, who receiveth not the things of Thy Spirit, can not comprehend Thee. In his pride he refuseth to permit Thy Spirit to enter his heart and convince him of sin and of righteousness and of judgment. In his blindness he sometimes doth imagine that he doeth God a service when he warreth against Thee and Thy holy name. Grant that the natural man may lose all his power in us, lest we fall into the error of blindness and unbelief, or of unholy zeal. Show us, by numberless examples of men who have erred and strayed from Thy ways like lost sheep, what folly our own benighted reason can work in our lives unless Thy holy Spirit come and regenerate it. But preserve us not only from the crime of outspoken enmity against Thee: free us likewise from that thoughtless nature which causeth us, even while we are in name and confession Thy devoted followers, to hurt Thee and Thy work by our lack of true love for Thee. If we are not for Thee we are against Thee. When we do not gather with Thee, we scatter. Often have we persecuted Thee by our negligence and lukewarmness. Grant us deliverance from our own heedless selves, for Thy great mercy's sake. *Amen.*

JULY 3

Read Psalm 61: 1-8

VERSE 2 — *"Lead me to the Rock that is higher than I."*

GREAT GOD, almighty Ruler and Governor of the universe, how small are we when we look upon Thy majesty and infinity. Thou art like the mountainous rock, and we are like insignificant grains of sand. Thou art immovable and glorious: we are shifting and perishable. All our days we spend in anxiety and fearfulness: Thou art a safe Shelter, a strong Tower. Thou dost spread out Thy protection like the giant wings of strong eagles, and under their covert there is security from all harm and every danger. Always our feet turn their way again to Thee, after we have tried to stand in our own thought and might. From the farthest end of the earth we cry to Thee, knowing Thou art a very present Help in time of trouble. We would have Thee lead us to the Rock that is higher than we. Our own strength can not suffice. Life hath too many hard places, our souls have too many foes, eternity's judgment hath too many terrors, for our feeble powers. We come to Thee with all boldness and confidence. Though Thou art immeasurably high, Thou hast condescended to us men of low estate. Thou hast made of Thy Son, our Lord Jesus Christ, a Way on which we may come to the Rock that is higher than we are. In Him Thou hast made it possible for us to bear every evil of soul and body, of time and eternity. Keep us near His side, close in the shadow of His cross, and may He ever be our Rock of defense, our Tower of safety. We ask it for His love's sake. *Amen.*

JULY 4 (Independence Day)

Read Psalm 46: 1-11

VERSE 9 — *He maketh wars to cease unto the end of the earth.*

LORD GOD JEHOVAH, before Thine awful throne the nations must all bow. Grant that they may bow there with sacred joy; for Thou art God alone: Thou canst create, Thou canst destroy. Never hath nation so mighty arisen, but Thou couldst humble it to the dust. Thou didst cast down Chorazin and Bethsaida, Thou didst crush Jerusalem, the city highly favored by Thee and chosen for the dwelling-place of Thy holy temple. This Thou didst because they rejected Thy Son. We come before Thee on this day on which we celebrate the birth of our nation, and beseech Thee above all other things to make us a nation of humble, God-fearing people. Thy favor hath smiled upon us, giving us liberty and prosperity. Our boasted independence is not our own achievement: it is Thy gift, wholly by mercy. We know Thou wilt continue to bless our land, its institutions, its governors, its people, if we will be true to Thee. Though all the earth be removed, Thou canst give our land stability. Oh, safeguard our people against unbelief. Work in their hearts not only a belief that God is, but the faith which maketh them penitent sinners at the feet of their only Savior, Jesus. Arrest the power of heathen cults within our borders. Teach our citizens to see the need of rearing our youth in Thy fear. Destroy the spirit of lawlessness, violence, ungodly socialism, and anarchism. Let Thy kingdom come and Thy will be done among us, for our Redeemer's sake. *Amen.*

JULY 5

Read Titus 2: 9-15

VERSE 10 — *That they may adorn the doctrine of God, our Savior, in all things."*

GRACIOUS GOD, whose salvation hath appeared unto all men, who hast given all the sons of men a blessed hope: Thou hast bestowed upon us faith in Christ, and in this faith the certainty of our eternal salvation. We know in whom we have believed, and are persuaded that He is able to keep that which we have committed unto Him against the great day of Thy judgment. We are righteous in Thy sight, cleared in the court of Thy justice, because Christ's ransom delivereth us from every demand of the law. Lead us on now, deeper and deeper into that clean and pure life with which Thou wouldst have us adorn our profession of faith in Thy Son. Thou wouldst have us be Thy peculiar people, belonging to Thee alone, servants of no other master. Thou wouldst find in us the bold courage to deny all ungodliness. Thou wouldst have us live as though our faces were ever set, looking for the appearing of our Lord and Savior. But the enemy of Thy throne goeth about, never ceasing in his temptations to lead us back into his service. Do Thou enlighten us so that we may behold and value the beauty of the Christ-like life. Reveal to us the hideousness of sin, even though it may come to us in the guise of that which is attractive and beautiful. Let us see the beauty of Thy service in all things, in the little acts of godliness as well as in the more heroic; and let us never weary of wearing the garb of our Master, modest and humble though it may seem. Help us, for His sake. *Amen.*

JULY 6

Read First Samuel 7: 5-13

VERSE 12 — *"Hitherto hath the Lord helped us."*

LORD, Thou unconquerable Helper in every hour of distress, in every day of battle, in every time of seeming calamity: why do men, why do Thine own children, doubt Thy power to rescue and deliver? The way of human history is marked all along its windings by ebenezers, memorial stones which proclaim, "Hitherto hath the Lord helped us." There is not a human life, however harassed and beset, whose journey is not marked by numberless signs of Thy presence and effectual help. Oh, for a faith that will not shrink, though pressed by many a foe, that will not tremble on the brink of poverty or wo! We confess, O Lord, that our happiest moments in life have always been our moments of unhesitating faith; and our sorriest moments have always been those in which we have been led to doubt Thy care and guardianship. But, fickle and foolish as we are, we need daily reminders of Thy continued goodness. Let them not be lacking in our lives. Train us in the wisdom which impresseth upon our minds indelibly the memory of days when Thy help hath been marvelously in evidence. Especially do Thou rear up in our hearts an imperishable remembrance of the great facts of our Savior's salvation: of His birth, His death, His resurrection. As we look upon these mighty deeds, let our hearts shout aloud, "Hitherto hath the Lord helped us." Then let us gird on the armor of His truth the more firmly, and go forward with Him unterrified. We ask it in His name. *Amen.*

JULY 7

Read Acts 9: 13-22

VERSE 16 — *I will show him how great things he must suffer for my name's sake.*

LORD JESUS CHRIST, who dost call men and women into Thy service, how often we would fain turn away, as though Thou hadst no claim upon our lives. How often we conduct ourselves as though it were ours to receive from Thee, but not Thine to take from us. It is our old sinful nature which maketh us unwilling to heed Thy plea for laborers in Thy vineyard. Thou hast made it plain that if we would come after Thee we must take up our cross daily and follow upon the same path which Thou Thyself didst tread. Thou showest every one who cometh to Thee how great things he must suffer for Thy name's sake, even as Thou didst show it unto Saul, when Thou didst call him out of his blindness into the light of Thy kingdom and its service. We can not be so mighty as he in Thy great work; yet we would bid Thee call us and impose upon us the labor which Thou needest for the upbuilding of Thy Church and the welfare of our fellow men. Suffering with Thee is happier than having delights and pleasures in the arms of the world. Self-denial for Thee is happier than satisfaction of the appetites of the sinful flesh. Humble toil in Thy cause is happier than reigning in the domains of the devil. Moreover, as Thou requirest that we suffer for Thy name's sake, Thou also givest us strength to bear the suffering and to profit by it. Each day will have its share of Thy grace, making itself mighty in our weakness. We ask only to be kept Thine, for Thy mercy's sake. *Amen.*

JULY 8

Read Hebrews 4: 11-16

VERSE 16 — *"Let us therefore come boldly unto the throne of grace."*

JESUS, Thou great High-priest, eternal in the heavens, Thy throne is a throne of grace. Thou art touched with the feeling of our infirmities. We know Thee as the High-priest of tender mercy and infinite pity. For Thyself Thou didst not need to be tempted in all points as we are. Thou wast with the Father from eternity, and when Thou didst come into our flesh Thou wast anointed with the Holy Spirit and with power. Yet Thou hadst come to live and die in our stead, to fulfil all righteousness for us. Oh, what comfort cometh into our hearts, what intimacy with Thee we feel, as we view Thy life's way, and note how Thou didst enter into all of our experiences of suffering and temptation, except that Thou didst remain without sin. In Thy name and at Thy gracious invitation we come boldly to the throne of grace. Nothing on earth or in hell shall separate us from that wondrous salvation which Thou didst make possible for us. We know all things which we have done amiss are naked and open in the sight of the just God with whom we have to do. We know His word is quick and powerful and sharper than any two-edged sword, and that it doth pierce, even to the dividing asunder of soul and spirit, and that it is a discerner of the thoughts and intents of the heart. But with Thee and Thy blood interceding for us, O great High-priest, we still come boldly, knowing that we shall be accepted for Thy name's sake. *Amen.*

JULY 9

Read Hebrews 6: 10-20

VERSE 19 — *Which hope we have as an anchor of the soul, both sure and steadfast.*

RIGHTEOUS GOD, Thou hast promised that if one giveth a cup of cold water to one of his suffering fellow men upon earth, he shall have his reward from Thee, if he but render the service in Thy faith and fear. Thou art in truth not unrighteous, that Thou shouldst forget what we do for Thee, although it is only by Thy direction and with the strength Thou in mercy givest us that we are able to do even the slightest tasks. Thou art likewise patient with us, when we render Thee imperfect service, bearing with us, and gently training us into better accomplishment of Thy will; and, as Thou art patient with us, Thou dost ask that we wait patiently, whenever the unfolding of Thy purpose maketh us weary. We do not come to Thee to ask praise for what we have done, but only to ask Thy further forbearance and Thy continued supply of the strength we must have. Found us immovably upon the true Corner Stone, which is Christ, our Lord. Let our hopes in Him be like anchors, sure and steadfast, holding our ships secure in the midst of driving storm and destructive tempest. As we go forth to meet the dark wave of death, banish all thought of self-righteousness from our minds, and let our souls rely upon that anchor which entereth into that within the veil, whither the Forerunner is for us entered, even Jesus, made a Highpriest for ever. Our only hope is in Him. We plead His life and death. For His sake forget us not. *Amen.*

JULY 10

Read First Samuel 15: 13-23

VERSE 22 — *To obey is better than sacrifice, and to hearken, than the fat of rams.*

O JEALOUS GOD, of whose Word not one jot or tittle shall fail until all is fulfilled, before whom all we are as bond-servants in the presence of their lord and master: direct our thoughts to the holiness and immutableness of Thy will and Word. When Thou dost send us to do Thy bidding, may we heed Thy will alone, not permitting our own desires or our own judgment to enter and to persuade us that we dare follow our own choice instead of Thine. In our flesh we perceive this weakness, that it desireth liberty in the compliance which Thou dost require of us. It hath not learned the lesson of true submissive obedience. It is willing to have the form of obeying Thee; but, under pretense of doing Thy will, is minded to have its own will. Thus it doth lead us into hypocrisy, then into neglect, then into open rebellion, then into utter unfaithfulness, and thus into misery and wretchedness. Oh, guard us against the beginnings of disobedience. Help us to watch and pray at every step we take. Keep before us the example of the perfect obedience and unquestioning submissiveness of Jesus, our Savior. Deaden the influences of our flesh by the regenerating power of His blood. Insure to us the constraining power of His love. Close our ears to the insidious false suggestions of the world and the devil, and make us bold to crucify our own flesh. We ask this of Thee in Thy mercy and goodness. *Amen.*

JULY 11

Read Hebrews 7: 19-28

VERSE 19 — *The bringing in of a better hope, by which we draw nigh unto God.*

LORD JESUS, how can we ever sufficiently thank Thee for bringing into our world a better hope than that which men tried to find in their fulfilment of the law. Dead in trespasses and in sins, men had lost hope; and yet they knew they must find righteousness, or be cast away from God's presence forever. What pitiful toils and pains they endured as they sought to find reconciliation with God through their own efforts. Then didst Thou come, and didst bring the better hope. Thy new covenant made possible what before had been impossible. By Thy covenant, written in Thy precious blood, we draw nigh unto God. Nor need we fear we must again go under the domination of the law; for Thou hast been given an unchangeable priesthood, and Thou dost ever live to make intercession for us. Better than the blood of Abel, Thy blood crieth out unto God for our pardon and eternal peace. Thou wast holy, harmless, undefiled, separate from sinners, and Thy blood is the perfect price for our redemption. Neither is there need that Thou shouldst again be sacrificed, for Thou didst once for all offer Thyself for us, and Thy sacrifice is eternally effectual. Now do Thou make us willing subjects of the new law of love. As Thou hast redeemed us, renew us daily into higher and better life, lest we dishonor Thee and Thy glorious priesthood. We ask it, our Lord, not for our own merit, but only for Thine. *Amen.*

JULY 12

Read Mark 10: 1-12

VERSE 9 — *What, therefore, God hath joined together, let not man put asunder.*

ALL-WISE GOD, who didst not only bring into being this world and all that is therein, but didst in wisdom order all things for Thine own pleasure and for the delight and profit of Thy creatures: we bless Thee for the institution of wedlock. It was not good that the man should be alone. Therefore Thou didst create a companion for him, and didst order the wedded life, in which two souls may be as one and two hearts may taste of the bliss which is nowhere else to be found. But, since sin hath come and hath worked havoc in the paradise of marriage, putting evil unspeakable into human hearts and leading them to make impure and unholy what Thou hast hallowed, we pray Thee to save this Thy gift from utter destruction. Let the love of Jesus, which doth constrain us to live as Thou wouldst have us live, order us also in the paths of wedlock. May that which Thou hast hallowed and set apart not become common and unholy in our sight. Have us bear in mind that marriage can not be happy unless Thy blessing resteth upon the home, and that Thy blessing can rest only where Thy will is followed. Grant to those who are wedded constancy in love and affection, and mutual respect and helpfulness. Preserve our homes from the destruction which must surely come when the holiness of marriage vows is forgotten. May every home rear an altar of devotion to Thee, where Thou art feared and worshiped, and where Jesus Christ is loved and trusted. *Amen.*

JULY 13

Read First Samuel 17: 32-49

VERSE 45 — *"I come to thee in the name of the Lord of hosts."*

ALMIGHTY GOD, what deeds men in all times have performed when they went forth to their tasks with a great trust in Thee. How plainly Thou showest us, both in Thy holy Word and in the history of this world, that Thou lovest to join Thy strength to our weakness, and through us to accomplish the purposes which Thy wisdom hath in view. Thou delightest in using us as Thine instruments. Sometimes Thou almost persuadest us to believe Thou couldst not gain Thy purposes without us, so closely Thou unitest Thy power with our poor effort. But never hast Thou poured Thy strength through the channels of a heart which wavered or doubted. Always hast Thou required that they through whom Thou wouldst work Thy mighty will must put their trust entirely in Thee, having no confidence in their own goodness or in their own ability. Grant that the lesson of Thy use of us as Thy agents may not be lost to us. May we not think Thou didst thus work in days gone by, but in our day Thou no longer workest thus. Make us useful members of the human family by making us trustful members of Thy household. And let us not be ignorant of the truth that our union with Thee is alone through the mediatorship of Jesus, who was David's Lord and David's Son. Through Him make us Thine; and, being Thine, we look to Thee for strength and wisdom to do all things. *Amen.*

JULY 14

Read Psalm 42: 1-8

VERSE 5 — *"Why art thou cast down, O my soul?"*

HOLY SPIRIT, Thou art called by our Lord the Comforter, and it is His promise that Thou wilt ever be with us, to lead us into His truth and to convert our sorrows into joys. But again and again we are cast down and our hearts droop as we try to go the way of life. There is so much to discourage us. Our lives seem to be filled with that which weigheth our spirits down. Cares and want attend our footsteps, disappointments are our daily experience. Not only do we ourselves suffer thus, but the whole world lieth in wickedness, and all its lands and peoples are burdened with sorrows and the things which distress. Thy Church, too, is harassed by ten thousand foes, and remaineth a little flock, going its way in fear and trembling. Thou canst not wonder we are downcast, that tears are our meat night and day. We come to Thee for comfort. Remember us richly with Thy consolations. As the hart panteth after the water-brooks, so our souls pant after Thee, thirsting for the living God. We know Thou canst raise us up. Yea, we know Thou wilt, and that Thou dost raise us up. Behold, we will not weep as do those who have no hope. Thou wilt command Thy loving-kindness in the day time, and in the night Thy song shall be with us. We hope in Thee, and we know we shall yet praise Thee, who art the Health of our countenances and our God. Surely, we can not ask amiss, for we come to Thee relying on the merits of Christ Jesus. *Amen.*

JULY 15

Read Matthew 19: 23-30

VERSE 26 — *With God all things are possible.*

DEAR LORD, again we come to Thee to ask Thee to clear the mists from our eyes and the ignorance from our minds, that we may see and know the way of life. Let Thy heavenly light fall across our paths, wherever we may roam, and do Thou grant us the perfect brightness of the day, that we may walk securely. Because we are in this world, we are inclined to use this world's judgments and wisdom; and this world is a world which is not only ruled by the love of money, but is blinded by the sheen of silver and gold. In men's minds here in the world there is no power like the power of earthly possessions. Be gracious unto us, and free us from this destructive delusion. Open our understandings to know that the riches of this world can not save one soul from damnation; nay, rather, that the love of money is the root of all evil, and that they who would be rich fall into temptation and a snare, and into many foolish and hurtful lusts, which drown men in destruction and perdition. Teach us how little money can do, and how great things Thou canst do. With Thee nothing is impossible. Thou canst without silver and gold fill the hungry soul with eternal treasures. So fill us with Thy heavenly wisdom that we will count our earthly gains but losses, and, losing all for Thee, will be confident Thou wilt recompense us a hundred-fold. We ask it in Jesus' name. *Amen.*

JULY 16

Read Acts 10: 34-44

VERSE 34 — *God is no respecter of persons.*

FATHER IN HEAVEN, of Thee the whole family in heaven and on earth is named. Thou hast made of one blood all the nations of the earth. Thou art no respecter of persons. Long years ago Thou didst make Israel Thy people, and didst entrust to their keeping the sacred ordinances of Thy tabernacle and the oracles of Thy revelation; yet Thou didst never reject those of any nation if they would come to Thee; and when the fulness of the time had come, and Thou didst send forth Thy Son, made of a woman, made under the law, to redeem them that were under the law, Thou didst include all mankind in the gracious redemption worked through His merits. Thou didst anoint Him to be the Prophet and Priest and King of all men's souls; and since the day of His rising from the dead many have come from the East and the West and the North and the South, and now sit with Abraham and Isaac and Jacob in Thy kingdom. We too have been called and gathered in by Thee, though we were not of Thy chosen people. Thou didst not despise us, although we sprang from gentile stock. Still doth Thy Word go out into all the earth, bringing all nations the testimony that Jesus is the risen Savior and that He will one day come to judge the quick and the dead. We thank Thee for this great mercy; and we beseech Thee to move our hearts with compassion for those who yet sit in darkness and the shadow of death, that we may have a part in their conversion. We ask it for Jesus' sake. *Amen.*

JULY 17

Read Psalm 84: 1-12

VERSE 2 — *My soul longeth, yea, even fainteth, for the courts of the Lord.*

GRACIOUS LORD, how well Thou dost fathom the needs of our hearts and minds. Thou didst know of old that Thy people must have hallowed places in this earth, which they might call Thy houses, where they might feel Thou wouldst meet them with special grace to help them on their ways. Lord, we love Thy house, and the place where Thine honor dwelleth. In every new distress we'll to Thy house repair, we'll think upon Thy wondrous grace, and seek deliverance there. Verily, our souls long, yea, even faint, for Thy courts, O Lord. Make Thy house our place of refuge from every ill. Let us delight in its shelter, and let us there seek counsel in the preaching of Thy holy Word. Thy tabernacles are amiable beyond all other places. Like birds seeking shelter and security for the nests they build, so we come to Thine altars to find a place where our souls may compose themselves and feel they have found abiding places. Do Thou protect Thy house as we have it in our midst. Make Thy people willing to supply it with their gifts. Let the pure truth of Thy Word ring forth from its pulpit. May Christ crucified be its joy and its song. May we count one day in Thy courts better than a thousand days elsewhere. And do Thou send us forth from Thy presence with such streams of refreshing in our souls that, as we pass through dreary deserts, we may make Thy life-giving water abundant there. Withhold no good thing from us in Thy house. Hear us for Christ's sake. *Amen.*

JULY 18

Read James 2: 10-17

VERSE 17 — *Faith, if it hath not works, is dead.*

SPIRIT OF GOD, sent by the Son, coming forth from the Father, Thou hast worked faith in our hearts, calling us away from our sinful estate, granting us the new birth from above, and creating in us a new spirit. We rejoice in Thy gifts, knowing full well we could never by our own reason or strength believe in Jesus Christ, our Lord, or come to Him. We know, if Thou hadst not worked faith in us, our lives would be drear and lonely, and we could have no hope of the life to come. We approach Thee to-day with shame and confusion, because we have hindered Thee in working in us so that our faith might be unconquerably strong. Despite all Thy goodness, we have not whereof we can boast, for our faith still wavereth and daily needeth Thy supporting hand. Nor can we point with pride to the fruits which our faith hath brought forth, for they are still few and imperfect. Were our faith living and strong, the community in which we dwell would be filled with the fame of our good works. Men, beholding the fruits of our companionship with Jesus, would glorify the Father in heaven and would give their hearts to Him. We pray Thee to enrich our faith, as Thou alone canst enrich it. Give it strength to bring forth in their beauty the fruits of patience and love and good will. Let sweet charity abound in our lives, and make us a blessing to all those with whom we company. We ask it in our dear Redeemer's name. *Amen.*

JULY 19

Read Romans 15:1-7

VERSE 2 — *Let every one of us please his neighbor.*

BLESSED LORD JESUS, we know it is only through Thy selfless sacrifice that we are saved. Thou didst not seek to please Thyself, but Thou didst contemplate our need and didst desire our happiness. For this end Thou didst offer up Thyself, that we through Thee might have pardon and eternal happiness. How ungrateful would we be if we did not learn from Thee the lesson of unselfish love for others. Drive far from our minds the wretched delusion that we will not find happiness unless we take thought always for ourselves. If we are children, lead us on the delightful paths of loving service of our parents. If we are neighbors, move every one of us to please his neighbor. If we are citizens, fill us with zeal to labor and pray and spend ourselves in the cause of our country's welfare. If we have wronged others, send us to them to make amends. If others have wronged us, teach us the lesson of requiting evil with good and gathering coals of fire upon their heads. If we have weak companions, cultivate in us the sweet grace of bearing their infirmities. If we have heavy loads to carry, preserve us from making our companions unhappy by our discontent. In all ways, dear Lord Jesus, let Thy pattern be constantly before our eyes, and withhold not from us all the grace we need to follow Thee as our Example. Truly, then we may be assured we have not followed Thee in vain. Bless us, Lord, for Thy beloved name's sake. *Amen.*

JULY 20

Read Luke 2: 41-52

VERSE 49 — *Wist ye not that I must be about my Father's business?*

GOD, OUR FATHER, we have not come into this life of ourselves. Thou hast sent us into this world, and it is Thou who hast lengthened our lives unto this present, desiring that we accomplish that for which Thou hast commissioned us. Every day of our lives cometh from Thy hand as an added opportunity to do what Thou hast planned for us. Our times are in Thy hands, and we are but Thy servants, although Thou hast deigned to make us children of Thy household. Quicken within us the sense of our dependence upon Thee as well as the sense of our responsibility to Thee. Often we forget that we must be about our Father's business. Our own affairs, apart from the interests of Thy kingdom, draw us away from our highest duties. How faithful to Thee was our Savior, the Christ. In His very boyhood He knew He had come to do only Thy will and He must be about Thy business. Never did He seek His own. Always His question was what Thy will might be. Always He knew Thy will, always He obeyed it, no matter at what cost. We can not equal Him, Father, but we would strive to be like Him. Detach us from earthly concerns and draw us in deep consecration nearer to Thee. The cost may be great. We may need to offend those of our own household, our dearest earthly friends. Yet our path must be clear, and we pray Thee to make it a plain path, and to set our feet firmly upon it. Hear us, for we pray this in Jesus' name. *Amen.*

JULY 21

Read First Peter 2: 1-10

VERSE 5 — *Ye also, as lively stones, are built up, a spiritual house.*

O CHRIST, Thou art called the chief Stone of the corner, and upon Thee we are to be built up, a temple of God, a house in which His name shall be glorified. Us who were spiritually lifeless the Holy Spirit hath converted into living stones, and in His hand we are being fitted into that structure which Thou didst come to found. Fill us with a sense of the great worth which Thou hast placed upon us. What honorable names Thou hast given us in Thy Word. Thou dost call us a chosen generation, a royal priesthood, a holy nation, a peculiar people. Thou wouldst not share our allegiance with any other. We are to be peculiarly Thine. Oh, let us feel the greatness of the privilege which is ours because Thou hast chosen us. Let us rejoice in being of the seed royal. Let us be willing to lay aside all that displeaseth Thee, and that doth not befit us as Thy holy nation, which Thou hast called out of darkness into Thy marvelous light. Let us lay aside the passions which adhere so closely to human nature — malice, and guile, and hypocrisies, and envies, and all evil speakings; and let us, as new-born babes, desire the pure milk of Thy Word, that we may grow thereby. Forbid that we should ever find in Thee a stone of stumbling and a rock of offense. We are Thy people, we have obtained mercy through Thy blood. Do Thou remain our chief Corner Stone, elect and precious, for Thy mercy's sake. *Amen.*

JULY 22

Read Second Samuel 1: 17-27

VERSE 25 — *How are the mighty fallen in the midst of the battle!*

GOD OF TRUTH and grace, how merciful are Thy counsels to us erring ones. What folly, for any of us, whatever his might or his station, to imagine he can prosper without Thy favor. What folly, for us ever to look to helpers other than Thou. It is better to trust in Thee than to put confidence in men; it is better to trust in Thee than to put confidence in princes. Thou canst lay the mightiest low, and often Thou hast done thus. What is man's might, that we should make it our stay? It doth vanish like a shadow. What is man's wealth, that we should trust in it? It taketh wings and flieth away. What is man's life, that we should expect much of it? It may endure three score years and ten, or mayhap four score, but it is soon cut off and he flieth away. What is man's wisdom, that we should follow its guidance? It endeth in confusion and shame. How man doth love to boast of his prowess. How many voices there are in this day, extolling the genius of man's mind. How proudly reason doth prate of its achievements. How lightly Thine eternal Word is set aside to make room for men's vain imaginings. Yet soon their dirge will be sung, "How are the mighty fallen!" Our trust is still in Thee and in Thy Son. In the midst of countless temptations and enticements, do Thou maintain in us true loyalty to Thee. Thou wilt never fail, Thou wilt never fall. We know, abiding in Thee, we shall be saved forever. Bless us with the gift of Thyself, for our Savior's sake. *Amen.*

JULY 23

Read Luke 15: 1-10

VERSE 7 — *Joy shall be in heaven over one sinner that repenteth.*

LOVING FATHER, what are we, that Thou dost so earnestly and tirelessly seek us, not resting until Thou hast gathered us safe into Thy fold? What are we, that there should be joy in the presence of Thy holy angels in heaven when one of us doth repent? Beyond all understanding is the mystery of Thy love for us. Yet, Thou canst not but love us, for Thou art Love, and to love others is Thy very essence. We are lost in the depths of contemplation, as we ponder over the tenderness and sympathy which are in Thy heart for us. We are lifted up out of our sinful selves, as the story of Thy redeeming love cometh into our comprehension. We are astonished and amazed at the message which hath told us of the sacrifice of Thy dear Son for us. We are humbled and prostrated at the thought that God could die because the welfare of sinful man requireth such awful ransom. When we survey the wondrous cross on which the Prince of Glory died, our richest gain we count but loss, and pour contempt on all our pride. Joy in heaven over one sinner who repenteth! We among the sinners over whom heaven hath burst forth in songs of joy! Father, hold our minds enchained with this thought. Make it the sobering, controlling force in our lives. Forbid it, Lord, that we should boast, save in the death of Christ, our God: all the vain things that charm us most — we sacrifice them to His blood. Have mercy, bless us, for His dear sake. *Amen.*

JULY 24

Read First Peter 2: 11-25

VERSE 11 — *Abstain from fleshly lusts, which war against the soul.*

HOLY GOD, can it be that Thou dost purpose so fully to deliver us from the stain of sin that we shall one day again possess Thine image, fulfilling Thy will that we be perfect, as Thou art perfect? Ecstatic thought — that we shall one day so triumph over sin that it shall have no dominion whatever over us or in us. Thy Son hath shown us the perfect life. He did no sin, neither was guile found in His mouth. But He hath done far more for us, for He hath made a way by which we may escape from the curse of sin. In His own body He bore our sins on the tree. We, who have gone astray as lost sheep, have now returned to Thee, saved by His blood. O God, now Thou dost ask us to follow in His steps. Thou wouldst have us, here and now in this tempted life, to abstain from fleshly lusts, which war against the soul. Be very gracious to us, and grant that we may heed Thy will. Gird us for the warfare against the power of evil. Heighten our courage so that, if our right hands offend us, we may cut them off; or, if our eyes offend us, we may pluck them out; and thus rather enter heaven crippled and blind than, remaining unmaimed, be cast into the outer darkness. Make us so zealous in doing Thy will that we may put to silence the ignorance of foolish men who deny the power of Jesus' blood. Keep us steadfast in our Savior's footsteps until the end, for His love's sake. *Amen.*

JULY 25

Read Revelation 19: 1-9

VERSE 9 — *Blessed are they which are called unto the marriage supper of the Lamb.*

MERCIFUL FATHER in heaven, we thank Thee for the visions Thou dost grant us of the land and the life which lie beyond this vale of tears. We can not understand the revelations Thou hast given us concerning the new Jerusalem, for our senses are dull, and that fair city is so far above this earthly habitation that we can not comprehend when Thou speakest to us of its beauty and glory. But Thou hast assured us perfect happiness is there in store for us. Thou dost tell us that they who are called unto the marriage supper of the Lamb are blessed. We hear the sound of the alleluias sung by the saints and the angels. The flash of the bride's glory, as she standeth forth arrayed in white, falleth upon our wondering gaze. It is enough. Oh, the transporting, rapturous scene, that riseth to our sight: sweet fields arrayed in living green, and rivers of delight. And this beauteous heaven, this land of life and light, of unspeakable joy and glory, is our home. We are but pilgrims and strangers in this earthly life. O our Father, hold us in Thy hand, that our footsteps slip not as we journey heavenward. Abide with us, preserving us steadfast in the faith unto the end; and, when the end cometh, may we fall asleep in Jesus, and awake yonder in His likeness, to be arrayed in spotless white, washed in His blood, and to partake of the blessedness of His marriage supper. Accept this prayer, for His sake. *Amen.*

JULY 26

Read Second Peter 1: 12-21

VERSE 16 — *We have not followed cunningly devised fables.*

CHRIST, Thou faithful Witness, what assurance we find in the Word given us through inspiration by Thy Holy Spirit, that sure Word of prophecy, which shineth like a light in a dark place. What testimony we find within the Word itself that it hath not been of any private interpretation, but that holy men of God spoke as they were moved by the Holy Spirit. Verily, we have not followed cunningly devised fables while we were following Thy Word. The world is filled with the fables which men have devised. Professing to have found new truth, they come to us ever and again, bringing with them the old fables invented by the father of all lies, the devil, who abode not in the truth. We still have Thy Word, Lord Christ, the Word of the Old Covenant and the Word of the New, the Word which pointeth to Thee as our Savior, the Word which is a light unto our feet and a lamp upon our path. By Thy grace we will contend earnestly for its possession. So fill us with the blessedness of Thy sure Word that we may be ready at any time to give a reason for the hope that is in us. Frustrate the wiles of men's intellects, who would lead souls away from the plain teaching of Thy Word. Place loyal watchmen on the towers of Thy Church. Purify our schools of the leaven of false teaching, and rear up for us a generation which looketh to Thee for guidance in all things. We ask it, relying upon Thine infinite grace. *Amen.*

JULY 27

Read Matthew 20:1-16

VERSE 4 — *Go ye also into the vineyard, and whatsoever is right I will give you.*

LORD, OUR GOD, Thou hast a work for us to do, and for this cause Thou hast called us into this life and dost daily grant us renewed health and strength. It is for this that Thou, Lord Jesus, hast redeemed us, that we might be Thine and serve Thee. Thou wouldst that we live not unto sin and the world, nor yet unto ourselves and our own selfish interests, but unto Thee, and unto those whom Thou hast placed into this world with us. Thou dost call Thy kingdom a vineyard, in which Thou art the Master, and in which we as Thy servants have a day's work to render. In goodness and mercy Thou hast promised us rich reward for serving Thee. Lord, not for reward's sake, but because Thou hast so dearly loved us, we offer Thee our dutiful service, asking Thee only to let us remain in Thy vineyard until the close of life's day, then to take us into the heavenly rest which Thou canst give us. Make us contented laborers in Thy kingdom. Let no thoughts of rank and preferment enter our minds. Let us rejoice when Thou dost reward others, and not complain when Thou art good to them beyond their deserts. We, too, are only unprofitable servants. We have nothing of which to boast, nothing for which to demand recompense. It is sufficient for us that we are Thine, laboring for Thee, knowing all will be well with us because Thou art our loving Lord. Hear us to-day and evermore, for we come to Thee at Thy command and relying upon Thy promises. *Amen.*

JULY 28

Read Haggai 2: 1-9

VERSE 7 — *"I will fill this house with glory,"* saith the Lord of hosts.

GOD OF ALL GLORY and eternal majesty, we know we could not, with the eyes which are now ours, look upon Thy brightness and live. Thou art too great and wonderful for us in this sinful state. We shall one day behold Thee in the infinite grandeur of heaven, and then Thou wilt have given us that perfectness which all those must possess who enter there. Perfected by Thee, we shall stand before Thy throne and rejoice in our nearness to Thee. But, thanks be to Thy great love, Thou hast means whereby to come to us and let us see the radiance which is Thine, even while we yet sojourn in this flesh. In Thy consecrated house, as it echoes to the blessed message of the gospel of Jesus, Thou dost glorify Thyself among us, and gatherest us round about Thee, to touch the hem of Thy shining garments. When He tabernacled in our visible flesh, His glory was beheld, the glory as of the Only-begotten of the Father, full of grace and truth. This heavenly glory is still with us, and it filleth the house which we have dedicated to Thy service. The glory of our poorest place of worship is greater than that of the temple of old, for in it Christ crucified is preached. Through the preaching of our Lord Thy Spirit remaineth among us. Through this preaching Thou still shakest the heavens and the earth, the sea and the dry land, the dominions of all the nations. We thank Thee for this inestimable gift. Preserve it unto us as long as time endureth, for Jesus' sake. *Amen.*

JULY 29

Read First John 2: 15-23

VERSE 15 — *Love not the world, neither the things that are in the world.*

FATHER OF OUR LORD Jesus Christ, and through Him our Father, take full possession of our worldly-minded hearts, and draw them from the futile things of this earth to the abiding things which are Thine. Thou knowest our frame, how frail it is: Thou knowest our hearts, how, by reason of our frailty, they cling to the things which are seen: Thou knowest our affections, how by reason of our sinfulness, they crave the forbidden pleasures of the world. The passing years have oft reminded us that the earth passeth away and the lusts thereof. Turn our affections away from earth's corruptible crowns to the incorruptible crown Thou wouldst give us in our Lord Jesus Christ. Thy will is that we see Him and believe in Him; and he that doeth this Thy will abideth forever. May we not be weakened in our faith because others have proved unfaithful, though they may have been of the foremost among us. Thou hast anointed us with Thy Holy Spirit. May He control our emotions and passions, kindling in us a burning zeal for Thee alone. Save us from the folly of a divided heart, that would serve Thee and yet enjoy the worldly things. Let not a wavering heart be ours, that is the world's, and would be Thine. To this end, grant us wisdom to avoid companionships and places in which the tempter hath his strength. Truly as we are in the world, let us not be of the world, while yet we strive to save men from the world. We bring this prayer to Thee in our Lord's all-prevailing name. *Amen.*

JULY 30

Read Second Peter 3: 3-15

VERSE 13 — *We, according to the promise, look for new heavens and a new earth.*

GRACIOUS GOD, seest Thou not how we are surrounded by those to whom this earth and its good things are real, but to whom Thou art unreal and unseen? Dost Thou not hear their mockeries? Thy saints have proclaimed that Thou wilt come to judge this earth and our humanity. Until now Thou hast delayed Thy coming. Behold, how men taunt us and speak scornfully of Thee and of Thy promises. We need Thine unbroken companionship, else we will fall prey to their wiles and violence. Pity us, and renew our faith, holding before us the eternal truths on which our hope is founded. With Thee, one day is as a thousand years and a thousand years are as one day. Thou hast not forgotten Thy promises. In Thine own season they have come true, one by one, all through the ages. When Thy time hath come, Thou wilt bring upon the earth that awful day, when, shriveling like a parched scroll, the flaming heavens together roll. Like a thief in the night it will come upon all who are upon earth. Then shall we lift up our heads and look up, for our redemption draweth nigh, our deliverance from every evil work of Satan. Then wilt Thou open to our eyes the sight of the new heavens and the new earth, where we shall be ever with Thee. We do not ask Thee to speed this day. It is not for us to choose the times or seasons. But, O God, when Thou dost bring these things to pass, we will gladly go with Thee, for we are redeemed by our Savior's blood. *Amen.*

JULY 31

Read Psalm 90: 1-17

VERSE 1 — *"Lord, Thou hast been our Dwelling-place in all generations."*

ETERNAL GOD, what is time to Thee? We count the dreary years and the weary days, we watch the dragging hours; sometimes the very minutes seem like a myriad tortures to us; for we are children of sorrow, shadows that fleet across the plain. But Thou art the Eternal, and of Thy days there is no end. Thou wast from everlasting, Thou wilt be unto everlasting. We spend our days like a tale that is told, Thou reignest omnipresent and unending. Our years are three score and ten, sometimes four score; yet always their strength is but labor and sorrow. What would our state be if Thou, the Eternal, wert not our God, our Savior, our Dwelling-place? We beseech Thee, let not Thy mercy depart from us. Hold up our goings in Thy paths. Shine upon us with Thy favor. Reclaim us early from the error of sin's way, and satisfy us with Thy mercy. Let Thy beauty be upon us, the beauty of the righteousness which Christ hath won for us, the beauty which alone can make our lives what Thou wouldst have them be. Though we ourselves are perishable, like grass, establish and make permanent the work of our hands as we labor in Thy kingdom. Make us daily mindful of the shortness of our time of grace, teaching us to number our days that we may apply our hearts unto the wisdom which is from above. Throughout our generations be Thou our Dwelling-place, a Shelter, a Defense, and at the last our eternal Home. We ask it alone through the merits of our Savior, Christ. *Amen.*

AUGUST 1

Read Luke 5: 1-11

VERSE 4 — *Launch out into the deep, and let down your nets for a draft.*

LORD JESUS, Thou who didst walk the weary ways of our life when Thou wast here among us, clothed in our visible flesh, surely Thou must know how our hearts fail us when discouragements come upon us, as they do every day. We can more easily bear the burden of hard toil than the sting of defeat in our undertakings; and defeat cometh upon us so often, for with our poor strength we can accomplish so little, and with our poor wisdom we undertake so much which lieth beyond our ability. Often we toil all the night, and for night after night, and our toil is all in vain. Then come the anxious cares of life. We wonder whether we with our loved ones will survive. We can not see our way through. Poverty or want threaten us. Then cometh the temptation to do wrong, to forsake the ways of honest toil, to stoop to means which are beneath us. But when Thou art near we are safeguarded. Thou always hast cheer for us; and, when we hear Thy voice near by, the prospect brighteneth and the clouds disperse. We are willing, dear Lord, to let down our nets whenever Thou commandest us, no matter whether our eyes see the prospect or not. We are willing to take up whatever duty Thou dost impose upon us, though Thou mayest call us away from occupations which promise us ease and wealth. Be and remain our close Companion, blessing us with the gift of Thy salvation and cheering us with the voice of Thy grace. We ask this for Thy mercy's sake. *Amen.*

AUGUST 2

Read First John 3: 1-12

VERSE 1 — *"Therefore the world knoweth us not, because it knew Him not."*

SAVIOR, strengthen our hearts, lest we feel the slight which the world and its lovers put upon us because we are Thine. Our eyes often stray with longing to the things of the world. We ask ourselves why, if Thou hast placed us into this world, we should not enjoy all its good things, knowing Thou art the Lord and Master of all the earth. We forget that Thou dost abundantly supply us with blessings, and that the things which are sinfully worldly are not good. Our poor hearts need the vision and the strength which Thou alone canst give them. The world knew Thee not when Thou didst appear among men, and it would not receive Thee. If we are Thy true followers, we must accept what was accorded to Thee. We are willing, dear Master, but our flesh is weak. Fix our eyes upon the exceedingly great glory which shall one day be ours because Thou hast bought us with Thy blood. Let our eyes often behold what manner of love the Father hath had toward us in sending Thee as our Savior and Friend. May we bear in mind we are in the truest sense the children of God, sons and daughters of the great King Eternal. Grant that the hatred of the world may not so affect us that we grow impatient and loveless toward one another. Let our minds often dwell on the glory which will one day be revealed in us, despite the slight which the world doth place upon us. Help us to return good for evil to those who love neither Thee nor Thy followers. We ask it for Thy name's sake. *Amen.*

AUGUST 3

Read Romans 7: 14-25

VERSE 24 — *"Oh, wretched man that I am, who shall deliver me from the body of this death?"*

MERCIFUL GOD, deeply as we feel our own wretchedness because of sin, Thou dost understand our plight better than we do ourselves. Thou knowest, more clearly than we do, the whole consequences of sin. Thou knowest, better than we do, the terrible weight of the curse which resteth upon us. We feel we can come to Thee with every burden which doth oppress us, and in Thee we will find sympathy and understanding of our inmost woes and needs. We know every outcry of our distressed souls will find its way to Thy listening ear, for Thou art not far away. We dare look to Thee for help, although we know that in our flesh dwelleth no good thing, since Thy law is spiritual, while we are carnal, sold under sin. O God, in Thy pity Thou hast looked upon us, and hast delivered us from the curse of the law. The wretchedness which still afflicteth us cometh by reason of the sin which still dwelleth in us. Do Thou hasten the death of the old man in us, and quicken in us the life of the new man, who is created after Thine image in righteousness and true holiness. When depression cometh upon us, as we view the weakness of our faith and the strength of sin in our members, do Thou bring us assurance. When Satan would drive us to despair, bestow upon us the power to banish the doubts which he planteth into our minds. Make us ever joyful and thankful in our possession of the merits of our Lord Jesus Christ. We ask it for His sake. *Amen.*

AUGUST 4

Read Luke 15: 11-24

VERSE 21 — *"I have sinned against heaven and in thy sight, and am no more worthy to be called thy son."*

HEAVENLY FATHER, what comfort stealeth into our hearts as we speak Thy name, and as we assure ourselves it is by Thine own teaching we call Thee our Father. We know why Thou hast taught us thus to call Thee. Thou wouldst thereby tenderly invite us to believe that Thou art in very truth our dear Father, and that we are without dispute Thy beloved children, so that we may with all boldness and confidence pray unto Thee, as dear children entreat blessings of their beloved father. Like as a father pitieth his children, so dost Thou pity them that fear Thee. Though we have sinned against heaven and in Thy sight, we know we dare to come to Thee at any time, if we but come repentant, contrite for our sins, throwing ourselves entirely on the mercy of Thy loving heart as it looketh upon us in Jesus. We must come back to Thee if we care to have happiness. Our hearts can find nothing but husks in the world, in its wisdom, in its philosophies, in its pretended sciences. The service of our own flesh and its appetites bringeth nothing but bitterness and poverty to our souls. At the last it biteth like a serpent and stingeth like an adder. Should we stray from Thee, O our Father, may we come to ourselves again and remember that in our Father's house there is plenty and peace, there is pardon and acceptance. Preserve us from hardened hearts, work daily repentance in us, and forgive us all our sins, for our Redeemer's sake. *Amen.*

AUGUST 5

Read Leviticus 26: 3-13

VERSE 6 — *I will give peace in the land, and ye shall lie down, and none shall make you afraid.*

O GOD, great Ruler of all nations and peoples, were it not for the earthly powers Thou hast instituted, our lives would be unsafe and our possessions insecure. We do not sufficiently and often enough thank Thee for discipline and order, for national peace and prosperity. Awaken in us a keener sense of the blessings we enjoy because Thou hast been the Governor and Provider of our land. No foreign foe invadeth our borders. Thou givest rain, the land yieldeth its increase, the trees bear abundant fruit, the threshing floors are scattered with nourishing grain, the vintage maketh the land fragrant with its sweetness. May we not forget all this is Thy bounty. Thou hast always admonished nations that destruction must come upon them if they depart from Thy statutes. Thou hast set Thy tabernacle among us, in order that we might be and remain a people fearing Thee and delighting to do Thy will. Bring home to every several one among us the responsibility he beareth for the welfare of the land. Not many of us are chosen to be the nation's leaders; but upon each of us resteth the land's welfare. Protect our faith, lest it fail by reason of earthly prosperity. Make us know that Thy goodness in earthly things should lead us to truer repentance and faith in Christ. Teach us that His blood flowed for the healing of the nations. Make His followers the salt of the earth. Make His Cross our country's light and guide. We pray this in His name. *Amen.*

AUGUST 6

Read Luke 5: 17-26

VERSE 20 — *When He saw their faith.*

LORD, why should we fear to have Thine eyes upon us, when Thou dost search us through only for our own good? Thou dost find hidden sins in our hearts which we ourselves do not discover. We must daily ask Thee to cleanse us from secret faults. But Thou dost also find in us the smallest spark of faith if it be there. Ofttimes, when we fear we have lost our confidence in Thee, Thou discoverest that our hearts are still leaning upon Thee and looking up to Thee; and, when Thou seest in us the weakest faith, Thou dost accept us, according to Thy promise. A bruised reed Thou wilt not break, and the smoking flax Thou wilt not quench. Be very tender toward us, and keep alive in us the spark of faith which Thy Holy Spirit hath kindled there. Grant to our faith the exercise which will increase its strength. Direct us in the ways which will be for the growth of our trust in Thee. Incline our hearts to avoid those things and those companions and those places which may imperil our confidence in Thee. Guard us against the assaults of human reason and learning, when they cast doubt upon the revelations of Thy Word. Make our discouragements stepping-stones on which we cross the turbid stream to reach Thy side. Break down every barrier which might separate us from the healing power of our Lord Jesus Christ, who hath power to cure our diseases and to forgive our sins. Hear us for His sake. *Amen.*

AUGUST 7

Read Romans 8: 1-10

VERSE 6 — *To be spiritually minded is life and peace.*

MIGHTY SAVIOR, Lion of Judah, Jesus, anointed with the Holy Spirit and with power: our newest experiences have but made clearer to us that we have not sufficient power of ourselves to live our life as we should, still less to fulfil the eternal destiny which Thou hast planned for us. We have come into this world with the corruptness of sin in our natures. Our minds are by our birth carnal minds, intent upon satisfying the appetites and desires of the unregenerate earthly nature. Yet our souls feel there can be no blessedness for us until their hunger hath been satisfied. In them there is a cry for deliverance. We are afraid, O Lord. Our thoughts accuse one another. We know there must be reconciliation with One with whom we have to do. We see the traces of His wrath everywhere in our world. Condemnation must come upon us unless Thou dost rise as our Deliverer, able to save to the uttermost. If Thou canst make us spiritually minded there will be life and peace for us. We rejoice, because Thy Word assureth us Thou art indeed the Savior, with power to destroy the works of the devil, with power to raise the fallen, to heal and to help all. Since Thou camest there is no more condemnation, if we but believe in Thee and trust in Thy power to save. Come in unto us, O Christ, and dwell with us. Restore us when we fail, lift us up when we fall; and let not the carnal mind again take possession of us. We ask it for Thy love's sake. *Amen.*

AUGUST 8

Read First Chronicles 17:1-12

VERSE 7 — *I took thee from the sheep-cote, even from following the sheep, that thou shouldst be ruler over my people Israel.*

ALMIGHTY GOD, convince us anew of our entire dependence on Thee. We owe Thee our life and being. Thou providest us with all that we need to support this body and life. Thou defendest us from all danger and guardest us against all evil. The air we breathe, the food we eat, the sunshine and the rain, the frost and the heat, the earth and the sea, all are Thy gifts. When we rise from humble station to power and influence among our fellow men, it is because we have enjoyed Thy favor, and Thou hast preserved us from the snares and pitfalls along the way. We look upon our paths of life to-day, to view the journeys Thou hast led us from childhood to our present station. We recount the numberless benefits which have been showered upon us. We look out upon the pleasant prospects to which we have come. The lines have indeed fallen unto us in pleasant places. The least favored of us must acknowledge he hath not lacked the good things. The most afflicted of us must still confess he is blessed beyond compare. Whatever we have gained in life, keep us in the spirit of humility and thankfulness. Fill us with a live sense of Thy providence. Save us from thoughtless use of possessions and power. Above all else, let us never value the earthly blessings above the heavenly, but ever acknowledge Thy greatest gift to us is our salvation from sin by the blood of our Lord and Savior, Jesus Christ. *Amen.*

AUGUST 9

Read First Chronicles 22: 6-16

VERSE 16 — *Arise, therefore, and be doing, and the Lord be with thee.*

LORD GOD, Thou who dost never sleep nor slumber, Thou who never tirest, who never withdrawest Thyself from the great operations of this universe which Thou hast created: behold, how indolent we are in the performance of our daily duties. We love ease and comfort, luxury and self-indulgence. We fail to see how brief our life will be and how much there is for us to accomplish. When Thy dear Son was here, visible in the flesh, He did not weary in the work Thou hadst sent Him to perform. We hear His words to-day, "I must work the works of Him that sent me while it is day: the night cometh, when no man can work." Do Thou impress these words upon our minds. As the king of old admonished his son, "Arise, therefore, and be doing, and the Lord be with thee," so let our ears hear the call of duty as it seeketh to arouse us day by day. What if the night should come, Lord, and our work be still unfinished? Behold, now is the acceptable time, now is the day of salvation. Save us from neglect and procrastination and the evil which cometh in their train. Especially do Thou arouse us to the importance of seeking to-day the things of Thy kingdom. Let not our faith in Christ slumber. Let us see the need of daily strengthening of the ties which bind us to Him, who is our only Hope. But let us also have a care to redeem our time of life with industry and zeal in good works, which may be to Thy glory and the eternal welfare of our fellow men. Do this, for Jesus' sake. *Amen.*

AUGUST 10

Read Matthew 21: 18-22

VERSE 22 - *All things, whatsoever ye shall ask in prayer, believing, ye shall receive.*

JESUS, Thou didst teach Thy followers to pray. Thou didst instruct them how to approach the throne of grace, with what spirit to come to their God and Father, what things to ask of Him. Thou didst form the very words Thou wouldst have them say when they went to their God, asking Him for all that pertaineth to the welfare of soul and of body. Yet we must confess unto Thee, we still have not learned to pray as we should. We do not approach our Father's throne with confidence. We have not, because we ask not as we should ask. We can not doubt Thy Word when it saith the effectual fervent prayer of a righteous man availeth much; yet many a prayer which leaveth our lips is neither effectual nor availing. It is because our faith is yet too weak. Thou hast made the hearing of our prayer dependent upon the faith in which we offer it. The speaking of doubting lips is not pleasing to Thee. If we are to pray as Thou wouldst have us pray, and if our prayer is to prevail and be effectual, we know we must first of all attain unto that perfect trust which taketh Thy promises at their full value, and that boldness which believeth without shadow of doubting. Lord Jesus, do Thou hear our prayers even though they be imperfect. If Thou canst not, because of our imperfect prayer, grant us all we ask, do not withhold Thy blessing entirely from us. Without Thee we can do nothing. We cast ourselves wholly on Thy mercy. Amen.

AUGUST 11

Read Job 38: 1-12

VERSE 4 — *Where wast thou when I laid the foundations of the earth?*

OUR FATHER IN HEAVEN, how good it is for us to contemplate Thy majesty and great glory, as Thou hast manifested Thyself in the marvelous work of creation. We are lifted up to the sublime heights of omnipotence as we gaze upon the numberless works of Thy hands and realize Thou didst call all things into being by the power of Thy resistless will; and we are deeply humbled as we compare the sweep of Thy creative might with the littleness of our own wisdom and resources. Ages ago Thou didst order our universe, before our race was brought into existence; and Thou didst order it all wisely and beneficently, without the aid of our counsel. Never hast Thou forsaken the work of Thy hands. The spheres go on their ways through space, directed by Thy mind, balanced by Thy judgment. We can not fathom the depths of skill which Thou didst display in this marvelous work. We do not know what forces operate to continue the course of all things. But we rejoice that we live in a world in which Thy hand ruleth. We know Thou art as truly present in this earth to-day as Thou wast when the morning stars sang together and all the sons of God shouted for joy. Still Thou speakest in the whirlwinds, still Thou commandest the proud waves of the sea. Most blessed of all, Thou didst bring new hope and life into the world after the coming of sin marred Thy handiwork. We thank Thee for our world, we thank Thee for Him who bringeth it back to Thee, Jesus Christ, Thy beloved Son. *Amen.*

AUGUST 12

Read First Kings 2:1-12

VERSE 2 — *"I go the way of all the world."*

GOD OF AGES, great and mighty, mysterious and marvelous, who wast from all eternity, whose years never end: Thou hast the keys of life and of death. The course of every one of us is planned by Thee, and Thou watchest over us step by step throughout the way. When other helpers fail because death standeth at our door and knocketh, Thou art still with us, and death hath no terror for Thee, nor for us when Thou dost hold our hands. We go the way of all the earth, dying daily, drawing nearer and nearer to that solemn hour when we go out upon the journey from which none of us ever returneth; but we go with our fears all laid upon Thee and our cares all reposed in Thy bosom. We know how Thou hast robbed death of its terror for us. How Thou couldst send Thine only-begotten Son into the shame and pain of the cross we can not comprehend; but that Thou didst send Him we know, and we know Thou didst this because Thou didst love us; and that Thou didst through Him make death a happy experience for Thine own, instead of an hour of destruction and hopelessness, we know full well. When we are gathered to sleep with our fathers, may we fall asleep in Jesus, blessed sleep, from which none ever waketh to weep, a calm and undisturbed repose, unbroken by the last of foes. Then hold Thou Thy cross before our closing eyes, shine through the gloom, and point us to the skies. We ask it of Thy mercy, knowing none can save us as Thou canst. *Amen.*

AUGUST 13

Read Ephesians 3:13-21

VERSE 19 — *Know the love of Christ, which passeth knowledge.*

GOD OF ALL WISDOM, look in mercy upon us as we poor mortals follow after the things which seem to us to be wise and discreet. Day after day we seek for knowledge, night after night we use our senses and our minds to gather store of that which, as we deem, may enrich our intellects and make us able to gain profit for our lives. But oh, how often we fail of true wisdom. How often what we consider wise Thou dost look upon as folly, and what we consider foolishness Thou hast commended as the truest of wisdom's treasures. We would bow low before Thee to-day, not only bending our knees in Thy presence, but subjecting our reasoning powers to Thine influences. Work in us cheerful assent to Thy direction and make us see that knowing the love of Jesus passeth all earthly knowledge. Strengthen us with Thy might in the inner man, O Christ, by dwelling within us and giving us wisdom to comprehend what is the breadth and length and depth and height of Thy redeeming love toward us fallen creatures. Thou art able to do abundantly above all we ask or think. Endue us with courage, likewise, that we may not faint under any burden, that we may not flinch before the difficulties of any service which Thou dost require of us. May we love Thy Church, the communion of Thy saints here upon earth; and may we according to Thy command and in Thy grace love all our fellow men as we love ourselves. Attend unto this our prayer, dear Lord, in lovingkindness. *Amen.*

AUGUST 14

Read John 10:11-18

VERSE 14 — *I am the good Shepherd, and know my sheep, and am known of mine.*

JESUS, tender Shepherd of us all who own Thy name, who leadest us wisely and well, who gatherest the lambs with Thine arms and carriest them in Thy bosom, who seekest the lost sheep and, when Thou hast found it, layest it on Thy shoulder and bearest it home rejoicing: forbid that we should ever so far stray from Thee that Thy love can not recall us to Thy side and again enfold us with Thy flock. Our greatest blessedness is to know we are Thine, that Thou knowest us, that Thou callest us by name, that we are precious in Thy sight. Thy goodness toward us knoweth no bounds. Whatever we may need, Thou dost supply. When danger neareth, before we can discern its approach, Thou dost see and dost warn us. When the wolf cometh to devour and scatter, Thou goest forth to meet him and deliverest us out of his power. When Thou didst lay down Thy life for Thy sheep, it was not because Thou couldst not save Thyself. Thou hadst power to escape death; but Thou didst of Thine own free will lay down Thy life; and, glory be to God, Thou didst have power to take it up again. As Thou providest for us, Thou dost also care for countless thousands in every nation and clime. Have us bear in memory that they and we are one fold, and let our hearts go out to them in feelings of fellowship and willing service. Lead us safely through this life, and gather us into the fold above, for Thine infinite mercy's sake. *Amen.*

AUGUST 15

Read Psalm 103: 1-22

VERSE 2 — *Bless the Lord, O my soul, and forget not all His benefits.*

GRACIOUS LORD, teach our hearts and lips the songs of praise and thanksgiving. All the earth lifteth up its myriad voices to the honor of Thy great name. Shall man be dumb when even inanimate nature raiseth the song of jubilee to its Creator? Stifle the old nature within us, which would have us believe that it is by skill and might of our own that we have what we enjoy. Humble the reasoning power within us, which would have us imagine that when Thou providest for us it is no more than our desert. We were rebels against Thy majesty, this we know right well. Our own consciences convict us of the wrongs we have done against Thee. We have not deserved that Thou shouldst forgive us, or redeem our lives from destruction, or crown us with loving-kindness. We have deserved that Thou shouldst chide with us and cast us off in Thy hot displeasure. But Thou hast permitted mercy to go before justice. As high as the heavens are above the earth, so great is Thy mercy toward us. As far as the East is from the West, so far Thou removest the curse of sin from us. We bless Thee, O Lord, with all our hearts and souls. All that is within us shall unite to glorify Thy name. We will not forget Thy benefits. With the voices of angels our voices shall unite, in all places of Thy dominion, praising Thee evermore. May our praise be acceptable to Thee, and may we join with it obedience to Thy commandments. Accept our praise and our hearts for Jesus' sake. *Amen.*

AUGUST 16

Read Luke 7: 11-17

VERSE 13 — *He had compassion on her and said unto her, "Weep not."*

BLESSED JESUS, how gentle is Thy voice and how tender is the touch of Thy hand when Thou dost minister to us in our days of affliction and trial. No friend among men can be so loving as Thou art. No voice among those which come to our ears can be so assuring as is Thine. Whatever the tempest that tosseth in our hearts, Thou canst with authority command it, saying, "Peace, be still." When Thou speakest, there is a great calm. Earth hath no sorrows which Thou canst not heal. We know not what clouds and thick darkness may lie over our pathway, through which we must travel in the future. We know not what losses and bereavement, what heart-breaks and calamities, may fall to our lot. We know not in what form death may come to us. War and pestilence, fire and sword, may cross our way as we press on. But this we know that, whatever may befall, Thou art willing to journey with us wherever life may lead, and Thou wilt in every disaster which may overwhelm us be always the same, calm and commanding, able to rescue and to bear us through to deliverance. May we seek no other helpers. May we delight in Thy comradeship. May we keep our hearts free from foolish fears and anxious dread. Mighty Savior, King of life, Conqueror of death, be Thou our Friend and Counselor. Make us braver to meet misfortune, more cheerful in the midst of suffering. Yea, and make us gentler and tenderer toward others who are in distress — for Thy name's sake. *Amen.*

AUGUST 17

Read Isaiah 1:.10-20

VERSE 18 — *Though your sins be as scarlet, they shall be white as snow.*

O GOD MOST HOLY, we tremble at the thought of our many transgressions of Thy perfect law. Our lives are filled with sins of omission and commission. The good which we ought to do we leave undone; the evil which we should despise we commit again and again. There is no hope for us except in Thy free grace and pardoning love. We can not put our confidence in any sacrifices we may bring to Thee. What we offer Thee of earthly goods is but Thine own. It is not ours to give. Moreover, when we bring Thee sacrifices with our hearts not cleansed, our offerings, however rich and great, are but an abomination to Thee. Thou desirest clean hearts and hands: and Thou alone canst so cleanse us that we will be acceptable before Thy righteous throne. Thanks be to Thee that Thou hast given us the promise of pardon and purification. Though our sins be as scarlet, Thou hast said Thou wouldst make us white as snow. Though our sins be red, like crimson, Thou hast promised Thou wilt make us purer than bleached wool. We know Thou canst keep Thy promise. for Thou hast given us a Savior, who shed His precious blood for our redemption. Through Him we can have the righteousness which availeth before Thee; through Him we can obtain the uprightness which pleaseth Thee. Then, when we have accepted justification through His merits, Thou wilt also be pleased with our offerings, brought to Thee in spirit and in truth. Oh, make us acceptable by the virtue of His blood. *Amen.*

AUGUST 18

Read First Corinthians 9: 24-27

VERSE 26 — *"So fight I, not as one that beateth the air."*

JESUS, Thou Victor in the strife which Thou didst wage against the kingdom of darkness: Thou art the Captain of our salvation, Thou art the Leader of the hosts which Thou hast gathered together beneath Thy banner, into which Thou hast mercifully called us. We rejoice that Thou dost deign to accept us among Thy warring followers. The time for peace hath not yet come. Thou camest to bring peace to troubled hearts, but Thou didst not come to bring peace to the kingdom of Satan. Wherever wrong and untruth lift up their crests, there Thou wouldst have the battle go forward, blow for blow, and thrust for thrust. Close our ears to the unholy songs of peace which many to-day would have us join. Impress upon us that there can never be peace until the last enemy hath been laid low. Teach our hands and hearts the true skill of warfare against error and unrighteousness. Let us not fight as do those who beat the air. Order our lives so that by temperance and chastity, by uprightness and industry, by close touch with Thee and Thy holy Word, we may always be ready for the fray. Let not the yearnings of our bodily appetites interfere with the discipline of our souls. Oh, save us from ever being cast away because of unfitness for Thy service. To this end keep in our view the incorruptible crown which we shall one day wear if we remain steadfast. We ask it, Master, relying on Thy grace. *Amen.*

AUGUST 19

Read Isaiah 48:12-19

VERSE 18 — *Then had thy peace been as a river, and thy righteousness as the waves of the sea.*

MERCIFUL CHRIST, Thou didst once say of one of our fellow men that it were better if he had not been born. He was one who had permitted the day of Thy grace to pass, leaving him in the bonds of wickedness, untouched by Thy pardoning love, because he had hardened himself. Thou didst once weep over Jerusalem, lamenting that its people, whom Thou wouldst have gathered as a hen gathereth her brood under her wings, would not. Thou didst indite for us the parable of the virgins who, having no oil for their lamps, were shut out from the wedding feast. Grant that we may heed Thy repeated warnings, and that Thou needst never say to us, "Oh, that thou hadst hearkened — then had thy peace been as a river!" Lord, Redeemer, Holy One in Israel, Thou who art the First and the Last, purge out of our hearts the disposition to trifle with holy things. May we not tamper with sin. May we not deal thoughtlessly with our opportunities. Peace like a mighty river, righteousness like the waves of the sea — these shall be ours if we but listen to Thy pleading voice, calling us to repentance, inviting us to faith in Thy shed blood. Peace like a river! How beautiful our lives can be when Thou art permitted to have Thy way in us. Peace like a river! What strength might be ours, if Thou couldst make us channels of Thy grace. Peace like a river! Pour it into our souls, dear Lord Christ, from Thy riven side, peace, perfect peace — for Thy mercy's sake. *Amen.*

AUGUST 20

Read Luke 9: 51-62

VERSE 62 — *No man, having put his hand to the plow, and looking back, is fit for the kingdom of God.*

O PEERLESS CHRIST, crystal Christ, like whom there is no other: how perfect Thou wast in all Thy virtues, on all Thy ways, in all temptations, despite all Thy misery and wretchedness. In poverty and want Thou didst undertake the most stupendous task. In the face of enmity most bitter Thou didst set Thy face steadfastly to go wherever the way of Thy great mission might lead. Never once didst Thou show Thyself reluctant. Never once did Thy heart divide itself, seeking to serve self while serving God. Never once didst Thou yield to temptation to do Thy task otherwise than was proper for the Son of God. When Thou callest us to follow Thee Thou dost not conceal from us that to be Thy followers we must be like Thee and must suffer as Thou didst suffer. Take our wavering selves into Thy steadfast keeping and make us firm and fixed in purpose. We are not fit for Thy kingdom if, having put our hands to the plow, we look back. What lieth back there in our past is not worthy of our glances since Thou hast given us the prospect of blessedness and usefulness in Thy kingdom. Nothing in all the attractions of the alluring world is worthy of our attention, once we have entered the ranks of Thy followers. Yet our eyes often stray from the path. We need Thy correcting hand and the full power of Thy grace to keep us whole-heartedly with Thee. Be gracious to us, O Christ, and keep us steadfast to the end, in mercy and pardoning love. *Amen.*

AUGUST 21

Read Second Corinthians 6: 14-18

VERSE 17 — *Come ye out from among them, and be ye separate.*

O GOD, HEAVENLY FATHER, Thou dwellest in purity and light. We live in the midst of sin and ungodliness, in a world where Thou art not received. If we desire to dwell with Thee in this life and in the life to come, we must not be of the world, it must have no part in us. Our flesh inclineth to evil and the nature within us leadeth to the sinful lusts which our worldly fellow men enjoy. It is hard for us, weak and unstable as we are, to keep ourselves unspotted by the world. Do Thou make strong in us the sense of the uncleanness of the world's lusts and ambitions. Recall to our minds that we are Thy temples, and that no unclean thing should be permitted to defile the temple of God. Show us that friendly association with anything which is sinful is the wearing of an unequal yoke. Thou hast made us to be light: help us shun the fellowship of darkness. Thou hast led us to the spotless Christ: may we despise the friendship of Belial. So fill our hearts with a delight in Thee and in Thy Son, that we may not feel a sense of loneliness when we separate ourselves from the world and its unclean things. Thou dost not command us to shut ourselves off bodily from our fellow men, but Thou dost command us not to be in spirit like those who have not believed in Jesus. May Thy fellowship be so sweet and wholesome to us that we may never regret our surrender to Thy love. We ask this in Jesus' name. *Amen.*

AUGUST 22

Read Revelation 21: 1-8

VERSE 4 — *The former things are passed away.*

ETERNAL GOD AND FATHER, God of the heavens as well as God of our earth, God of the future as well as God of the past: it is often with fainting hearts we view the passing of all things earthly. The perishableness of this world and the things of this world is hourly before our eyes. We feel within ourselves that we are being hastened on to a future into which our eyes can not peer. But Thou hast given Thine inspired prophets vision of the land which lieth beyond, and Thou hast through them granted us to know of its beauty. We believe, dear Father, that there cometh a time when Thou wilt wholly change the order of this earth. All these former things shall pass away by Thy will, by Thy power, for Thy wise purposes. New heavens and a new earth shall greet our sight. There shall be a holy city, a new Jerusalem, Thy tabernacle. No sin shall enter there, nothing which Thou abhorrest. Death and sorrow, crying and pain, shall be no more. They whom Thou dost receive into the holy city shall gather about the fountain of life and drink freely; and everlasting life and happiness shall be theirs in body and in soul. Let this Thy revelation of things to come awaken in us an earnest yearning to be among those who are Thine. May we remember it is alone through the Lamb slain on Calvary we can be cleansed and made fit for the eternal blessedness. Give us the mind which detesteth sin and loveth the Savior. We ask it all in His blessed name. *Amen.*

AUGUST 23

Read Jeremiah 22: 11-19

VERSE 13 — *Wo unto him that buildeth his house by unrighteousness.*

HOLY GOD, have mercy upon us when Thou seest we are still often in the bondage of covetousness. We are indeed saved by the blood of our Lord, and His blood purifieth our inner life and bringeth forth fruit in our thoughts and words and deeds. Yet we must confess unto Thee that the love for earthly gain still maketh itself felt in our hearts, and often hindereth us in the pure service we should render Thee because we are Thy children, reborn by the creating grace of our Lord. We build our houses by unrighteousness. We forget the rights and the needs of our neighbor. We imagine that because we occupy higher stations we are freed from the restraints of honor and duty. We flee to Thee for refuge from the insidious love for gain and the sensuous enjoyment of wealth. Fold us deep in Thy love, and save us from our own selves and the baser nature which still holdeth us in its captivity. Make us see that whatever of earthly goods we hold in our possession by a show of right, whatever we gain by crafty dealing, whatever we withhold from Thee or from our neighbor whose need crieth out to us, is stolen property, and can not prove a blessing to us. If we are to be clean of the great transgression, Thou must utterly change our inmost nature. This Thou alone canst do. We pray Thee, work Thy saving, cleansing will within us, until we are truly righteous, through the redeeming blood of Christ. *Amen.*

AUGUST 24

Read Ephesians 4: 11-20

VERSE 14 — *That we henceforth be no more children, tossed to and fro, and carried about with every wind of doctrine.*

LORD, OUR GOD, Thou delightest in steadfastness of mind and of purpose. Thou wouldst not have us be reeds shaken by the wind, children unsteady in their steps, waverers, tossed to and fro and carried about with every wind of doctrine. Behold, the world is filled with the winds of false teaching. Men depart from Thy holy revelation as though it were fable. They heed the call of superstition and its mystifying folly, or they listen to the voices of those who call themselves scholars and scientists, but who deny the truth of Thy sacred record. In this time of many men with many minds, place our feet again upon the firm foundation of the Word. It is a blessed thing for us to be firmly grounded in the faith. Deliver us from the unhappiness of uncertainty. Grant us the nourishing power of the truth, that we may come unto the measure of the stature of the fulness of Christ, growing up into Him in all things. Preserve us from the fate of those who, having the understanding darkened, are alienated from the life in God through the ignorance that is in them because of the blindness of their hearts. Professing to be wise, they are foolish; and, forsaking the truth of Thy Word as it speaketh of Thee, they sink into lasciviousness and uncleanness and greediness. Watch with jealous eye over the rising plant of faith in our souls, shelter it from the heat and the frost, and let it, arrived at full stature, yield abundantly to Thy good pleasure, through our Lord and Savior. *Amen.*

AUGUST 25

Read Ezekiel 34: 11-22

VERSE 16 — *I will seek that which was lost, and bring again that which was driven away.*

JESUS, gentle Shepherd of our souls, watch over us and all Thy flock, for we need Thy shepherd's eye to guard us every day. The dangers come so suddenly, the storms arise when we least expect them. We go on our way rejoicing, and we think the time hath come when care and distress will no longer vex us — only to discover they are coming upon us with redoubled weight. We walk along Thy ways, and delight in the thought that now our feet have at last learned the path of peace, when presently we see we have strayed from Thee and are lost in the wilderness. Nothing can comfort us then until we hear the sound of Thy voice again, as Thou comest to seek and to save. How good it is to know Thou hast given Thy life, Thy precious sinless life, for the sheep. How blessed to know Thou art not a hireling, tending the sheep merely for sordid gain, but that Thou watchest over us and guidest us and feedest us and leadest us because Thou truly lovest us. How comforting to know Thou givest Thy precious care to every one of us; that when one lamb is missing from the fold Thou goest out to seek it and bear it back again. Let us ever seek safety in Thy fold upon the high mountain. Be specially near us in the dark and cloudy day. Safeguard us against presumptuous trifling with Thy gracious goodness. We ask it for ourselves and all other souls, for the sake of Thy suffering and death in our stead. *Amen.*

AUGUST 26

Read Luke 10: 38-42

VERSE 42 — *Mary hath chosen that good part, which shall not be taken away from her.*

ALL-WISE GOD, knowing all things, forgetting nothing in the most distant past, viewing all things in the farthest distant future, exercising unerring judgment in every crisis, always counseling and directing us surely: what unwisdom we display in the choices which it is ours to make. How few of us choose the good part. Wilt Thou not in kindness direct our minds to the loftiest things which are to be found in Jesus, our Lord? We know that every service pleaseth Him. He hath revealed to us that even a cup of water given to one of His little ones in His name is an offering which delighteth Him. Nothing which we may bring Him in our love remaineth unseen by His eyes. Yet we likewise know we should grow in our intimacy with Him, and that He desireth to lead us higher and higher in our enjoyment of Himself. Do Thou grant us wisdom always to know this is the best and highest. Lead us to understand we must seek first to let Him be our All-in-all. Take us to His feet and place us there as humble willing beneficiaries of His redeeming love. Keep ever clear in our minds that not what we may do for Him but what He hath done and still doeth for us is the source of our blessedness and the way to our acceptableness. Constrained as we are by His love to do our poor best for Him, may we always comprehend that we must not close the channels of His grace as it sendeth its refreshing streams to us. We ask this wisdom of Thee in His name. *Amen.*

AUGUST 27

Read Ephesians 4: 22-32

VERSE 30 — *Grieve not the Holy Spirit of God.*

O HOLY SPIRIT, how often we forget Thee and Thy loving ministry. Our thoughts are so deeply attached to our Savior, Christ, that we fail to remember Thee, of whom He so often spoke. Thou wast His constant Companion in His life in the visible flesh. He was anointed with Thy fulness and abundance. When He was taken from those whom He loved most dearly, He promised them, as the highest and most precious which He could impart to them, Thy coming and Thy continued presence. Have we grieved Thee by forgetting Thy love and watchful care over us? Have we grieved Thee by unfaithfulness to Him who hath sent Thee to us? Have we grieved Thee by profaning ourselves after we have become the temples in which Thou dost yearn to dwell? Thou knowest the secrets of our hearts. Thou knowest why we are weak, forgetful, sinning. We have put off the old man by Thy grace, yet he still clingeth to us and hindereth our way. Grow mightier in us, Spirit Divine. Root out the sinful inclinations and habits which have fastened themselves so strongly upon us. Drive out the spirit of untruthfulness, the spirit of vengefulness, the spirit of uncleanness, the spirit of unkindness, the unforgiving spirit. Remind us that when we entertain these evil spirits in our hearts we are grieving Thee, and that when we grieve Thee we are grieving our true Friend, our God. Help us, O Spirit of God, who livest and reignest with the Father and the Son, world without end. *Amen.*

AUGUST 28

Read First Kings 17: 10-16

VERSE 16 — *The barrel of meal wasted not, neither did the cruse of oil fail.*

FATHER, teach our hearts and lips the wondrous secret of the assurance that we have never wanted for any good thing. Thou seest how hard it is for us to look upon good things as Thou dost. We speak of want and lack and hunger and poverty, only because our hearts are set upon the wrong things. Were we minded as Thou art minded, how different our words would be. Then our funeral dirges would be transformed into songs of triumph, our tears into glistening pearls of wealth. Have patience with us and come to us again to convince our hearts Thou dost always provide that which is necessary and that which is best. Of old Thou wast Thy people's Stay in every time of need. Thy messengers, the holy prophets, trusted Thee, and never were they put to shame. Why can we not fully trust Thee? Why can we not learn to speak and deal with Thee as a friend dealeth with his friend? Surely, Thou dost possess sufficient supply for all our needs. Surely, Thou hast love for us sufficient to move Thee never to see evil come upon us. How can we ever doubt Thee? All that Thou sendest us is given in mercy. Our very griefs Thou permittest to come in order that in them we may be drawn nearer to Thee. When Thou dost pillow our heads upon stones it is that we may behold ladders reaching up to heaven and Thee. When Thou dost show us the emptiness of the barrel and the cruse, it is to make us see Thy bounty. Renew our faith, Father, through Jesus Christ. *Amen.*

AUGUST 29

Read Luke 12: 13-21

VERSE 15 — *A man's life consisteth not in the abundance of the things which he possesseth.*

DEAR LORD CHRIST, how often Thou wast tempted to regard the possessions of this world, and its power and pomp, its rank and station, its glitter and gold, above the unseen and eternal things which Thou didst bring within our reach by Thy sinless life and Thy guiltless death. It is the devil's constant purpose to draw God's children from His love by making that which is of the earth seem more delightful in their eyes than that which is of heaven. How steadfastly Thou didst set Thy face against all the appeals which Thy human nature might have made to Thee. Thou couldst not be swerved from Thy divine conviction that a man's life consisteth not in the abundance of the things which he possesseth. Thou mightest have possessed all the world instead of living the wretched life of privation. At Thy temptation in the wilderness Thou wast offered all the kingdoms on earth. The men of Thy nation came to Thee and purposed to make Thee their king. But always Thou didst set Thy face toward the higher goal. Give us this mind, dear Lord. What shame if, after Thou hast redeemed us with Thy blood, we turn to the worthless riches of earth and deny Thee! What shame if, purchased by Thy blood, we know not how to deal with the earthly goods Thou dost permit us to have in our stewardship. Let not temptation steal our hearts from Thee. We ask it of Thee, trusting only in Thy power to save us. *Amen.*

AUGUST 30

Read Philippians 4: 4-13

VERSE 13 — *I can do all things through Christ, which strengtheneth me.*

O CHRIST, Thou Lamb of God, that takest away the sins of the world, have mercy upon us in our weakness and wilfulness. Hast Thou not won for us the victory over sin and devil and death and hell? Surely, Thou wilt not let us fall by the way, but wilt give us succor in the hour of our trial and strength for every day of our pilgrimage. We need Thee, precious Jesus, for we are very poor: but strangers here, and pilgrims, we have no earthly store. We need Thy love, O Jesus, to cheer us on our way, to guide our doubting footsteps, to be our Strength and Stay. Grant us the assurance that Thy strength is at all times available to us. Save us from the folly of thinking we must rely upon our own might and wisdom. Cheer us with evidences that Thou art not far away, and that Thou art never unwilling to let us touch the hem of Thy garment and to have virtue flow from Thee unto us. Make us happy, rejoicing servants of Thy Cross, never doubting Thou art at hand, and convinced that, though a host should encamp against us, in Thee we can be confident. Possess our minds with the peace of God, which passeth understanding, and which maketh us calm and self-controlled in every crisis of our lives. Endue our souls with so rich a supply of cheerfulness and patience in Thee that, whether we abound or suffer want in bodily things, we may still pursue our way joyful and unafraid. Hear us, Lord, for we ask it in faith and trust in Thee. *Amen.*

AUGUST 31

Read Isaiah 64: 1-9

VERSE 8 — *We are the clay, and Thou our Potter; and we are all the work of Thy hand.*

OMNIPOTENT GOD, who canst create and destroy at will, who dost build mountains and cast them into the depths of the sea, who dost call worlds into existence and bid them vanish in vapor: we look up to the grandeur of Thine infinite might, and stand in awe of Thy resistless will. We are the clay, and Thou our Potter. We are all the work of Thy hand. Yet we know that, after Thou hadst created us pure and holy, without flaw or blemish, and hadst shown us every kindness which might bind us to Thee, it was not of Thee but of our own wills we turned from Thee and went the way of vanity. Then Thou mightest have destroyed us in Thy power. But Thou didst rather let mercy go before justice, and hast continued our time of grace until this present. Though all of earth's people were as unclean things, though what they called righteousness was as filthy rags, though iniquity, like stormy winds, carried men and nations away in its nadness, though Thy prophets wondered that Thou didst not rend the heavens and melt the mountains in anger because of earth's abandonment in wickedness, Thou hast been patient, and Thou wouldst, as a loving potter, mold our clay back again into an image of Thyself. When Thou didst rend the heavens, it was to send us Thy Son, to die for us. We stand in awe of Thy might, but in deeper awe at the sight of Thy love to us in Him. Thanks be to Thee for Thy marvelous gift, our Savior, Jesus, who again maketh us the work of Thy hand. *Amen.*

SEPTEMBER 1

Read First Kings 18: 30-39

VERSE 38 — *Then the fire from the Lord fell and consumed the burnt sacrifice, and the wood, and the stones.*

GREAT GOD of heaven and earth, we ask Thee to make our faith in Thee a living trust, which putteth all doubts to flight. Forbid that we should consider Thee powerless to interfere in the course of nature. Thou hast created all things which are made, and Thou hast laid down the laws by which they are governed. Thou canst with perfect ease change nature's course and suspend or annul the laws by which Thy universe doth operate. Thou art willing at any time when the honor of Thy name requireth, or when the welfare of Thy people maketh it necessary, to alter the ways of nature's working. Preserve us from becoming bound in our opinions that the things of this earth must always be governed by the same laws. Show us the reasonableness of the belief that He who established the rules by which the physical world is governed surely hath authority and power to do with them as it pleaseth Him. Prove to our minds that Thou hast not bound Thyself, and that there is no God besides Thee. Have our eyes opened to the vanity of the idols which men's minds still set upon thrones. Purge away the superstitions which cling to our nature. Send into our lives Thy holy fire, that it may destroy all that hindereth us from coming to Thee and may kindle in us a divine yearning. Warm our hearts with the miracle of all miracles, the coming of Thine eternal Son into our mortal flesh, and the working of Thy saving grace through Him. We ask it in His name. *Amen.*

SEPTEMBER 2

Read Colossians 3: 12-21

VERSE 13 — *Forbearing one another, and forgiving one another, if any man have a quarrel against any.*

LORD JESUS CHRIST, through Thee all our sin and guilt is freely forgiven. All that was needful in our perfect deliverance from the curse of sin Thou hast rendered. Without merit on our part Thou hast made Thyself the Propitiation for all our transgressions. Thou hast made the peace of God to rule in our hearts, quieting all our fears, allaying all our sorrows, assuaging all our griefs. Thou hast put psalms and hymns of happiness into our hearts and upon our lips. Can we receive the message of Thy salvation, can we accept the benefits of Thy redemption, can we enter into the enjoyment of Thy blessed companionship, and still harden our hearts against a fellow man? Oh, flood our hearts with tender mercies, kindnesses, meekness, long-suffering, forbearance, and charity, which is the bond of perfectness. May those with whom we come into contact see and feel that we are ruled by the peace of God. May our love to them be so great and true that they must comprehend that Thou dost dwell in us richly. Whatever station in life, whatever relation to one another, we may occupy, whether that of parent, or that of spouse, or that of child, help us to forbear one another and to forgive one another. Make us understand that to whatever degree we fail to live in Thy spirit, to that degree do we fail to thank Thee for Thy forbearing, forgiving love. Lord Jesus, move us to abhor unthankfulness and hypocrisy. Hear us in mercy. *Amen.*

SEPTEMBER 3

Read First Thessalonians 5: 12-24

VERSE 19 — *Quench not the Spirit.*

O HOLY SPIRIT, who hast lived and reigned with the Father and the Son from eternity, who dost come in flames of fire, who bringest light and warmth into cold human hearts, who movest among men to bring forth in them the fruits of repentance: grant that we may not oppose Thy ministration in our souls. Thou comest unto us in the Word, Thou comest very near to us in the blessed Sacrament. Deliver us from that carelessness which maketh men's hearts unresponsive to Thy gentle influences. May we be diligent and earnest in our search in the Scripture, may we be devout and eager in our approach to the Supper of the Lord. Bestow on us the mind and the will to pray without ceasing, always to bear with us a longing to be in communion with our God, always with thoughts of Him uppermost in our minds. Stimulate us to keen watchfulness, lest error, coming to us in new guise, gain an entrance. Equip us with the understanding which hath power to prove all things and to hold fast only that which is good. Teach us that peace among ourselves is needful if we would have Thy presence remain among us. As for evil, strengthen us so that we may avoid even its appearance. Sanctify us wholly. Apply the saving cleansing blood of Christ to our souls, and may we never lose its blessings. We know Thou wilt hear us, for Thou hast called us, and Thou art faithful. Accept our prayer in Jesus' name. *Amen.*

SEPTEMBER 4

Read First Kings 19: 9-18

VERSE 15 — *Go, return on thy way.*

FATHER IN HEAVEN, despite all Thy goodness and faithfulness shown unto us, we Thy children can not escape the hours when we are discouraged to the utmost. Our faith in Thee and in our mighty Savior doth waver, for we permit ourselves to lose sight of Thee. Often when Thou hast been most clearly present with us, to help and to deliver, we forget that it was not by might or wisdom of our own that we have been enabled to stand. Then cometh other danger, and we fear our own strength will not be sufficient, and forget that Thou, who hast helped us in six troubles, wilt not forsake us in the seventh. Often, too, our impatience overcometh our better judgment, and we grow discouraged because we can not wait for the slow unfolding of Thy wise purposes. We need the lessons which Thou canst teach us; we need them not once, but many times. Foster in us the will to submit all things to Thy divine direction and the disposition to be hopeful when the enemy seemeth to be gaining the victory over us. Have us remember that our resources are never exhausted. Should Satan league his forces Thy purpose to withstand, may we not think his rage and curses can stay Thy lifted hand. When Thou makest known Thy pleasure, the counsels of Thy will, that in its utmost measure wilt Thou at last fulfil. When we have fled the field in hopelessness, command us to return on our way, and, in the strength of our Savior, to carry Thy cause forward. We ask it in His name. *Amen.*

SEPTEMBER 5

Read Luke 16: 1-9

VERSE 2 — *Give an account of thy stewardship.*

LORD GOD, Thou art God, great and mighty, our Master. We are Thy servants, subjects of Thy kingdom, bond-servants in Thy household. What have we that we have not received from Thee? If we have received all our possessions from Thee, why should we glory, as though we had not received them? We brought nothing into this world, and it is certain we can carry nothing out. Thou givest us this world's good things to have and to hold while we remain in the land of the living. When we leave this earth we must leave all here below. We are but stewards, to whom Thou hast committed Thy goods in trust, and Thou dost demand of us that we deal faithfully with what is Thine. Enlighten us to know that the highest purpose for which we can employ these earthly possessions is to do our part in the great work of saving souls, of bringing to men the eternal gospel of their only Savior, our Lord Christ. We ask Thee for a sufficient portion of this world's goods. We ask Thee to keep poverty and severe want from our hearths and homes. But with the earthly goods Thou dost apportion to us give us a deep sense of our responsibility. Never forgetting Him who had not where to lay His head, may we use Thy gifts to His honor and glory. Detach our hearts from any thoughts of selfishness. Keep before us the judgment, at which we must render account unto Thee, and grant that we may be able to stand, for the sake of our Lord and Savior. *Amen.*

SEPTEMBER 6

Read Matthew 22: 2-14

VERSE 11 — *He saw there a man which had not on a wedding garment.*

RIGHTEOUS GOD, who in Thy righteousness canst not excuse our transgressions, whether it be that we have done those things which we ought not to have done, or have left undone those things which we ought to have done: we would tremble at the thought of Thy judgment if we had not Thy merciful promise that through Jesus Christ we are justified in Thy sight. May Thy boundless mercy shown to all mankind in Him not be in vain in us. Many there are who despise the righteousness Thou hast offered them, who are determined to clothe themselves in garments of their own uprightness. Thou dost provide for every guest who will attend the wedding feast of the Lamb a garment which maketh acceptable before Thee. Christ's crimson blood and righteousness our beauty are, and glorious dress. Yet this garment is an offense to some and a folly in the eyes of others. We do not chide with Thee because Thou dost demand that we must appear before Thee arrayed in Jesus' merits. We know He alone could atone for our sins, and Thou couldst not accept us if we came to Thee with our sins unatoned. Help us to bear the world's scorn as we press on our way arrayed only in Jesus' righteousness. May nothing ever move us to give this wedding garment for the robes with which others ask us to attire ourselves. We know Thou wilt receive us, however great our sins, if we come to Thee through Him. Hear us now, for we ask it relying on His love. *Amen.*

SEPTEMBER 7

Read First Kings 21:15-24

VERSE 20 — *I have found thee because thou hast sold thyself to do evil in the sight of the Lord.*

HOLY, RIGHTEOUS GOD, how often and in what various ways hast Thou endeavored to impress upon us the stern truth that the way of the transgressor is hard. We can not escape Thine all-seeing eye. Nothing is so carefully concealed that Thou dost not see it as though it were openly revealed. Do Thou clear our minds of the delusion that we can ever deceive Thee. Do Thou instruct us to know that Thou canst never look upon sin with favor, that Thou wilt surely punish iniquity, that wealth and station and power can shield no man when he hath transgressed Thy holy laws. Behold, O God, what power sin doth exercise, and with what craft and cunning it doth seek to ensnare us. Thou must be very strong in us to guard us against its lure. Always it doth promise us that in its service there is great reward. Always it doth lull us into the secure feeling that, somehow, Thou wilt not visit our sins upon us. But always Thou dost find us when we have sold ourselves unto sin. Renew a right spirit within us. May no reward seem sufficient in our eyes to cause us to barter our souls away. What doth it profit us if we gain the whole world and lose our souls? Work in us the thoughts which filled our Savior's mind when He was tempted. Keep us safe by the power of His precious blood. When we fail, grant us forgiveness for His sake. We ask it only in His all-prevailing name. *Amen.*

SEPTEMBER 8

Read Leviticus 26: 14-20

VERSE 17 — *Ye shall flee when none pursueth you.*

MERCIFUL HEAVENLY FATHER, ofttimes Thou seemest very austere to us. Thou art terrible in Thine anger, and Thy threatenings are like a roaring of the mighty storms and the breaking of many waters. Terrors and consumptions and burning agues Thou dost send upon those who will not hearken unto Thy will. Thou dost visit the land with famine, and the seed which is sown is sown in vain. Throughout the centuries Thou hast overthrown great kingdoms and humbled mighty kings. Thou hast so terrified great nations that they have fled when none pursued. Thou hast broken down the pride of the haughtiest. Thou didst not spare even Thy chosen people. Though they enjoyed Thy brightest favor for long seasons, Thy day of wrath did come and Thou didst scatter them to the four winds of the heavens. Ah, Thou art indeed terrible in Thy wrath; but only to them who will not hearken to Thy voice. Be gracious unto us, lest we be found among them that resist Thy will. Show us ever again the blindness of opposing our wills to Thine. Convince us that Thy yoke is not grievous. Make plain to us that, great as Thy wrath is against sin, Thy kindness toward sinners is equally great. Let us behold Thee as Thou hast manifested Thyself in Thy Son when He became flesh and offered Himself up for us. In Him grant us full pardon, and in Him make sin so abhorrent to us that we may always choose to follow Him in strict obedience to Thy holy will. We pray this in His name. *Amen.*

SEPTEMBER 9

Read Second Timothy 2: 11-19

VERSE 15 — *Study to show thyself approved unto God, a workman that needeth not to be ashamed.*

JESUS, we love to name Thy name. We love to call ourselves Thy followers, Thy brethren, Thy friends. No happiness is greater than that which cometh into our souls when we contemplate what Thou hast done to redeem us, and when we know Thou art indeed our Lord, that we belong to Thee, and that no man can pluck us out of Thy hand. Thou knowest them that are Thine. Ah, how intimately Thou dost know them. We feel, blessed Jesus, that all our secrets are Thine; that Thou and we are groom and bride; that Thy love and our devotion is our very life. We were dead, but now we live in Thee. Living in Thee, we desire to show ourselves approved unto God. It is our will to make Thy will our own. It is our pleasure to show ourselves workmen who need not be ashamed. Thou hast promised to give us Thy life, as a vine giveth life to its branches. Thou canst not and wilt not deny Thyself, for Thou art the faithful God. We know Thou wilt dwell in us if we remain in Thy Word, for Thou hast said if we continue in Thy Word then are we Thy disciples indeed. May we have wisdom to avoid the profane babblings of false teachers. May we store our minds with the golden treasures of Thy gospel. Then will we have Thee, and Thou wilt give us life and strength. Should faithfulness to Thee bring with it suffering and loss, we will remember that if we suffer with Thee we shall also one day reign with Thee. Accept our prayer, dear Lord, in Thy great mercy. *Amen.*

Read Second Chronicles 18: 6-17

VERSE 13 — *Even what my God saith, that will I speak.*

O THOU FAITHFUL GOD, who dost never err from the path of truth and right, it is a good thing for us to have our hearts fixed, and our souls established in the courage which cometh to those who place their confidence solely in Thee. It is a good thing for us thus courageously to be established in the truth although we know the world hateth the truth. Because our Lord loved the truth the world hated Him. Because the world hateth the truth it hateth us when we are true to Thee. We are an offense unto this world. Our conversation in Thee is a reproof unto the world in its wickedness and deceit. Often the tempter cometh to us to break down our love for truth. Grant us the wisdom to bear in mind that if we resist the devil he will flee from us. Teach us always to be brave enough to say, "What my God saith, that will I speak." Point us to the example of our Savior, who in the darkest hour of His wo spurned the tempter's enticement and was faithful unto Thee. Remind us that by His faithfulness He brought salvation unto us. The Son of God went forth to war, a kingly crown to gain — His blood-red banner streamed afar — who followeth in His train? We, O God, we follow in His train, by Thy grace; and, as we stand steadfast in every time of threat and danger, grant that we may strengthen our tempted brethren, that they too may speak only what their God saith. We beseech Thee to hear us of Thine infinite mercy. *Amen.*

SEPTEMBER 11

Read First Corinthians 13:1-13

VERSE 13 — *Now abideth faith, hope, charity, these three; but the greatest of these is charity.*

JESUS, Lover of our souls, what a blessed commandment Thou didst bring into the world, that we love one another, that we love even those who do not love us. Thou hast bidden us to love our enemies, to bless them that curse us, to do good to them that hate us, to pray for them that despitefully use us and persecute us. Thou hast revealed to us that in so doing we shall show we are children of the Father in heaven, who maketh His sun to rise on the evil and on the good and sendeth rain on the just and on the unjust. Thou dost warn us that, no matter what seeming good deeds we may perform or what seeming great sacrifices we may bring, if our deeds and sacrifices do not come from true love in our hearts, they are vain and idle. Yet, in spite of all Thy words, how often we are still loveless. We ask Thee to melt these obdurate hearts of ours and make them tender and considerate. Without Thy redeeming love we would all be lost forever. Canst Thou not so influence us that we will have compassion on our fellow men and love them more? Open our hearts to all who may need our love. Enable us to experience the joy of spending ourselves freely for the sake of others. Lead our minds away from any thought of reward for our service. Fill our world more and more with that good will which was proclaimed when Thou wast born. We ask it Lord, for Thy love's sake. *Amen.*

Read Luke 17: 11-19

VERSE 17 — *Were there not ten cleansed? But where are the nine?*

O JESUS, our loving Master, how can it be that Thy kindnesses are so often forgotten by us? We see and know Thou art the great Helper. We realize that without Thee there is no hope for us. We experience the uselessness of seeking other helpers. Yet we forget Thy loving-kindness, receive Thy blessings as though they were our due, and live as though we owed Thee naught for Thy wondrous mercy toward us. We crave Thy forbearance and pardon. Quicken in us again the sense of our dependence on Thee. Impress upon us the truth that God did not spare Thee, because He willed to spare us. Convince us of our utter unworthiness. Attune our hearts to the songs of praise and thanksgiving which the angels sing. Then make us understand that our thanks can never be acceptable unless they express themselves in deeds as well as in words. Show us our numberless opportunities to do good to others. Come to us in our home life, and move us to radiate sunshine in our own families. Make us useful members of our communities. Speed us on the way of service in Thy Church, especially in our own congregations. Out of the abundance of the heart the mouth speaketh. May our mouths speak much of Thy grace and goodness. Fill us with the missionary spirit. Let nothing daunt us when we set out to proclaim Thy mercy. Keep us in the faith, and let us one day join the jubilant throng above, where Thy praises never end, for Thy great mercy's sake. *Amen.*

SEPTEMBER 13

Read Psalm 1:1-6

VERSE 3 — *He shall be like a tree planted by the rivers of water, that bringeth forth his fruit in his season.*

FATHER ON HIGH, lift up our eyes unto Thee, away from the erring reasonings of this world and its learned men, and let us see in all its clearness and beauty the delight of owning Thee as God and Lord, and the blessedness of serving Thee with true hearts fervently. Daily we are bidden to walk in the counsel of the ungodly, and to stand in the way of sinners, and to sit in the seat of the scornful. The world into which Thou hast placed us is filled with the voices of those who proclaim the rich rewards of the service of sin. Our own eyes deceive us, for it seemeth to us that those who err and stray from Thy ways are blessed with exceedingly great treasure, while those who refuse to walk after their manner of ungodliness are forsaken and distressed. We need to have Thy Spirit show us that no true blessedness can come except by delighting in Thy law and meditating on Thy holy Word day and night. When Thou openest our understanding, we see that they who heed Thy Word are like trees planted by the rivers of water, bringing forth their fruit in their season, their leaf never withering. Despite all contrary appearances, it is what the godly man doth that prospereth. Lead us on the path of true godliness, the path of contrition and faith, the path of trust in Thy Son, Jesus Christ. When the day of judgment cometh and the wicked is driven away like chaff before the wind, grant unto us to stand in Thy judgment, through our Redeemer and Lord. *Amen.*

SEPTEMBER 14

Read Second Chronicles 20: 14-24

VERSE 15 — *The battle is not yours, but God's.*

O HOLY SPIRIT, do Thou favor us with the wisdom which showeth us that our God is mighty and merciful, and that it is He who will lead us, and carry us, and make all things work together for our good. Thou wouldst not have us be indolent, that we know right well. Many a duty Thou dost lay upon us, and Thou canst not approve us unless we are found faithful in the least and in the greatest things which Thou hast committed to our trust. When Thou givest us talents, it is that we may deal with them, and bring Thee ten-fold in return. But Thou dost never ask of us that we take upon our own shoulders the burden which resteth on God. Again and again Thou hast said to Thy people, "Ye shall not need to fight in this battle: set yourselves, stand ye still, and see the salvation of the Lord with you." Teach our minds the heavenly lesson that the battles are our God's, not our own. Persuade us to ask great things of Him, expecting great things, knowing that we dare expect infinite things of Him, for He is infinite, omnipotent, omniscient, omnipresent; and His mercy and grace are so endless that He will have pleasure in delivering His children from all their enemies. Help us realize that, if our Father could bring us salvation from the curse of sin through His Son, Jesus Christ, surely with Him He will also freely give us all things else that are needful and helpful to us. Oh, increase our faith and give us a great confidence, for Jesus' sake. *Amen.*

Read Titus 3: 3-11

VERSE 5 — *Not by works of righteousness which we have done, but according to His mercy He saved us.*

HEAVENLY FATHER, Thou hast been so good to us that Thou didst permit Thy saving grace to reach us when we were yet in our infancy. By the washing of regeneration Thou didst make us Thine own. We can remember no time in our lives when we were not with Thee. But Thy Word doth reveal unto us that we are born in sin, that we are by nature the children of wrath, resting under the curse, all of us as an unclean thing, without righteousness in Thy sight. Were it not for the saving grace which sought us in our infancy, we might be in our natural bondage under sin at this day. Help us to understand how gracious Thou hast been unto us. Especially do Thou forbid the thought to enter our hearts, that it is by works of righteousness which we have done that we are saved. The natural man receiveth not the things of Thy kingdom, for they must be spiritually discerned, and he is carnal, sold under sin. So we also would be, hadst Thou not come to us and remembered us early with Thy mercy. Maintain in us the humble spirit which recognizeth Thee as the sole Source of all our righteousness. Free us from the pride which so easily entereth the heart, the pride which is minded to persuade us that it is unmanly for us to confess our unworthiness and impotence. He that humbleth himself shall be exalted, but he that exalteth himself shall be abased. Exalt us, dear Father, by the way of humility beneath Thy merciful hand, for the sake of our Lord Jesus Christ. *Amen.*

SEPTEMBER 16

Read Psalm 115: 1-15

VERSE 3 — *Our God is in the heavens: He hath done whatsoever He hath pleased.*

O LORD, not unto us, but unto Thy name give glory, for Thy mercy, and for Thy truth's sake. Thou art in the heavens. Thou hast done whatsoever Thou hast pleased. Still Thou art enthroned on high, still dost Thou work Thy sovereign will, without let or hindrance on the part of any man, or any king, or any nation. May this faith be strong in us, and may no philosophy of men and no lust of our own flesh dislodge it from our minds. Many gods have been worshiped by men, many great ones have been trusted by men; but they have all fallen into nothingness; Thou alone remainest, ever the same, the God who art in the heavens, doing whatsoever Thou dost please to do. Thou art our Help and our Shield; Thou hast been mindful of us; Thou dost increase us more and more. Thou art the living God: all other gods are the work of men's hands, having mouths, but speechless; having eyes, but sightless; having ears, but not hearing; having hands, but working nothing; having feet, but never moving to battle or to the aid of those who trust in them. Dear Lord, as Thou hast freed us from the folly of worshiping idols made with hands, free us all the more from idols made by our own imaginations. Holding to Thee as the true God, may we not forget that the only way to Thee is through Jesus Christ, slain for us on Calvary. Be Thou our true God, Father, Son, Holy Spirit. We pray this in the Son's name. *Amen.*

SEPTEMBER 17

Read Luke 16: 19-31

VERSE 31 — *If they hear not Moses and the prophets, neither will they be persuaded, though one rose from the dead.*

SPIRIT DIVINE, attend our prayer, and make our hearts Thy home. Descend with all Thy gracious power — oh come, great Spirit, come! We know how it pleaseth Thee to make Thy way into our hearts. It is through that precious Word from God in heaven, full of blessedness, wherein by the law Thou dost bruise our hearts and by the balm of the gospel dost heal them again. O Holy Spirit, we desire so to fear and love God that we may not despise preaching and His Word, but hold it sacred and gladly hear and learn it. We know God's name is hallowed among us when the Word of God is taught in its truth and purity and we as children of God lead holy lives according to it. We know His kingdom cometh when our heavenly Father giveth Thee unto us, so that by Thy grace we believe the holy Word and lead godly lives, here in time and hereafter in eternity. Now do Thou come, Holy Spirit, come, let Thy bright beams arise. Dispel the sorrow from our minds, the darkness from our eyes; and let us fully understand that only through the Word of truth can our souls possess that which is needful to them for this life and the life beyond. Many deceivers come to us, to turn us from Thy Word. They would have us believe that voices from the dead, or that revelations from other spirits, will guide us more securely than Thy Word. Keep us steadfast by that revelation which alone bears to us the saving grace of Jesus' blood. We ask it in the name which is above every other name, the name of Jesus, the Christ. *Amen.*

SEPTEMBER 18

Read Psalm 4: 1-8

VERSE 3 — *The Lord hath set apart him that is godly for Himself.*

LORD, lift Thou up the light of Thy countenance upon us. Hear us when we call. Have mercy upon us and hear our prayer. Thou dost send us out upon ways which are beset with dangers, and among men who are ungodly. Satan and his hosts war against us, trying always to turn our glory into vanity. It enrageth him to see that Thou hast set us apart for Thyself, and that Thou hast enlarged us. He doth not stand in awe of Thee. We are mocked and scorned at every turn by him and his powers, by the world and its mighty ones. Thou who hast set us apart unto Thyself, forget us not in our trials. Grant us composure of mind and ease of conscience, so that we may both lay us down in peace and sleep, knowing that Thou makest us dwell in safety. Put gladness into our hearts, a gladness which is better than the joy of the worldling when he seemeth to prosper. Let all Thy saints in all the earth have deliverance from all their foes. Be with every struggling mind, as it laboreth its way through doubts and evil suggestions. Protect our youth in their ways, lest the enemy beguile them into unfaith. Bless the preachers of Thy Word, that they may remain brave and fearless in every time of apostasy. We have not chosen Thee, Thou hast chosen us and set us apart from the world. It is Thine to keep us and guard us. Thine is the kingdom and the power and the glory. To Thee we commit ourselves and all Thy Church fully, through Jesus Christ, our dear Lord. *Amen.*

SEPTEMBER 19

Read Second Kings 2: 9-18

VERSE 11 — *A chariot of fire, and horses of fire: and parted them both asunder.*

DEAR HEAVENLY FATHER, God of glory and splendor, enthroned in light; preserve us, in this workaday world, from losing our touch with the unseen and eternal things. We know Thou hast created us for eternal fellowship with Thee. So fervently didst Thou desire to have us with Thee, Thou didst pay the price of Thy beloved Son's life in order to win us back again to Thee. Now do Thou, through Him and by the operation of Thy Holy Spirit, protect us against the inroads of any worldliness which would tend to harden our minds and hearts and make them earthy. We know full well we have a life to lead which is here upon earth. We know full well that pure religion and undefiled bringeth us many duties which must concern us with earthly conditions. But we know as surely that Thou dost bid us hourly have our thoughts on the world and the life which are to come. It is Thy will not only after our course here on earth to translate us into that other world, but Thou wouldst have us now lift up our thoughts in daily meditation to the new heavens and the new earth. There Thou hast gathered those who put their trust in Thee. From that world Thou didst send chariot of fire and horses of fire to take home Thy servant in days gone by. Fill our minds with confidence in what Thou hast revealed of yonder world. May we not deem Thy revelations vain imaginings. It is there our Savior sitteth at Thy right hand. Take us there, for His mercy's sake. *Amen.*

SEPTEMBER 20

Read Psalm 27: 1-14

VERSE 5 — *In the time of trouble He shall hide me in His pavilion.*

ALMIGHTY GOD, what joy it is to know Thee and to feel the nearness of Thy presence as we go on through this life with its thousand dangers, its dread darknesses, its dismal disappointments, its numberless enemies. Thou art our Light in the darkness, Thou art our Salvation in danger. Thou art always faithful. Our closest friends, father and mother, may forsake us, so inconstant is human friendship; but Thou art ever with us, to take us up when others cast us aside. Thy strength is sufficient for us, though a host of enemies should encamp against us. In the time of trouble Thou wilt hide us in Thy pavilion, enfolding us in Thy love, Thy might thrown like a great wall around us. We have not deserved such grace on Thy part. We have often merited that Thou shouldst hide Thyself from us and deny us the least of all Thy blessings. Yet we come to Thee, confident Thou wilt still be with us, waiting on Thee as our Deliverer and Protector. Our greatest joy is this, that Thou canst and dost rescue us from the damnation of sin. Thou hast prepared for us a pavilion where we may seek refuge from the justice of God, which would condemn us. It is the Rock of Ages, cleft for us, Jesus Christ, Friend of sinners. One thing we desire, that will we seek after: that we may dwell under the shadow of His righteousness all the days of our lives. There and there alone can we hope to be safe. Light our path, that it may lead us to Him, that He may be our Salvation. We ask it in His name. *Amen.*

SEPTEMBER 21

Read Matthew 22: 35-46

VERSE 42 — *What think ye of Christ? Whose Son is He?*

LORD JESUS CHRIST, Thou art He who was set aside for the fall and rising again of many. Thou art the Sign which was spoken against. As touching Thee, the thoughts of many hearts will be revealed. Thou camest as a Light into the darkness, and the darkness did not comprehend Thee. Thou art in the world to-day, and the world was made by Thee, but the world knoweth Thee not. Thou hast hidden Thyself from the wise and prudent of this world, and hast revealed Thyself unto babes. We rejoice that we are of those whom Thou hast brought to a knowledge of Thyself. Thou hast touched our hearts with Thy constraining love, and we own Thy lordship over us in all things. Thou art in truth the Son of David, having in truest sense made Thyself a member of our human family. Yet hast Thou been Lord of all from all eternity, and wast David's Lord while Thou wast His Son, very God of very God, begotten of the Father from eternity. Great is the mystery of Thy person; yet we believe in Thee as the God-man. This is our faith; and we are minded to hold it firmly against all the wiles of Satan to deceive us and to lead us into misbelief, despair, and other great shame. Help us, Lord, by Thine almighty power and in Thine endless grace, to stand in our fight for our own faith and the faith of others. Make us bold witnesses of that which Thy Spirit hath witnessed in our hearts and lives. Answer our prayers above that we are able to think, for Thy great name's sake. *Amen.*

SEPTEMBER 22

Read Hebrews 10: 19-29

VERSE 23 — *Let us hold fast the profession of our faith without wavering.*

O GREAT HIGH-PRIEST, forget us not, though we have often Thee forgot, but give us strength for all the strife and all the toil and pain of life. May we in faith Thy promise hold, and never wander from Thy fold. Thou hast redeemed us with Thy blood, and washed us in the mystic flood: let not this grace be all in vain, nor let us pierce Thy side again. To Thee we humbly raise our eyes. Do not our sinful souls despise. Perfect the work Thou hast begun, and let Thy saving will be done. Thou hast given us boldness to enter the holiest place, the very presence of God. Thou hast made Thyself a new and living Way of approach unto an outraged God. Forbid, dear Lord, that we should let slip from our hold the faith which Thou hast called forth in our hearts. Forbid that we should not hold fast the profession of this our faith. Forbid that we should waver. Guard us against the insidious beginnings of doubt and unbelief. To this end teach us to provoke one another to faithfulness and good works. May we not neglect the assembling of ourselves together, as the manner of some is. Give us grace and wisdom to exhort one another. May Thy warnings against wilful sin startle us into watchfulness and prayer without ceasing. Oh, show us the horror of wilful sin, that it is as though we trod Thee under foot and accounted Thy blood an unholy thing. Hear us, and save us, Master, for we are helpless. We cry to Thee, trusting in Thy power and love to save us. *Amen.*

SEPTEMBER 23

Read Acts 16: 4-15

VERSE 10 — *After he had seen the vision, immediately we endeavored to go.*

FATHER IN HEAVEN, at the price of Thy Son's blood and life Thou hast adopted us as Thine own. Now dost Thou seek in Thy children obedience and willing service. We are slow to render Thee our whole-hearted compliance with Thy will. Where our treasure is, there our hearts are also; and too often we make the things of this world our treasure still. Teach us by the example of Thy servants in times past the secret of immediate submission to Thy commands. May we profit by the example of their ready obedience, and by the story of the blessings which rested upon them because they were subservient to Thy will and Word. Thou hast promised that Thy Spirit will guide us, and Thou hast called Thy Word spirit and truth. We know it is a safe guide in all the perplexities of our lives. To see the visions Thou wouldst in our day vouchsafe to us, we need but search the Scriptures, for in them we know we have eternal life, and they are they which testify of our Savior. Grant us to look deep into the revelations Thou hast given us in the Word, then fashion our hearts into ready obedience to all Thou requirest of us. Let us learn that our highest purpose in life must be to keep alive the knowledge of Thy Word. May we spare no cost or sacrifice to keep it in our own hearts and to bear it to others, though they may dwell in the farthest corners of the earth. Speed the day when all shall know Thee, from the least unto the greatest, for our Redeemer's sake. *Amen.*

SEPTEMBER 24

Read Second Kings 6:10-17

VERSE 17 — *The mountain was full of horses and chariots of fire round about Elisha.*

GREAT GOD, who rulest in the heavens, what endless resources Thou dost possess. Thou makest Thine angels spirits, Thy ministers a flaming fire. Thou sendest them forth to minister for them who shall be heirs of salvation. Our angels do always behold Thy face, looking to Thee for commands to bring about our greater safety and welfare. Thine angels excel in strength, doing Thy commandments and hearkening unto the voice of Thy Word. Oh, that our eyes were ever open to behold how near Thou art to us with Thy help and salvation. How many an hour of anxiety and suffering we might avoid, if we but had the sight of faith to view the nearness of Thy deliverances. What heroes we might often be, instead of timid cowards, if we but real ed that the mountains round about us are filled with the horses and chariots which gleam with Thy splendor like flames of fire. How often we might spare ourselves the desolateness of loneliness, if we could but believe that Thou with Thy heavenly hosts art never far away. Convince us more fully of our entire security when we are in Thy service. Make us unafraid to confess our faith in Jesus in the midst of those who deny His name. Embolden us to cheer others who are about to faint because of the numbers of the enemy. Give us the grace to open their eyes, directing them again to the visions Thou grantest us. We pray this, looking to Jesus, the Author and Finisher of our faith. *Amen.*

SEPTEMBER 25

Read Acts 16: 23-35

VERSE 25 — *At midnight Paul and Silas prayed and sang praises unto God.*

BLESSED JESUS, we look back into the lives of Thine apostles and stand amazed at the strength which Thou didst cause to be so mighty in their weakness. We thank Thee that Thou didst entrust Thy kingdom to men whom Thou couldst make so bold, whom no terror could frighten, whom no threat could intimidate, whom no pain could conquer. Canst Thou not permit a double portion of their spirit to come upon us? Oh, that we possessed their unyielding faith. Oh, for a faith that will not murmur nor complain beneath the chastening rod, but in the hour of grief or pain can lean upon its God; a faith that shineth bright and clear when tempests rage without, that, when in danger, knoweth no fear, in darkness feeleth no doubt; that beareth unmoved the world's dread frown, nor heedeth its scornful smile; that sin's wild ocean can not drown, nor Satan's arts beguile. Lord, give us such a faith as this; and then, whate'er may come, we'll taste e'en here the hallowed bliss of an eternal home. But ah, how far we yet are from such faith. Yet, with Thee nothing is impossible. Thou canst in Thy mercy lift us up to sublime heights of indifference to all earthly pain and danger, and of absolute trust and joy in Thee. Dear Master, pity Thy poor timorous followers. Be with us in the midnights, in the prisons, in the midst of heartless foes. Be with us as a very present help in trouble, making us certain of Thy close presence. Do this, for Thy mercy's sake. *Amen.*

SEPTEMBER 26

Read Psalm 139: 1-12

VERSE 1 — *O Lord, Thou hast searched me and known me.*

OMNISCIENT GOD, should we not live more circumspectly, knowing Thou dost search us and see our inmost thoughts? Should we so often forget that Thou knowest our downsitting and our uprising, that Thou understandest our thoughts afar off, that Thou compassest our paths and art acquainted with all our ways? Wherever we go, Thou beholdest our paths. Whatever companions we may select, Thou seest we are with them. Whatever places we visit, Thou perceivest we are there. Whatever words we speak, Thou hearest them. Whatever passions surge through our hearts, Thou takest note thereof. Whether in light or in darkness, Thou searchest us through, for before Thee the night shineth as the day, and the darkness and the light are both alike to Thee. Such knowledge is too wonderful for us. We can not comprehend how past and present and future lie before Thee like an open book. Whither shall we go from Thy Spirit, or whither shall we flee from Thy presence? Lord God, we will flee to Thy side, not away from Thee. Thou hast shown us Thy face, kindly and fatherly. We have felt the touch of Thy hand, leading us and holding us. The blood of Thy dear Son hath made a way for us to come unto Thee, weary and laden with sin, and to find forgiveness and love awaiting us. Behold the faith in our hearts, and accept us for His sake. *Amen.*

SEPTEMBER 27

Read James 3: 3-12

VERSE 8 — *The tongue can no man tame: it is an unruly evil, full of deadly poison.*

HOLY SPIRIT, Thou whose office is to regenerate and sanctify us through the cleansing blood of Jesus, what labor Thou dost find in our unruly hearts. What spirit of rebellion Thou dost discover in the gentlest of us. What long seasons of toil are required to fashion us again and to restore in us the image of God, which we so completely lost when we first transgressed God's holy command. We pray Thee not to grow weary, but to bear patiently with us. If we fail seventy times seven times every day, do Thou still remain with us. If Thou shouldst forsake us, there is no help, and we must perish in the fires we ourselves have kindled. Do Thou take control of our passions, and make them obedient to our Master, Christ. Do Thou take control of our wills, and guide them into the paths of Jesus' will. Do Thou take control of our members, and forbid that they should be made the instruments of malice or impurity or any other form of ungodliness. Do Thou rule our tongues, lest they lay snares which will prove our undoing. With them we bless our God, but with them we wish evil to our fellow men. Out of the same mouth proceedeth blessing and cursing. We know it ought not so to be. Place Thou a heavenly guard before our lips, and let no unholy thought find expression there. May we see the greatness of the destruction which one wicked word may bring to pass. We ask it for His sake who never uttered one word amiss, Jesus, our Savior. *Amen.*

SEPTEMBER 28

Read First Peter 3:8-18

VERSE 15 — *Be ready always to give an answer to every man that asketh you a reason of the hope that is in you.*

OUR FATHER, Thou who must new-create us, else we are of the kingdom of darkness: do Thou unite within our hearts the spirit of firmness and the spirit of gentleness. Make us firm in our faith. Make our belief in Jesus Christ a mighty rock, a foundation on which our hope resteth secure and untroubled. So instruct us in the wisdom of faith in the Cross, that we may be ready always to give an answer to every man that asketh a reason of the hope that is in us. Many minds come to us, some in doubt, some in scorn, to ask us why we hope in Thee. May we be ever ready to answer without reluctance and without hesitation. Lord Jesus, may Thy rich grace impart strength to the fainting heart. Our zeal inspire. As Thou hast died for us, oh, may our love to Thee pure, warm, and changeless be, a living fire. In our love and faith make us all of one mind. Make us to be pitiful and courteous in this cruel, cold, heartless world, not rendering evil for evil, or railing for railing, but, contrariwise, blessing. Make us confident no one can harm us if we are followers of that which is good. Convince us that good days can come only through our eschewing of evil and cleaving to that which is right and good in Thy sight. Help us to sanctify our God in all our conversation. Our Father, give us the inestimable blessing of a good conscience. Increase our patience when we must suffer innocently. Mature in us a likeness to our Savior. Hear us for His sake. *Amen.*

SEPTEMBER 29

Read Second Chronicles 26:14-21

Verse 16 — *When he was strong, his heart was lifted up to his destruction.*

ALMIGHTY GOD, Thou desirest to be honored by Thy creatures, the work of Thy hands. When Thou liftest man up and dost give him positions of greatness and influence, helping him marvelously, making his name great, Thou dost require that before Thee he remain humble. But our hearts are treacherous and unstable. Often, when Thou hast clothed us with honor, we deprive Thee of the glory due unto Thy name. Our hearts grow haughty and we neglect Thee, forgetting to heed Thy commands, and choosing our own ways. Protect us against the wily approach of such folly to our hearts. Teach us that, if we lift ourselves up in vanity, it is for our own destruction. Ever remind us of the impotence of human imaginations. Steady us when we rise to greater heights, lest we fall and perish. Bring Thy warnings into our consciousness before it is too late. Bless us with a more abundant portion of the spirit of Jesus, who was humble, even to the death of the cross. May we behold in His resistance to temptation a source of strength for ourselves. As we walk humbly before Thee, may we also walk humbly in the presence of our fellow men. May we not hurt them by overbearance and inconsiderateness. Give us greater faith in Thy promise that he who humbleth himself shall be exalted. Enable us to bide Thy times and seasons. Exercise us in the art of self-examination, and may our search of our own inner selves be pitiless and honest. We ask it in our Savior's name. *Amen.*

SEPTEMBER 30

Read Second Chronicles 29: 3-11

VERSE 10 — *It is in my heart to make a covenant with the Lord God.*

DEAR LORD, in Thy condescending love Thou dost invite us to come to Thee and enter with Thee into a covenant, sacred and inviolable. Thy blood is the blood of the covenant. Sprinkled therewith, we have taken upon ourselves the vows of the covenant. Thou didst put it into our hearts to enter into covenant relationship with Thee. Thou wilt uphold Thy promise, this our hearts know right well. But Thou must grant us steadfastness, that it may be in our hearts every day to keep covenant faith with Thee. Take our lives, and let them be consecrated, Lord, to Thee. Take our moments and our days, let them flow in ceaseless praise. Take our hands, and let them move at the impulse of Thy love. Take our feet, and let them be swift and beautiful for Thee. Take our voices — let us sing always only for our King. Take our lips, and let them be filled with messages for Thee. Take our silver and our gold, not a mite would we withhold. Take our intellects, and use every power as Thou shalt choose. T ke our hearts, they are Thine own, they shall be Thy royal throne. Take our love, Lord, we will pour at Thy feet its treasure store. Take our selves, and we will be ever, only, all, for Thee. Take us to-day, to-morrow, all the days of our lives. Take us for time, take us for eternity. This is the covenant we desire to make with Thee. This is the covenant we desire to keep by Thy grace. *Amen.*

OCTOBER 1

Read Acts 17: 22-32

VERSE 24 — *God dwelleth not in temples made with hands.*

O GOD, Thou art a Spirit, and they who worship Thee must worship Thee in spirit and in truth. Sin hath come over our senses and over our minds, and we feel in us the inclination to make Thee a God with whom we can deal as with our visible fellow men. Our reason, which Thou didst give us holy and sinless, striveth in its sinful condition to comprehend Thee. Our spirits, daily dealing with things of the body, strive to bring Thee down to the level of physical creation. If Thy Spirit were not our guide and strength, we would to-day be found among those who labor under the delusion that idols made by their own hands are gods, and who imagine Thou canst be confined in temples built by men's hands. Do Thou continue Thy saving grace within our hearts, and keep us from making our communion with Thee anything less than the communion of our spirits with Thee in spirit and in truth. Preserve us from formality in our religious life. Guard our church against the inroads of those religions which would rob Thy gospel of its beautiful spirit and make it only a new law. Lift us up from the plane of the baser and bodily things into the realm of spiritual contact with Thee. Make Thyself real to us, yet real not to our senses but to our souls. Thou hast made this all possible in Jesus, Thine eternal Son, who in the fulness of time became true man for us. For His blessed name's sake, grant us to live the life which He lived for us in our flesh. *Amen.*

OCTOBER 2

Read Job 41:1-10

VERSE 10 — *Who, then, is able to stand before me?*

OMNIPOTENT GOD, great and glorious Ruler over all, having dominion over every creature in the heavens and on earth and under the earth: the footsteps of Thy almighty power are visible wherever our eyes may rest. Thy path hath been marked through the trackless skies, across the huge mountains, through the mysterious depths of the oceans. How marvelous are the works of Thy hands. We stand awestruck before the grandeur of Thy creation. We join our voices with those of the angels and the morning stars, who sang Thy praises when Thou hadst brought all creatures into existence. May we bear with us constantly the conviction of Thine immeasurable power. It is good for us, as we read Thy Word, to remember it is the Word of Him who can do all things. It is good for us, as we listen to the voice of the skeptic and the doubter, the false scientists and the wrong interpreters, to recall that Thou art He with whom nothing is impossible. It is good for us, as we read the words of men who vaunt great learning, but who know not the beginning of wisdom, to remember Thou art the Maker of heaven and earth. Refresh our knowledge of Thee and Thy power. And show us that, because Thou art the Almighty, it is Thou alone who canst send the eternal Son into our flesh to be our mighty Deliverer. We pass from contemplation of Thy greatness in the kingdom of power to that of Thy greatness in the kingdom of grace, and worship Thee with deeply moved hearts, through Jesus, Thy Son, our Lord. *Amen.*

OCTOBER 3

Read Second Kings 20: 1-7

VERSE 1 — *Set thy house in order, for thou shalt die and not live.*

LORD GOD, do Thou engrave deep into our consciousness the thought that we are mortal, that we must leave this earth and this life, and that not one of us knoweth how soon the summons may come to him. We know Thou art indeed very merciful and Thou dost extend men's time of grace and opportunity; yet there is for none of us a continuing city here below. Wo unto us if death cometh and we have not set our house in order. So teach us to number our days that we may apply our hearts unto wisdom. We can not die in peace without the saving gospel of Jesus. Make it our highest concern day by day not to hinder Thy Holy Spirit as He worketh in us a stronger and purer faith in our Savior. Make us mindful, too, that faith without works is dead, and that the night cometh when no man can work. Whatever we purpose to do in thankfulness to Him must be done while it is still day for us. Do Thou make us a blessing to all with whom we come in contact. Move our hearts to go out in sympathy and helpfulness to all who suffer and are distressed, whether near or far away. Make our feet tireless on errands of kindness, make our hands generous in scattering bounty. Ward off from us the careless moments and hours in which we seem to live without purpose. Impress upon us the seriousness of every day in our lives. We ask Thee never to leave us alone to our own devices, but always to be near us, through our Lord and Savior, Jesus Christ. *Amen.*

OCTOBER 4

Read Second Peter 2:1-9

VERSE 9 — *The Lord knoweth how to deliver the godly out of temptations.*

JESUS, Thou who wast so often and so severely tempted: Thou didst teach us to pray that we be not led into temptation. Grant us the wisdom to make this our prayer earnest, and conform our wills to the words we pray. Have we not often called to Thee to deliver us from temptation, and at the same time made it easy for the tempter to overpower us? Ah, how we neglect to give ear to Thy many warnings. Ah, how we risk the welfare of our souls. Thou knowest how to deliver the godly out of temptations; but if we are not godly at heart even Thou canst not deliver us from the tempter's wiles. Make us more sincere in our profession of love for Thee and of hatred for sin. Grant us the spirit which despiseth sin in every form. Place us on guard against the efforts of the evil one to lead us into temptation. May we look for the tempter's hideous form not only where gross sin openly disporteth itself, but likewise where outward decency hideth secret wickedness beneath its fair garments. Keep us on guard against false teachers and their heresies, which lead to damnation. Frighten us by the example of those who in times past fell beneath the hand of Thine avenging justice because they refused to heed Thy warning voice. Hold us near Thy Cross, Thou wondrous Savior, who wast tempted in all points like as we are, yet didst remain without sin. It is because of Thy merits Thou canst deliver us from all temptation's destroying power. Hear us in mercy. *Amen.*

OCTOBER 5

Read Psalm 91:1-16

VERSE 5 — *Thou shalt not be afraid for the terror by night, nor for the arrow that flieth by day.*

GREAT GOD, dear heavenly Father, and Thou, beloved Christ, and Thou, almighty Spirit, who art one with the Father and the Son: what a glorious God Thou art in Thy sublime majesty, what a precious Friend Thou art in Thy gracious intimacy with us. What mercy is Thine, to prepare for us a secret hiding-place, where we may dwell in safety, where we are delivered from the snare of the fowler and from the noisome pestilence. Day by day we see men going to destruction; but, though a thousand fall at our side, and ten thousand at our right hand, we shall not be afraid for the terror by night, nor for the arrow that flieth by day, nor for the plague that walketh in darkness, nor for the destruction that wasteth at noonday. There is no harm from which Thou art not able and willing to preserve us. The most dread enemy, our own sin, Thou hast robbed of its power by the shedding of the blood of the Lamb of God without blemish. Accept our humble thanks for Thy saving mercy. Stir up our hearts, that we may make our daily lives songs of praise to Thee. As Thou hast been our Refuge and Fortress, may we lead others into the shelter of Thy pardoning love. As Thou dost give Thine angels charge over us to keep us in all our ways, do Thou make us messengers of Thy salvation unto many of our fellow men. When our end cometh, let Thy grace sustain us and bear us into the eternal place of refuge, for the sake of our Lord and Savior, Jesus Christ. *Amen.*

OCTOBER 6

Read Deuteronomy 6: 3-12

VERSE 6 — *These words, which I command thee this day, shall be in thy heart.*

HEAVENLY FATHER, Thy Word is like a garden spot, with flowers bright and fair, and every seeking one may pluck a lovely cluster there. Thy Word is like a deep, deep mine, and jewels rich and rare are hidden in its mighty depths for every searcher there. Thy Word is like a starry host: a thousand rays of light are seen to guide the traveler, and make his pathway bright. Thy Word is like an armory where soldiers may repair and find, for life's long battle-day, all needful weapons there. Oh, may we love Thy precious Word. May we explore the mine. May we its fragrant flowers glean. May its light upon us shine. Oh, may we find our armor there, Thy Word our trusty sword. We'll learn to fight with every foe the battle of the Lord. We know, heavenly Father, nothing delighteth Thee more than to have us come unto Thy Word and find in it all we need for this life and for the life to come. Thou wouldst have us bear Thy Word always in our hearts. Thou wouldst have us teach it unto our children. When we lie down and when we rise up, Thou wouldst have our last thoughts and our first to be of Thy Word. How precious Thou hast made this Word, by making Jesus Christ its very Heart and Soul. It is because of Him it hath its wondrous charm and power, Thy power unto salvation to every one that believeth. Let us be always wise, seeing the beauty of Thy Word, feeling its power, and holding it very close to our hearts in life and in death. We ask it for Jesus' sake. *Amen.*

OCTOBER 7

Read John 2: 1-11

VERSE 5 — *Whatsoever He saith unto you, do it.*

LORD JESUS, Thou knowest the secret of happiness is obedience, and Thou knowest the secret of obedience toward God is the merging of one's will with the will of God. Thou didst come into the world to do Thy Father's will. Whatsoever He willed Thou didst will. Now wouldst Thou teach us the lesson of obedience, ready, cheerful, entire obedience. Whatsoever Thou sayest, that we, as Thy followers, must do, without questioning why or wherefore, without delay, without arguing it might be done otherwise. If we are truly Thine, we can not question. If we truly trust Thee, we can not desire to interpose our own wisdom instead of Thine. If we are truly consecrated to Thee, we can not select our own times for the performance of that which Thou wouldst have us do. Grant us so intimate a relation with Thyself that our obedience can not but follow. In every crisis of our affairs, may our first question be what Thy will saith. When compliance with Thy will seemeth to expose us to the scoffing of the world, grant us composure to bear its ridicule. When compliance seemeth to require that we deny our own power to reason, grant us courage to lay a strong hand on our pride in our own knowledge. When submission to Thy desires seemeth to bring upon us earthly loss and suffering, grant us the vision which looketh through things as they appear and seeth them as they are. Ever make us able to do Thy bidding, for Thy dear name's sake. *Amen.*

OCTOBER 8

Read First John 3: 13-18

VERSE 16 — *We ought to lay down our lives for the brethren.*

GOD, OUR CREATOR, who hast given us this life, and with this life the desire to preserve our lives: grant that our love of life may never be so strong that it maketh our lives worthless. We know from the teachings of Thy Word and of the example of our Lord Jesus Christ, if we love life more than we love Thee, we are unworthy of Thee. We know, if we love life more than the truth and purity and charity which Thou seekest in us, we are not living aright. We do not know whether it may happen that Thou wilt require our death as a service to Thee and to our fellow men; but, O God, if this should be, we ask Thee now to instil into our souls the sublime godliness which maketh submission to Thee seem dearer and more delightful than life itself. This one thing Thou dost desire of us, that we love Thee above all else, and that we love each other as we love ourselves. Thou wouldst have us love even unto the sacrifice of life, as Thy Son loved us and gave His life a ransom for us all. How this world needeth love! How this world needeth our love! Thou wouldst have us love, even though we are hated. Come to us with the full power of Jesus' love and fashion us into the image of His selflessness. Through Him we have passed from death unto life; but, if we do not love, our life is nothing. Enrich us with Jesus' salvation, unto the forgiveness of all our sins and unto the giving of ourselves for others. We pray this in His name alone. *Amen.*

OCTOBER 9

Read Isaiah 37: 33-38

VERSE 35 — *I will defend this city, to save it for mine own sake, and for my servant David's sake.*

MIGHTY GOD OF HEAVEN, Defender of Thy people, Deliverer of the oppressed, Helper of the needy: except Thou keep the city and the land, the watchman watcheth in vain. We look back through the story of the nations, and see Thy finger tracing their rise, their prosperity, their doom, their fall, their ruin. Thou who dost mark the sparrow's fall art not far away when a mighty nation trembleth and staggereth and falleth. Thou who dost number the hairs of our heads, though we be the least of the great family of men, art not far away when mighty deliverances come to city and state. Oh, teach us through the lessons of the past; and, as we strive to build a world which may enjoy Thy favor, let us heed the voice of Thy warnings as they come to us from the story of days gone by. Not armies nor navies nor squadrons in the skies can safeguard ; if Thy hand is against us. No foe, however numerous and powerful, can harm us if Thou art with us to do battle with our forces. Fill our land with souls who trust Thee to the utmost. Govern our citizenship so that we may be led by men who have placed the fear of Thee foremost in their lives. Should wickedness grow bolder, grant that there may always be found among us enough of Thy faithful followers to move Thee to spare our land for their sakes. To this end glorify the name of Jesus in our nation. Oppose the plan and power of those who would rob Him of His kingship. We offer Thee our prayer in His name. *Amen.*

OCTOBER 10

Read Ephesians 6: 10-18

VERSE 13 — *Take unto you the whole armor of God, that ye may be able to withstand in the evil day.*

O CHRIST, who hast come to earth not to bring peace but a sword: Thou hast placed the sword of Thy truth into our hands. Redeemed by Thy blood, we have been brought to Thee and made soldiers of Thy Cross. We know we have vast hosts opposed to us, not flesh and blood, but principalities and powers, and the rulers of the darkness of this world, and spiritual wickedness in high places. If we are to stand in the evil day we shall need the whole armor which Thou canst give us. Preserve us from the folly of attempting the battle without Thee and Thine armor. Gird Thy gospel truth firmly upon our hearts, and the breastplate of Thy righteousness. Place upon us the helmet of that salvation which is by Thy blood and death. Place into our hands the shield of faith, wherewith we may be able to ward off the fiery darts of the devil; and the sword of the Spirit, the immutable, unconquerable Word. Make us strong, strong in faith, strong in purpose, strong in patience, strong in endurance. Forbid that we should be content when we have won the battle for ourselves. As our brothers' keepers, move us to continue in the battle for their sakes. Fortify us against the enemy's surprises. Put us ever on watchful guard. May we not, after we have gained victories over gross sins, fall a prey to the finer forms of wickedness. Grant us complete victory over sin in every guise, for Thy mighty name's sake. *Amen.*

OCTOBER 11

Read John 3: 1-12

VERSE 3 — *Except a man be born again, he can not see the kingdom of God.*

O HOLY SPIRIT, Thou art the Spirit of truth and purity. Thou dost work in our hearts in order to bring forth in them the growth of true Christian faith and the fruits of an abiding Christian life. Often we hinder Thee in Thy divine operation. Our worldliness is unwilling to have its reign in us interrupted. Our shallowness in unwilling to be disturbed by the plow-share of the law, with which Thou wouldst go deep beneath the surface. Anxious and watchful as we are in our earthly concerns, we are thoughtless and care-free in our spiritual concerns. Thou wouldst regenerate us through and through, our intellects, our feelings, our wills. Thou wouldst not leave one power within as untouched when Thou dost come to lead us to faith in our Lord and Savior. Thou wouldst work a total change in us, a new birth. Grant that we may not prevent Thy blessed work in our behalf. Come Thou, and have Thy will with us. Make us wholly new, in mind, in heart, in soul, in life. Drive out the old distrust, the old self-reliance, the old self-conceit. Produce in us a faith which doth surrender us unresignedly into the arms of our Savior. Plant and foster in us the seeds of a life so new that all our thoughts and words and acts may prove we have passed from darkness into light, from ignorance into wisdom, from death into life. We ask it all because Thou art sent by our Lord Jesus Christ. *Amen.*

OCTOBER 12

Read Psalm 14: 1-7

VERSE 1 — *The fool hath said in his heart, "There is no God."*

O GOD, the Father in heaven, we shudder at the thought that we might one time deny Thee. We have those among us who say there is no God. Enjoying the bounties of Thy universe, hearing the speech of the passing days and the knowledge of the succeeding nights, they close both eyes and ears and refuse to acknowledge Thee. Breathing the air Thou createst, they breathe forth defiance of Thy power. Truly, they have gone aside, they have erred, they have fallen into the arms of folly unspeakable. Only the fool can say Thou dost not exist. We bless Thee for instructing us in true wisdom. We know that Thou art, and that Thou art eternal and almighty, all-wise and everywhere present, holy and righteous, merciful and truthful. We know Thou art triune, Father, Son, and Holy Spirit, one God in three persons, indivisible and immutable. We know Thou hast created all things which are made, Thou hast redeemed us through the blood of the Son, Thou dost work in our hearts for our sanctification. We know Thou, Lord Jesus, wilt one day come to receive us all unto Thyself. Lord God, will we persevere in this faith? Thou alone canst bring it to pass. We are dependent wholly on Thy mercy. Guard us against the beginnings of doubt in our hearts. Purify our faith, lest it be a faith of the lips only. Be faithful unto us until our end, and make us faithful unto Thee, for the sake of our Redeemer, Jesus Christ. *Amen.*

OCTOBER 13

Read First John 4: 9-21

VERSE 18 — *There is no fear in love, but perfect love casteth out fear.*

GOD OF LOVE, we desire to love Thee truly, fervently, steadfastly. Thou hast breathed upon our loveless hearts and hast kindled in them the flames of divine love. We love Thee, our Father, who hast made us and all other creatures. We love Thee, O Christ, who hast redeemed us from sin and death, and purchased us free from the power of all evil. We love Thee, O Holy Spirit, who dost come so intimately into our souls and dost sit down with us and sup with us, bringing us the Father's love and the Son's salvation. We love Thee for all Thy loving-kindness. But our love is mixed with impurity. There is fear in our love, and we know perfect love must cast out all fear. In our love there is a desire for the things which are seen, and we know that no man hath seen God at any time. Be patient with us, and labor in us toward the purifying and cleansing of our imperfect love. Banish from our minds the sophistry that we can love Thee while yet we fail to love our fellow men. May our love not come grudgingly, from compulsion, but let us rejoice in its exercise. Move our love to go forth and relieve the sorrow and suffering of others. Let love flourish in our own households. Bless and brighten the love of husband and wife, of parent and child, of sister and brother. Let Thy Church be one fellowship of mutual love. Grant that love may more and more control the hearts of men in this world. We ask it for Jesus' sake, who loved us unto His death. *Amen.*

OCTOBER 14

Read Luke 18:9-14

VERSE 14 — *This man went down to his house justified rather than the other.*

HOLY AND RIGHTEOUS GOD, who art worthy to be adored and worshiped, to be feared and served, by all men: keep Thou our feet when we approach Thy throne with our petitions. We have not because we ask not; and often, when we ask, we have not because we ask amiss. How it doth offend Thee when we, laden with sin and bent upon iniquity, come before Thee pleading our own righteousness and worthiness. How we do err when we come before Thy presence with thoughts of our own goodness. What ignorance on our part, when we compare the poor deeds of our morality with the strict standard of Thine eternal uprightness. What ingratitude on our part, when we come to Thee to point our fingers in lofty superiority at other men, of whom we judge they are wicked while we are perfect. What will all our self-sufficiency profit us when it is Thou who must justify, and when we know Thou findest no pleasure in our pretended goodness? No man can come to Thee except through the righteousness which our Savior hath won for us. No man can stand in Thy presence except he come humbly confessing his own insufficiency and pleading the merits of Thy Son. Speak to these stubborn hearts in us and break their trust in self. Speak to these loveless breasts and soften them into considerateness for our brethren. So let us come into Thy presence, with hearts bowed down with the weight of our own sins, with hearts yearning for the welfare of others. We ask it in our Savior's name. *Amen.*

OCTOBER 15

Read Second Chronicles 33: 11-16

VERSE 12 — *When he was in affliction, he besought the Lord, his God, and humbled himself greatly.*

LORD GOD, if Thou canst not humble us except Thou send us grievous affliction, spare not, but cover us with stripes and weigh us down with a load of misery and wretchedness. Thou knowest our frame, Thou knowest the imaginations of our hearts. They are evil from our youth. We need Thy correcting hand laid heavy upon us from our earliest infancy. No one can bring us to ourselves as Thou canst. Oh, keep us from straying; but, if we should leave Thy side and spend our substance with the world and the flesh, humble us under Thine almighty hand, and grant us grace and a day of acceptance in which we may beseech Thee for forgiveness and may humble ourselves unto our own salvation. Should the possession of money and goods lead us from simple faith in Jesus, humble us by sending loss and poverty. Should ambition and success in seeking earthly station make our hearts grow godless, humble us by sending failure and disappointments. Should discouragement and untoward circumstance rouse us to murmur and rebel against Thee, humble us by sending us into the valley of tears and loneliness. But ever, if Thou must deal severely with us, be merciful, and work in us by Thy Spirit, lest we be hardened and abandon ourselves utterly to despair. Show us Thy kindness, and lead us back to fellowship with Thee and the joy of serving Thee in humble submission. Hear us for our Savior's sake. *Amen.*

OCTOBER 16

Read Psalm 145: 8-21

VERSE 17 — *The Lord is righteous in all His ways, and holy in all His works.*

RIGHTEOUS LORD, we need Thine assurance that Thou art righteous in all Thy ways and holy in all Thy works. Our blunted sinful minds tempt us to believe Thou often dealest with us unrighteously. Thou seemest to bless the wicked above the godly. Thou sendest us sickness, while our neighbor hath good health. Thou multipliest the money and the store of our neighbor, while we, with toil more faithful and methods more honest, lag in the race and eat the bread of sorrows. Often, when we have endeavored most earnestly to serve Thee, Thou permittest loss and distress to visit us. Often, when we have prayed most earnestly, Thou failest to give us that for which we have cried unto Thee. Verily, we need Thine assurance that Thou art holy in all Thy works. Lay Thy restraining hand upon our hasty impulses and make us pause. Give us wisdom to consider that Thy thoughts are not our thoughts, and that Thou often hast purposes in view of which we are ignorant. Remind us that whenever we choose our own ways we fall into misfortune. Point us to Thy grace and long-suffering. Thou art nigh unto all that call upon Thee, even when Thou seemest to be distant. Thou art good unto us. Thou upholdest us when we fall. Have us remember we are to walk by faith and not by sight. If Thou didst not love us, if Thou wert not seeking our welfare, wouldst Thou have offered Thine only-begotten Son? Help us bear our crosses in the strength of His name. *Amen.*

OCTOBER 17

Read John 3: 25-36

VERSE 30 — *He must increase, but I must decrease.*

HOLY SPIRIT, one with the Father and the Son in the eternal Godhead, pour Thyself into our hearts as Thou didst anoint the hearts of holy men of old. We do not ask Thee for the wonder-working powers they possessed. We do not ask Thee for the gift of tongues and of healing, for power to change the course of nature. Only, do Thou give Thyself to us abundantly, transforming our hearts into the likeness of Jesus, and emboldening us to fight the good fight of faith and in the end to lay hold on life eternal. Make us conquerors over ourselves. Let the strength of Christ increase in us, as the strength of the old man decreaseth. Let our confidence in Him grow daily, let our trust in our own powers daily disappear the more. Let the love of our Savior possess us so mightily that our love of self may vanish. Let our attachment to His Word become closer, while our attachment to the wisdom of the world groweth less and less. Let our delight in His service become the highest fascination to our hearts, while our pleasure in the joys of the flesh and the world fadeth away. If we are truly His, He must increase, we must decrease. Do Thou further and foster the good work in us, until we have grown to the perfect stature of manhood in Him; and let our advance in His favor incite those who behold us to follow Him and to receive from Him strength for strength. Hear us for His sake. *Amen.*

OCTOBER 18

Read Romans 8: 24-31

VERSE 28 — *We know that all things work together for good to them that love God.*

GRACIOUS FATHER IN HEAVEN, Thou hast all things in Thy power. No creature can withstand Thee. Throughout this universe Thou dost bend all to Thy will and compel them to accomplish Thy purposes. The creatures that serve Thee are a numberless host, as the sands of the sea, and the stars of the skies. Now Thou dost assure us they must all work together for our good if we love Thee. To what heights hast Thou exalted us, that all is made to serve the purposes of Thy love toward us. Truly, we are unworthy of the least of all Thy mercies and loving-kindnesses; yet Thou dost continue them to us every day. Nor can we doubt Thou speakest truth in this Thy promise; for, if Thou didst not spare Thy Son, but didst give Him into death for us, wilt Thou withhold any good thing from us? Wilt Thou not rather in Him freely give us all needful things? Verily, we dare not doubt or distrust Thee. Oh, make us joyful in the contemplation and possession of Thy goodness. Make us very penitent of our every sin. Make us very humble before Thee. Make us very anxious lest we offend Thee by thought, word, or deed. Make us very fearful lest we withhold from Thee the gifts which we know we owe Thee. Make us supremely defiant of all that any enemy may attempt against us. Make us immovably hopeful of what eternity holdeth in store for us. Keep us with Jesus in the true faith, for His blessed name's sake. *Amen.*

OCTOBER 19

Read Mark 13: 28-37

VERSE 31 — *Heaven and earth shall pass away, but my words shall not pass away.*

ETERNAL GOD, Thy Word is eternal. It shall not pass away. Countless minds have arrayed themselves against Thy truth, but today it standeth fast, while they have been swept away, and the place that once knew them knoweth them no longer. We look about us upon the changeableness of all earthly things, upon the unfaithfulness of friends, upon the uncertainty of our own lives, and we bless Thy great name for giving us that which can not pass away. We look into the future, and we see approaching the great day when heaven and earth will pass away, when all this ordered creation will again lapse into chaos, and again we thank Thee that Thou hast given us Thy Word, which will outlast both heaven and earth. With Thy Word as our treasure, we can look forward to the day of judgment without dismay. We do not ask Thee to reveal to us the day or the hour when the end of all things will be. We do not need to know. We have Thy Word, and it sufficeth us. With this Word as a lamp unto our feet and a light unto our paths we will watch and pray. In this Thy Word we have found Him of whom the prophets spoke, Jesus, our Guide through all the terrors of judgment. He will guide, He will guard, He will protect till our journey shall end. He hath power to forgive all our sins, and to make us acceptable in Thy sight even on that great day. Be merciful to us, for we plead His wounds and blood and death, His perfect righteousness. *Amen.*

OCTOBER 20

Read Romans 8: 32-39

VERSE 35 — *Who shall separate us from the love of Christ?*

CHRIST JESUS, dear Lord and Savior, wilt Thou always be ours? Other friends prove faithless. When dark days come into our lives and we look to earthly friends for cheer and help, we often find they have forsaken us. Wilt Thou remain true to us? We know Thou wilt. Nothing can separate us from Thy love. Jesus, Thou art ours forever, dearer far than earth can be: neither life nor death can sever those sweet ties that bind to Thee. Thou alone art all our treasure, who hast died that we might live. Thou conferrest noblest pleasure, who dost all our sins forgive. Jesus, Thou art ours forever, let us never from Thee stray, let us in our weakness never cast our priceless Pearl away. Lamb of God, we do implore Thee, guard, support us, lest we fall. Let us evermore adore Thee. Be our everlasting All. Only we ourselves can separate ourselves from Thee by our own unfaithfulness. Tribulation, persecution, distress, famine, nakedness, peril, sword — all are powerless to come between Thee and us if we will only let Thee hold us fast. We are persuaded Thou wilt preserve us steadfast; and if we remain in Thee, none can lay anything to our charge, none can condemn us, none can banish us from our heavenly Father's presence. Even death can not dissolve the tie which bindeth us to Thee, for Thou hast conquered death and every other foe, and in Thy grace we shall be more than conquerors in every battle of life. Lord, keep us in Thy faith. *Amen.*

OCTOBER 21

Read Proverbs 1: 7-19

VERSE 10 — *If sinners entice thee, consent thou not.*

KIND HEAVENLY FATHER, Thou watchest over us with the tenderness of a true father. Thou understandest all our weaknesses, and Thou knowest the cunning and the attack of our enemies. We would long since have fallen a prey to their might if Thou hadst not kept guard over us. We ask Thee not to forget or forsake us, for our need groweth with each new day. Sinners all about entice us, desiring to lead us away from Thee and Thy paths of uprightness into their slippery ways of dishonor and uncleanness. Strengthen Thou our purpose not to yield to their enticements. Give us the firmness of Jesus, who remained faithful in all the attempts of the wicked one to mislead Him. Bring under our control that ally of the world, our own flesh. Prevent it from becoming the occasion of our defeat. Preserve us from the influence of godless companions. Should we be joined to such by ties of relationship or business, make us courageous enough to resist their sinful examples. Preserve us from the foul influence of unbelieving literature. The mind of Satan, who is a liar from the beginning, lurketh in many a page of that which is given us to read. Fortify us against his most insidious attacks. Forbid that we should ever sell ourselves at any price into wrong-doing. May we through our example be able to save others from the evil influence of sinners. Hear us for Jesus' sake. *Amen.*

OCTOBER 22

Read John 4: 31-38

VERSE 34 — *My meat is to do the will of Him that sent me, and to finish His work.*

DEAR LORD GOD, who didst fashion our bodies of the dust of the ground, and didst breathe into us, so that we became living souls: cure us of the folly of considering our bodies greater than our souls. What care we bestow upon the mortal bodies we bear about with us, clothing them, feeding them, providing them with every necessity and with many a luxury. Meantime our souls often suffer neglect. Starved and shriveled, they cry out for nourishment. Thou dost not withhold it. Thou hast made it possible for our souls to eat and drink, and to go in the strength of that which Thou providest on all the journeys of life. But ah, how neglectful we are. Instruct us in the things which pertain to our souls' welfare, lest our souls die, and we perish eternally. Teach us to strive for the meat which perisheth not, and for the water which, if we drink it, will so satisfy us that we shall never thirst again. May our meat and drink be to conform our faith and life unto Thy holy will. Thou hast placed within our reach the richest treasures of Thine infinite bounty. Thou didst send Thy Son, whose flesh is meat indeed, and whose blood is drink indeed, for our weary hearts. Grant that we may taste and see how good He is. Deprive us not, on account of our neglect, of the needful things for our souls' welfare. Thy will is that every one that seeth the Son believe on Him and have everlasting life. Let this Thy will be done in us, for His dear sake. *Amen.*

OCTOBER 23

Read Ecclesiastes 11: 1-6

VERSE 1 — *Cast thy bread upon the waters, for thou shalt find it after many days.*

MERCIFUL FATHER IN HEAVEN, how slow we are to commit the keeping of ourselves and our affairs to Thy hands. What couldst Thou do more than Thou hast done, to make us understand we may safely trust Thee, leaving all things to Thy discretion? What further proof do we need than our past experiences to make us comprehend that our own thoughts lead only to disappointment? Oh, that we might more closely walk with Thee, receiving of Thy Spirit, breathing the atmosphere of Thy presence. Then would we more readily make of our lives the full surrender to Thy will which alone can lift us into the sphere in which lieth our glory. Come to us again, and draw us to Thyself by the power of Thy love. Remove the anxious cares from our minds. Enable us to cast our bread upon the waters, fully trusting Thee, and believing we shall find it after many days. Drive out the fears which prevent us from sharing with our needy brothers. Help us to view the future with Thine eyes, all its prospects, all its threatening dangers. Increase our reliance upon Thy many promises. Comfort us with the thought that Thou wilt prosper our ways even though we must come to Thee again and again to confess we have sinned against Thee. Convince us that we can never fully trust Thee for earthly gifts unless our consciences rest easy in the knowledge of the forgiveness of all our sins; and show us that the blood of Christ hath merited our full pardon. Hear us for His sake. *Amen.*

OCTOBER 24

Read Daniel 1: 8-19

VERSE 8 — *Daniel purposed in his heart that he would not defile himself.*

O HOLY GOD, who art perfect in purity and righteousness: behold how the power of sin worketh in us, inclining us to defile ourselves again and again. How can we ever trifle with evil? Only because sin hath robbed us of our wisdom, darkened our understanding, corrupted our desires, and perverted our wills. What wonder that Thou canst not look upon a single sin with tolerance, seeing it hath prostituted Thy children in such degradation. Be near us, O God, as we live our lives in this sin-ridden world. Hear our cry as we confess our misery unto Thee. But behold, Thou hast heard the cry of our wretchedness. Thou hast sent deliverance. Thou hast made a way for our escape. Thou hast given us help in Jesus. Thou canst justly command us to overcome all sin and to stan ', for Thou hast given us power through Him. May we purpose in our hearts that we will not defile ourselves with sin. We know that in weakness we shall still do things which we ought not to do and leave undone things which we ought to do; but in wilfulness we will no more defile ourselves, for we are Thine, bought by the blood of Jesus. Embolden us in this our resolve. Make us eager for the fight of uprightness. Influence us so that we will detest all impurity and wickedness in every form. So fill us with the good Spirit that wrong will find no room within us. Give us the pure mind of our Savior, for His holy name's sake. *Amen.*

OCTOBER 25

Read First Corinthians 10: 1-12

VERSE 12 — *Let him that thinketh he standeth take heed lest he fall.*

GOD IN HEAVEN, Thine is the kingdom and the power and the glory forever and ever — not ours, only Thine. Thou rulest, we are Thy subjects. Thou art the Almighty, we are frail children of dust. Thou hast eternal glory, unto us belongeth confusion of faces. Yet with each insignificant evidence of goodness in our lives we are ready to lift up our hearts in vainglory. Make us know that when we display unholy pride we give proof that there is nothing good in us. Rule our hearts so that we will give Thee the honor and praise for whatever good is engendered in our souls. Write deep upon our memories' tablets the warning, "Let him that thinketh he standeth take heed lest he fall." Recall to our minds the millions who, by lifting up their hearts in pride and self-sufficiency, have paved their way to destruction. Cleanse us of all hurtful conceits. Order our ways so that our steps will lead often to the cross on which our Savior died. Let us draw true strength from His bleeding wounds. As His cross towereth over the wrecks of time, may our only glory be in it and in Him who died thereon. Glorying in Him, we shall never fall. Glorying in Him, we shall praise Thee and become acceptable in Thy sight. Glorying in Him, we shall bring to our fellow men a blessing, and not the bane which followeth in the footsteps of those who grow proud in their own conceits. Help us to stand in our faith. We beseech Thee to hear us for Christ's sake. *Amen.*

OCTOBER 26

Read Proverbs 3: 11-24

VERSE 11 — *Despise not the chastening of the Lord, neither be weary of His correction.*

OUR FATHER, do Thou deal gently with us, because we are frail and inclined to err, and of Thy mercy there is no end. We have sinned against Thee, not only by outward and gross sins, but by inward blindness, wilfulness, anxiety, doubt, and other thoughts and feelings of our disobedient natures. We have deserved to be utterly cast away from Thy presence, into outer darkness, where there is weeping and gnashing of teeth. We throw ourselves upon Thy mercy, as Thou hast bidden us to do. We know Thou wilt receive us, we know Thou hast received us. Thou callest us Thy children, by faith in Jesus, our Lord. Yet we know that so much of our old nature still liveth in our flesh that Thou must chasten us, often and sorely. Bestow upon us so abundant a portion of Thy grace that we may never despise Thy chastening, nor be weary of Thy correction. **Thou correctest us only because Thou lovest us.** Truly, if we were not precious in Thy sight, why wouldst Thou labor and toil with us? We need Thy corrections and chastenings. Temper all our visitations with Thy mercy. Transform our misfortunes into fortune. In all the trials Thou bringest upon us, we will confide in Thy goodness. Thou wilt our souls deliver from deeps of troubled thought. Our graces wilt Thou nourish, with hope our hearts employ, till faith and hope shall flourish and yield their fruits of joy. Increase our trust, for our Savior's sake. *Amen.*

OCTOBER 27

Read Psalm 32: 1-11

VERSE 2 — *Blessed is the man unto whom the Lord imputeth not iniquity.*

OUR FATHER IN HEAVEN, we pray Thee to continue in us Thy saving work, until Thou hast broken down every resistance of our natural self against Thee. Though we have experienced the blessedness of Thy pardoning grace, we still are apt to forget, and to seek happiness and peace elsewhere. There come times when, instead of freely confessing our transgressions and casting ourselves upon Thy mercy, we keep silence, and purpose to stand in our own righteousness. Our hearts are very treacherous, and we need Thy constant guardianship to keep us from our own undoing. Blessed are we in having Thee as our God, who art so plenteous in mercy and loving-kindness. We know Thou forgivest our transgressions and coverest our sins. Thou imputest not our iniquity unto us, but imputest the perfect righteousness of Jesus Christ unto us all when we believe in Him. Only when we are unrepentant is Thy hand heavy upon us. May the Holy Spirit break down in us the pride which causeth us to oppose His gracious work. Do Thou not leave us to perish in our own folly. Make us pitiless in our self-examination, and forbid that we should try to conceal one sin from Thee. Bring forth in us so thorough a contrition that we will humble ourselves entirely under Thy correcting hand. Then, according to Thy promise, as we have often experienced, we will feel the blessedness which bringeth peace and comfort to the soul. Hear us for Jesus' sake. *Amen.*

OCTOBER 28

Read John 6: 60-71

VERSE 68 — *Lord, to whom shall we go? Thou hast the words of eternal life.*

JESUS, and shall it ever be, a mortal man ashamed of Thee, ashamed of Thee, whom angels praise, whose glories shine through endless days? Ashamed of Thee, our dearest Friend, on whom our hopes of heaven depend? Nay — when we blush, be this our shame, that **we no more revere Thy** name. Ashamed of Thee? Ah, yes, we may, when we've no guilt to wash away, no tears to wipe, no good to crave, no fears to quell, no souls to save. Dear Master, **many are going back** from following after Thee. Thy words have offended them. Their lofty spirits can not brook Thy message, that we must trust wholly in Thy redeeming blood. They can not bow their knees in repentance before Thee. They can not accept Thy words, that we must through much tribulation enter into the kingdom of heaven. But we have seen and believed that Thou art the Christ, the Son of the living God. There is none other to whom we care to go. Thou hast the words of eternal life. We will remain true to Thee, and follow Thee ever. Jesus, still lead on, till our rest be won; and, although the way be cheerless, we will follow, calm and fearless. Guide us by **Thy hand to our** fatherland. Jesus, still lead on, till our rest be won. Heavenly Leader, still direct us, still console, support, protect us, till we safely stand in our fatherland. There we will evermore praise Thee for Thy wondrous works in our behalf, for the way Thou didst lead us, for keeping us faithful unto the end. Accept this prayer for Thy mercy's sake. *Amen.*

OCTOBER 29

Read Second Corinthians 9: 6-15

VERSE 6 — *He which soweth bountifully shall reap also bountifully.*

GOD, Thou Lover of cheerful givers, why do we yet so grudgingly give unto Thee and for the welfare of those whom Thou hast committed to our trust? Thou hast shown us that we in this world are all, every man to every other man, neighbors. Thou hast made us all of one blood, whatever our clime or color may be. Thou dost place others in this same world with us in order that we may have opportunity to serve Thee in them. Thou dost make this world a field in which Thou desirest that we sow bountifully, and Thou hast promised, if we sow bountifully, we shall also reap bountifully. Soften our hearts into truer liberality. We give Thee but Thine own, whate'er the gifts may be. All that we have is Thine alone, a trust, O Lord, from Thee. May we Thy bounties thus, as stewards true, receive; and gladly, as Thou blessest us, to Thee our first-fruits give. What regret cometh into our hearts whenever we ourselves reap sparingly. Have us understand that it is because we have sown sparingly. What if Thou, Lord Jesus, hadst given grudgingly or sparingly? What if Thy blood had not flowed for our redemption? How unworthy we are of Thy name when we reluctantly give for Thy kingdom's sake and the relief of our suffering brethren. Open our hearts and our hands. Let Thy Church never lack the means wherewith to carry forward its work. May we never be of those who must be urged before they give. We ask it for Thy Name's sake. *Amen.*

OCTOBER 30

Read John 7: 40-53

VERSE 46 — *Never man spake like this Man.*

LORD CHRIST, Thou didst speak wonderful words when Thou didst company with men in the days of Thy visible presence on earth. Thou didst teach as one having authority. Thy words were spirit and life. Never man spoke as Thou didst speak. Thou didst hide the mysteries of the Kingdom from those who prized too highly the wisdom and prudence of this world; but Thou didst reveal them unto those who were but babes in the world's estimation. No one can speak to sinners as Thou canst, convincing them of sin, bringing them to repentance, humbling them in the dust. No one can speak to repentant souls as Thou canst, bidding them come to Thee, weary and heavy laden, telling them Thy yoke is easy and Thy burden light, lifting them up by the gracious sweetness of Thy gospel into the peace of reconciliation with God. No one can speak to the discouraged as Thou canst, cheering them on their way with words of strength and confidence. No one can speak to the tempted as Thou canst, making them bold to resist and hopeful of the victory. No one can speak to the erring as Thou canst, pleading with them to seek again an injured Father's face. No one can speak to the aging as Thou canst, giving them visions of the golden twilight of a life in Thy favor. No one can speak to the dying as Thou canst, filling them with joy as they go down into the valley which is flooded with the light of Thy cross. Wondrous Christ, incline us each day to listen to Thy voice, for Thy great love's sake. *Amen*

OCTOBER 31 (Reformation Anniversary)

Read Hebrews 11: 29-40

Verse 29 — *By faith.*

A MIGHTY FORTRESS ART THOU, God, a trusty Shield and Weapon. Thou helpest us in every need that hath us now o'ertaken. The old bitter foe meaneth us deadly wo. Deep guile and great might are his dread arms in fight. On earth is not his equal. With might of ours can naught be done, soon were our loss effected; for us fighteth the valiant One, whom Thou, God, hast elected. Ask we, "Who is this?" Jesus Christ it is, of sabaoth Lord. There is no other God. His is the field forever. Though devils all the world should fill, each watching to devour us, we tremble not, we fear no ill, they can not overpower us. Blessed be Thou, Lord Jesus Christ, for Thou hast taken away their power and hast placed the eternal victory into our hands. We lift up our glad voices to Thee for Thy glorious deliverance. We thank Thee because Thou dost unto this day maintain our liberty, according to Thy Word. We thank Thee for the open Bible, and for our free access to it and to the throne of grace by virtue of its blessed gospel truth. We thank Thee for the message which saith, "By faith." We are saved by faith, not by our own imperfect works. We rejoice in faith, faith in Thee and the blood Thou didst shed. We live by faith, we will one day die in the faith, the blood-bought faith which maketh Thee our only Hope. May we hold fast the profession of our faith in the face of every danger, and may our faith ever rest upon Thy Word and upon that alone. Hear us, mighty Savior, for Thy glorious name's sake. *Amen.*

NOVEMBER 1

Read Proverbs 11: 1-11

VERSE 11 — *By the blessing of the upright the city is exalted.*

O GOD, rich in loving-kindness and abundant in mercy, Thou hast revealed to us that when Thou dost favor the righteous, Thou art willing to make his blessings so great that thousands may derive benefits therefrom. Thou wast willing, when Abraham prayed to Thee, to spare the cities whose wickedness had doomed them to destruction, if Thou wert able to find in these wicked cities but ten righteous persons. By the blessings of the upright the city is exalted. May we bear this in mind, and may we by Thy grace become pillars upon whom the welfare of many others doth rest. Make us upright by the cleansing blood of Christ; righteous, first of all, in Thy judgment; but righteous also in our own lives, strengthened in every good work by Him who hath redeemed us. May our uprightness be so plain to men's view that they, seeing our light shine, may glorify Thee and Thy Son, our Redeemer. May our fellow men be lifted up to see better and higher things because we dwell among them. May the spirit of our land be impressed with the uprightness which Thou hast worked in our lives. Should wickedness increase, do Thou hear our prayers nevertheless, and extend the time of mercy allotted to our land and to our city. Help us to secure for our youth the one thing needful, their rearing in the nurture and admonition of their Lord. Make them useful citizens of this world, as Thou makest them fit subjects for the kingdom of heaven. We ask it of Thee in Thy loving mercy. *Amen.*

NOVEMBER 2

Read Galatians 6: 1-10

VERSE 2 — *Bear ye one another's burdens, and so fulfil the law of Christ.*

LORD JESUS, Thou didst bear the burdens of all of us. Thou didst take them all from our drooping shoulders and didst lay them on Thine own. Without murmur or complaint, Thou didst bear them all to the cross. We thank Thee for Thy gracious redemption. When Thou dost bid us bear one another's burdens, we can only feel constrained by Thy love to obey with all the strength and mind Thou dost give us. Make us Thy willing servants in bearing the burdens of others. May we help bear the burdens of those loving ones in our household who daily make sacrifices for us. May we help bear the burdens of those who preach Thy Word to us. May we help bear the load of those who are tried and tempted. May we help bear the burdens of those who are weak and without the experience which we have gained in Thy service. May we help bear the burdens of all those who are of our own faith, in whatsoever land they may be. Make us so cheerful as we lift others' burdens for them that our very willingness will make the load lighter for them. May we be ready to serve even when we have grown weary, knowing that Thy strength is mighty in weakness, and believing that as our day so shall our strength be. While we serve Thee not because we hope for rewards, do Thou yet cheer us with the thought that, as we sow, so shall we reap. Keep our eyes fixed upon the goal of all our service, eternal fellowship with Thee, which will not be denied us, because Thou hast died for us. *Amen.*

NOVEMBER 3

Read John 1: 1-14

VERSE 5 — *The Light shineth in darkness, and the darkness comprehended It not.*

O CHRIST, who didst suffer all things for us, was not this the bitterest of Thy pains, that they for whom Thou didst bear all things would not understand what wondrous mercy Thou wast showing them? How often Thou wast misunderstood. Thou camest as the Light, but they who sat in darkness did not comprehend. Thou wast from the beginning, but they to whom Thou hadst given the sure words of prophecy looked upon Thee as a mere child of their own times. In Thee was life, but they to whom Thou didst offer eternal life turned toward Thee to destroy Thy life. Thou camest to those who were Thine own covenant people to give Thyself fully to them, but they received Thee not. So dost Thou often come to us, only to be misunderstood. We pray Thee to open our understandings, lest we fail to receive and comprehend Thee unto our souls' salvation. Help us, dear Master, to understand Thy purposes. Safeguard us against the deception of those who do not love Thee and who desire that we cease loving Thee. We can not hope fully to understand Thee and Thy ways. Our hearts are yet gross and our understandings are yet darkened by the shadow of sin. But by grace we can and will understand Thy love, and, confiding in Thy love, will let Thy light shine in our hearts. Then shall we behold Thy glory as of the Only-begotten of the Father, full of grace and truth. Grant this unto us in mercy. *Amen.*

NOVEMBER 4

Read Deuteronomy 7: 1-6

VERSE 6 — *The Lord, thy God, hath chosen thee to be a special people unto Himself.*

LORD, how good it is of Thee that Thou art willing to have us. Thou mightest have passed us by, deeming us too impure for Thy presence. Thou mightest have cast us off forever, for we had rebelled against Thee. But Thou didst permit mercy to go before justice, and didst find a way on which Thou couldst lead our erring souls back to Thyself and couldst make them acceptable in Thy sight. May we be so thankful for this Thy kindness that we will not murmur when Thou askest us to forsake the companionship of those who are earthly-minded. Thou hast chosen us to be a special people unto Thyself. Thou hast signally honored us. May we heed Thy will that we keep ourselves separate from the worldly. Thou wouldst have us go to them to offer them Thy salvation. But Thou wouldst have us keep ourselves unspotted by the taint of their companionship. Make us brave enough to forego the world's friendships, although its friendships may mean our temporal gain. So fill us with Thy Spirit that what is worldly will have no power to win our hearts. Grant us grace always to conduct ourselves as Thy chosen people. Let us show in our kindness and purity and honesty and truthfulness and unselfishness that we are followers of Thee, and children of Thy household. Make us an honor to Thy holy name. Forgive us when we forget our station as citizens of Thy kingdom. We ask it boldly, because we know Thou lovest us in Jesus Christ, our Lord. *Amen.*

NOVEMBER 5

Read John 10: 22-33

VERSE 27 — *My sheep hear my voice, and I know them, and they follow me.*

JESUS, OUR SHEPHERD, may we ever bear in mind we are helpless sheep and lambs of Thy fold, and that Thou art our great and good Shepherd, upon whom we depend for all that is good, whether it be for our souls or for our bodies. We are so apt to forget our station, and Thine also. Like erring sheep, we stray from Thee because we have not made Thy voice and command our only guide. If we are in truth Thy sheep, we will listen to Thy voice, whether it uttereth generous promises or whether it revealeth hard sayings unto us. Lay Thy restraining hand upon our hearts when they trust in their own wisdom, or when they are inclined to listen to hirelings instead of giving heed to Thy words. It is not for us to choose our way. This is Thy task as our Shepherd. Stifle in us every desire to neglect Thy bidding. Truly, Thou hast merited our undying faithfulness in Thee. Thou art the Shepherd who laid down His life for His sheep. Thou art He of whom it was written, "I will smite the Shepherd." Thou wast stricken, smitten of God, and afflicted for us. Yet, in spite of Thine unspeakable humiliation, Thou and the Father are one. Thou hast so securely attached us to Thyself that no man can pluck us out of Thy hand, except we ourselves are willing to be misled. Keep us, dear Savior, within the sound of Thy voice, and make us ever more and more obedient to Thy call. We ask it in confidence, knowing that Thou lovest us. *Amen.*

NOVEMBER 6

Read Ephesians 5: 11-21

VERSE 11 — *Have no fellowship with the unfruitful works of darkness, but rather reprove them.*

HOLY SPIRIT, who didst come unto God's people with power, with a sound as of a roaring mighty wind, with the fervency of flames of living fire: come to us with Thy strength and make us bold and brave in our Christian faith and life. Grant us power to subdue the evil inclinations within ourselves. Rouse us from any lethargy which may steal over us when the way is hard and the day is long. Let not the idleness and self-indulgence of the world have place in our lives, but make us wise to redeem the time, seeing the days in which we live are evil days. Keep us on guard against the crafty approach of intemperance and all appetites of the flesh. Draw us away from the fellowship of the unfruitful works of darkness. Work within us the spirit which hath courage to denounce the deeds of darkness and to reprove those who commit them. May we not fear the loss of earthly friendships so much that we leave words unspoken which we should utter in censure of that which is wicked. May we be brave enough to risk position and favor and advancement and all other earthly advantage in our love of the right and the good, and in our determination to oppose all that is evil. Christ hath not redeemed us in order that we may serve sin or speed it on its way. As we are bought by His blood, do Thou hearten us to work for men's redemption from sin, if it be at the cost of our blood. We pray this in His holy name. *Amen.*

NOVEMBER 7

Read Jeremiah 33: 7-16

VERSE 14 — *"Behold, the day cometh,"* saith the
Lord, *"that I will perform that good thing
which I have promised."*

O GOD, what a dark world it is in which we poor sin-burdened mortals live and move. The wages of sin is death, and oh, how many things fell prey to death when Satan and man brought sin into Thy world. Thou hadst made earth a bright and happy place. There was life and growth, there was abundance and freedom, there was joy and peace. Then sin came, and death, and the blight hath been laid on all Thy glorious creation; and now we go our ways, eating our bread in the sweat of our faces, contending with thorns and thistles, terrified by the darkness and the storms. It is all the wages of sin. Amid sin's ravages, preserve our hearts from thoughtlessness on the one hand, and from hardness and bitter murmuring on the other. Thou knowest best, and Thou dost not desire the death of one sinner. Thou dost bring misery upon us for our good. Thou wouldst have our chastenings lead us to truer repentance, and thus to truer faith. To this end Thou hast given us this promise, that the days will come when Thou wilt perform good things for us. Work in our hearts in times of distress and visitation. Mold them after the pattern of our Lord's own mind, who bore Thy heavy hand so willingly. Point us to Him when our troubles grow thick and dark. Help us to believe that through Him Thou wilt at last restore to us all things which we have cast away by our sinfulness. We ask it for His sake alone. *Amen.*

NOVEMBER 8

Read John 11: 1-11

VERSE 4 — *This sickness is not unto death, but for the glory of God.*

MERCIFUL HEAVENLY FATHER, how Thou, through Christ, canst glorify all things even the dark days of our lives. We can not hope Thou wilt permit us to live our days upon earth without our portion of sickness and pain and suffering and all manner of affliction. We can not hope, as soon as we cry to Thee in our troubles, Thou wilt see fit to deliver us without delay. Teach us to commit ourselves into Thy keeping and guidance in the days when we are driven to gloom and sadness by our losses. Thou hast all things in Thy power, and canst bend them all to Thy will. Our most untoward experiences Thou canst overrule for our good. May we take fresh courage daily, even though the clouds which gather about us are black with dire threatenings. Show us that they are big with mercies, and that from their depths will come streams of refreshment instead of forked lightnings of destruction. Enable us to find in every circumstance which men's judgment would call misfortune only another opportunity for Thee to manifest forth Thine exceedingly great glory. Our extremity is ever Thine opportunity. But, Father, our faith is weak, uncertain. Strengthen us by the might of Jesus in our inmost hearts, and root our faith so deeply and firmly in Him that nothing can dismay us. Convince us that He who could deliver us from eternal death can deliver us from every evil of the body. May His cross, as we bear it, lift us nearer to Thee. Hear us in mercy, for His sake. *Amen.*

NOVEMBER 9

Read Psalm 16: 1-11

VERSE 5 — *The Lord is the Portion of mine inheritance and of my cup.*

O LORD, our Lord, how close Thou dost come to us, in that Thou dost permit us to call Thee our Portion, our Inheritance, and the Cup from which our lips drink deep of the water which refresheth unto eternal life. Truly, our lines have fallen in pleasant places because Thou art our God and our Redeemer. We will set Thee always before us, and daily will we draw from Thee the happiness and the confidence which we need to make the burdens of our lives bearable. How different all of life doth look when we remain near Thee. What a different purpose our lives have when we are drawn to Thee by the mercy of our Lord Jesus Christ, who died that He might reconcile us and Thee. What fulness of joy, what completeness of satisfaction, cometh into our hearts when we are convinced that Thou dost truly belong to us, that no one and no thing can dispute our possession of Thee and Thine everlasting love. The sorrows which afflict them who seek other gods and other helpers do not disturb us. Even in our woes we draw only nearer to Thee. When we must face the hour of death and leave all we have here on earth, we shall not be less confident, for Thou art with us to the end, and after the end. Even our flesh is under Thy protecting care, and Thou wilt raise it up again. Maintain unwavering confidence in us evermore. Let no deception rob us of our trust in Thee. We ask it in His name who hath redeemed us and made us Thine own. *Amen.*

NOVEMBER 10

Read John 11 : 17-29

VERSE 25 —*I am the Resurrection and the Life: he that believeth in me, though he were dead, yet shall he live.*

LORD JESUS, Giver of life, Conqueror of death, Savior from eternal death and darkness: we bring Thee our poor tired and frightened hearts, because we know that Thou hast the words of eternal life. No one else can comfort us as Thou canst. No one else can speak to us with the authority which Thou hast. We know the secret of Thy saving power: Thou art Thyself the everlasting God, although Thou didst appear among us in the garb of our own lowly flesh and didst take upon Thyself the form of a servant. With lips like ours, with lips which were soon to be cold and motionless in death, Thou didst call out into the hearts of all humanity, "I am the Resurrection and the Life." Thou hast given witness that Thou didst speak truth; for death could not hold Thee, and the grave could not remain Thy prison. Oh, we poor dying men and women thank Thee for bringing hope and light into our world. Lord, we believe in Thee. To us Thou art the Mighty One who hath entered into the palace of the strong one and despoiled him of all his goods. Death may lay its hands upon our bodies and hold them for a little while, but no death can have power over our souls, and eternal death can not claim our bodies. For us who trust in Thee as our Lord and Savior there is no death. What seemeth so is but transition. May Thine almighty hand and Thy gracious heart lead us into the dark portal, through the gloomy valley, across the black waters, into the realm of Thy light. Keep us in true faith, for Thy love's sake. *Amen.*

NOVEMBER 11

Read John 11: 33-44
VERSE 35 — *Jesus wept.*

LOVING SAVIOR, how deeply Thou wast touched at the sight of our infirmities. How Thy soul trembled, beholding the havoc which the curse of our sins visited upon us. Thou didst not create us that we might be children of darkness and death. We sprang from Thy hand clothed in life and in the image of our Father. When by sin man brought death into the world, Thou didst purpose to restore us unto life and happiness again if we would not hinder Thee in Thy merciful work. What a deep heart of love Thou hast. The price which Thou wouldst need to pay for our redemption was not unknown to Thee. The awful load which would be laid upon Thy shoulders when Thou didst come into our flesh was not concealed from Thee. Seeing all, knowing all, Thou didst nevertheless come and didst take it all upon Thee. Then, as Thou didst stagger forward beneath the terrible load, heart-breaks came to Thee, and Thou didst weep tears of sorrow for us. O Lord Christ, we can not comprehend it all. We do not know why God should shed tears for us. We can not measure the preciousness of the tears of Thy grief. We can only stand and wonder at the amazing work our sins have done and the infinite sympathy which Thou didst display. Let Thy sufferings in our behalf not be in vain. May we be moved by Thy tears to a faith and a love which will bring us in unconditional surrender to Thy feet, there to lie, humbly receiving blessedness from Thy hands. Hear us in mercy. *Amen.*

NOVEMBER 12

Read Proverbs 11: 24-31

VERSE 24 — *There is that scattereth and yet increaseth; and there is that withholdeth more than meet, and it tendeth to poverty.*

GRACIOUS GOD, who openest Thy hand daily to satisfy the wants of all Thy creatures, who providest for us everything which is good for us in soul and in body, who art loving and kind even to them who deny Thee: make us like Thyself in willingness to use our possessions for the benefit of others. Drive out of our hearts the littleness of faith which maketh us fear that, if we do not hoard our goods, we may suffer want and poverty. Teach us the manner of reckoning which obtaineth with Thee and with all those who have learned the secrets of Thy kingdom. Make us understand that, though we may scatter with lavish hand, we may yet increase our possessions, and, though we may close our hands fast upon that which we possess, it may tend to poverty. Make our souls liberal. Set clearly before our eyes the stupid folly of clinging to riches and loving them more than we love Thee and Thy service. Fill us with Thy Spirit, and through His influence take us farther away from earthiness and worldliness. Impress upon our minds that we are but stewards of our earthly goods. Show us the beauty of our Savior's great sacrifice for us. Without His sacrifice we could not have life. Let us use the life He hath purchased and won for us, making the lives of others happier and richer. Teach us to look for opportunities to spend and be spent in love to Him who died for us. We pray this in His name. *Amen.*

NOVEMBER 13

Read Daniel 3: 13-27

VERSE 17 — *"Our God, whom we serve, is able to deliver us from the burning fiery furnace."*

ALMIGHTY GOD, how lion-hearted we can be if we trust in Thee, and, trusting in Thee, laugh to scorn all the ills which Thine enemies may seek to bring upon us. Thou dost not conceal from us that sometimes it is Thy wise purpose to lead us through suffering into the larger, fuller life which maketh us more truly Thine own. We know Thou art always able to deliver us, no matter what the danger may be, no matter how strong the enemy may be. Yet we do not know where the path may wind and where Thou mayest choose to lead us. Grant us the faith which filled the hearts of Thy servants who said that, even though it were not Thy pleasure to deliver them from the fire, yet would they not yield to the commandments of the evil one. Let it be sufficient for us that Thy grace is mighty in our weakness. May we have the sublime courage which leaveth all to Thee, and which confesseth, "Though He slay me, yet will I trust in Him." Remind us that, if we distrust Thee and hearken unto the voice of the tempter, only unhappiness and loss can come. May the love of our Savior so constrain us that we may not even ask whether Thou wilt or wilt not deliver us — that we may ask only what Thy will is, and do it without doubting, believing whatever cometh will be for our own good. Fix our eyes upon Him as He went forth to war for us against all the powers of darkness, and give us grace to follow in His train. Hear us, O our Father, for His name's sake. *Amen.*

NOVEMBER 14

Read Matthew 25: 1-13

VERSE 6 — *At midnight there was a cry made, "Behold, the bridegroom cometh, go ye out to meet him."*

HOLY SPIRIT, Spirit of wisdom and truth, pity us in our ignorance and blindness, and help us gain heavenly wisdom ere it be too late. Of ourselves we can do nothing. Left to our own resources, we shall only fall into error and destruction. Thou must come and work within us if our eyes are to be made seeing and if our hearts are to be applied unto wisdom. We know how Thou art pleased to come to us: not in miraculous visions and mysterious dreams, but through the heavenly light of Thy holy Word. In this Word, according to the promise of our Lord and Savior, Thou dost lead us into all truth. We ask Thee through the wisdom of the Word to prepare us for the Bridegroom's coming. We know He cometh, even before the end of the world. To some of us He cometh in afflicting visitations. To all of us He cometh in the hour of death. To some of us death may come suddenly, without warning. We beseech Thee, give us the wisdom which maketh us always prepared to meet our Master, whenever He may elect to come to us. May we bear with us plentiful supplies of oil for the lamps which He desireth to find burning against His coming. Make us watchful of our own deceitful hearts. Keep us vigilant on account of our besetting sins. Give us minds which listen to the warnings of the watchmen who stand upon the towers of the Church, the faithful preachers of Thine unchanging truth. We ask it all in the name and for the sake of Jesus. *Amen.*

NOVEMBER 15

Read Daniel 5: 22-31

VERSE 27 — *Thou art weighed in the balances and art found wanting.*

GOD, Thou seest us at all times. Yet we live on as though Thine eyes were never upon us. Save us from the wretched carelessness which hath been the undoing of thousands of our fellow men, both low and high. Why should our spirits dare to lift themselves up in pride? Canst Thou not implant in us a lively sense of Thy nearness? Remind us, O God, that no man hath ever yet been able to hide himself from Thine all-seeing eye. Help us bear in mind that all our thoughts and words and deeds are known to Thee, and judged by Thee. Laid in the balances of Thy perfect righteousness, we know we shall be found wanting, and Thou wilt number our stewardship and bring it to an end — except an advocate appear, to turn the wrath of Thy justice away from us. Lord Jesus, we thank Thee that Thou didst come to supply that which is wanting in us. We thank Thee that Thy merit is laid into the balance for us when the justice of Thy Father weigheth us. Thy precious blood atoneth for all our omissions of the good and our commissions of the evil. Make us truly penitent and believing, so that Thy righteousness may avail for us. Be merciful, and continue us in the stewardship to which Thou hast called us. May we not die in our sins, but in Thy faith and fear. When Thou hast in Thy good pleasure ended our stewardship here below, do Thou continue us in Thy service in the glorious kingdom yonder, for Thy mercy's sake. *Amen.*

NOVEMBER 16

Read Daniel 6: 13-23

VERSE 22 — *My God hath sent His angel, and hath shut the lions' mouths, that they have not hurt me."*

OUR GOD AND FATHER, again we come to Thee, because the dangers have not ended. With each new day they seem to grow greater. With each new year of our lives they seem to be more frightful. In each new generation of the world they seem to take upon themselves more terrifying forms. Thou hast been our Help and our Refuge in ages past, Thou canst be an ever present Help to-day. Thou wast with Thy servants in olden times, lending their fainting hearts great courage, stopping the mouths of lions for them, delivering them out of deadly dangers. Convince our trembling hearts that, though the day of miracles may be past, the day of Thy saving love is never past. Thou dost still give Thine angels charge concerning us upon all our ways, and they will bear us up on their hands, lest we dash our feet against the stones. Not a sparrow falleth but its God doth know, just as when His mandate layeth monarchs low. Not a leaflet waveth, but its God doth see. Shall we doubt that Thou carest for us and watchest over us? Extend Thy guardian care over all our loved ones, near and far away. Be Thou the Protector of all who are in danger and distress. Let Thy mighty deliverances lead men's hearts to Thee. Above all else, do Thou, through the blood of Christ, continue to save men's souls from the jaws of eternal death. Rescue the perishing sinner from his doom. Revive our faith when it droopeth. Keep us brave and true in our confidence, for our Savior's sake. *Amen.*

NOVEMBER 17

Read John 3: 13-21

VERSE 16 — *God so loved the world that He gave His only-begotten Son, that whosoever believeth in Him should not perish, but have everlasting life.*

FATHER IN HEAVEN, we love to tell the story of unseen things above, of Jesus and His glory, of Jesus and His love. We love to tell the story because we know it true: it satisfieth our longings as nothing else can do. We love to tell the story. It is pleasant to repeat what seemeth, each time we tell it, more wonderfully sweet. And when, in scenes of glory, we sing the new, new song, it will be the old, old story that we have loved so long. Ah, how it toucheth our hearts, this story of Thy love and Thy Son's sacrifice for us. How it doth make us marvel when we hear that He, Thine only-begotten Son, the Son of Thine eternal love, came into our sinful world clothed in our own nature, so that whosoever believeth in Him should not perish but have everlasting life. Justly mightst Thou, Lord Christ, have condemned the world instead of coming to save it. Justly mightst Thou have cast it off when, after Thou hadst come, it would not receive Thee. But Thou camest to save, not to condemn. Thou wast lifted up, not to hurl destruction down upon us, but to draw us upward unto Thyself. Eternal praise and thanks and love be given Thee for Thine unspeakable gift of grace. Dear Lord, grant us the new life while we are yet here in the flesh, and grant us the eternal life when our time upon earth is past. We trust wholly in Thee. Other helpers have we none. Only Thou art our Savior and our King. Be merciful to us, for Thy name's sake. *Amen.*

NOVEMBER 18

Read First Timothy 6: 6-16

VERSE 8 — *Having food and raiment, let us be therewith content.*

LORD GOD, we pray Thee, draw our hearts upward from this earth and all earthly concerns, and let us dwell with Thee in the realms of the spirit. Cleanse us of all worldliness, relieve us of the bodily anxieties which make us forget Thy love and care. Impress upon us that Thou hast called us to fight the good fight of faith, and help us turn our weapons first against the fears and doubts in our own selves. Thou seest how we still have to do with the spirit of unrest and discontent which is in our own hearts. We forget Thou hast immortality. We forget Thou art a mighty Potentate, whom nothing can withstand. We forget that, if Thou art for us, no other power can prevail against us. Nor is it only our fear for our needs which maketh us weak in the faith. Often it is our love of the riches of this world. We are not content, having food and raiment. We forget that they who will to be rich fall into temptation and a snare. Help us bear in mind the poverty of our Savior, who, though He was rich, made Himself poor in order to become our Mediator and Savior. Possessing Him and His pardoning grace, may we be content, whatever may or may not come to us in this life. Enrich us in our souls, and teach us patiently to bear bodily privations, if this be Thy will. Fix our eyes upon the exceeding weight of glory which shall one day be revealed in us. We ask it in our Redeemer's name. *Amen.*

NOVEMBER 19

Read Revelation 22: 1-7

VERSE 5 — *There shall be no night there, and they need no candle, neither light of the sun, for the Lord God giveth them light.*

FATHER OF LIGHTS, with whom there is no variableness nor shadow of turning, who art the Source of all light and life and happiness: Thou dost direct our eyes to that world in which there will be no night, and where we shall have no need of candle or of sun. Though Thou didst make our own world a place of light, man by sin brought darkness into it, and all our lives we would be groping in darkness if Thou hadst not given us Jesus, the Light of our world. It is through Him Thou hast revealed to us the brightness of Thy face, and the endless brightness of the life we are one day to enjoy in Thy communion. Father, as we stumble on through the nights of this sorrow-laden life, fix our eyes steadfastly on the glory which Jesus, who shared our sorrows with us, now hath with Thee, and make us believe we shall one day partake of all the joys of His glory. Lighten the load which we must bear here below by showing us the pure river of the water of life which floweth from Thy throne. Let us find the water of life in the truth which Thou hast revealed to us in Thy precious Word. May we find in Thy holy book the leaves of the tree which will heal us and all nations. Permit us here in faith to behold the face of our dear Lord. Write His name upon our foreheads, as a token that we are His loyal servants and worshipers. Help us to bring light to those with whom we daily come in contact. We offer Thee this prayer in Jesus' name. *Amen.*

NOVEMBER 20

Read Psalms 5: 1-12

VERSE 11 — *Let them ever shout for joy, because Thou defendest them.*

LORD, ALMIGHTY GOD, Thou shalt hear our voices in the morning, nor will we be silent when the shadows of evening fall. In the heat of the noon-time we will find our refuge in Thee, and out of the blackness of midnight we will call upon Thee. We know that, at whatever time we may lift our prayer to Thee, Thou wilt hearken unto our cry. Thou wilt compass us as with a shield, and we shall rejoice because we have put our trust in Thee and in no other helper. Behold, we know Thou art not a God who hath pleasure in wickedness. He who doeth evil will not stand before Thee. Thou hast taken our sins away in the redeeming blood of Jesus. Through Him we ask Thee to keep us on the straight path which pleaseth Thee. Lead us ever to Thy house, where Thou dost prepare a rich feast for our strengthening, and where Thou dost give us light and guidance for our walk. Let not our enemies find cause for dishonoring Thee because we have failed to show forth Thine honor in our conversation. Let them not find in us a spirit of fear or doubting. Give us grace to manifest in our lives the joy and peace which have come to us through the blood which pardoneth us. Thou defendest us in every evil day. Thou preservest us against everything which might harm us in soul or in body. Make us not only thankful, but jubilant in the blessedness which is ours by reason of Thy gracious redemption. We ask it all, trusting in our Savior's mercy. *Amen.*

NOVEMBER 21

Read Second Timothy 3:12-17

VERSE 16 — *All Scripture is given by inspiration of God, and is profitable.*

O SPIRIT DIVINE, who livest and reignest with the Father and the Son, ever one God, world without end: we would have Thee breathe into our hearts and lives. We have a life to lead and a great work to do, and we can not trust in ourselves. We need to be anointed by Thee. We need the strength which can come to us only when we feel the everlasting arms underneath us. We need to be planted firmly on foundations which can not crumble or be moved. Thou hast given us power in the Word, that gracious revelation which Thou didst put into the hearts of holy men to write, inspiring them to place upon the sacred scrolls only what Thy divine wisdom dictated. Grant us a living trust in the utterances of Thy Word. Though evil men grow worse and worse, though their denials grow stronger and stronger, though we suffer the persecution which their stinging tongues may make very afflicting to our flesh, do Thou still keep us trustful. Give us steadfastness to continue in the childlike faith which was taught us in infancy. Let Jesus be and remain our All-in-all, as He is portrayed to us on the pages of the Scriptures. Lead us to this fountain of truth every day, and increase our love and devotion. Control all our being by the truth of Scripture. Make the Word our only rule of faith and living. We know in the hour of death it will not forsake us or let our hopes be put to shame. Hear us, we pray, for Jesus' sake. *Amen.*

NOVEMBER 22

Read Ecclesiastes 12: 1-7

VERSE 1 — *Remember now thy Creator in the days of thy youth, while the evil days come not.*

ETERNAL GOD, our Maker and Redeemer, Thou who art called the Ancient of Days: order our lives so that they may from beginning to end be consecrated to Thee in true faith and ardent love. Show us how frail we are. Remind us once more that we are but strangers and pilgrims, having here no continuing city; but do not let us despair of finding the abiding city which is to come. As we travel onward toward the days of old age, grant us to move forward joyfully, contentedly, resignedly, knowing Thou canst carry us to hoar hairs. Thou canst make our old age beautiful, like the glorious picture of the setting sun. Thou canst store our lives with treasure so rich that, when the days of unproductiveness come, we will have ample store, which will fill us with peace and happiness even though our bodily powers have failed and the sands of our life have run low. Teach us the wisdom of giving all our life to Jesus. May we not withhold from Him one day, one hour, of all the time of grace which Thou dost allot to us. Let us early seek His favor, early enjoy the blessings of His forgiving and cleansing blood. God, make our lives pure and holy. Lead us to abhor sin. Take away the love of evil pleasure. Remove the selfishness from us. Make us helpful to our fellow men. Move us to dedicate our best powers to humble service of our Master. Place us always under the direction of Thy holy and good Spirit. We ask it in His name who lived for us, Jesus Christ. *Amen.*

NOVEMBER 23

Read Hebrews 10: 30-39

VERSE 35 — *Cast not away, therefore, your confidence, which hath great recompense of reward.*

MERCIFUL SAVIOR, Thou who attendest us on all our ways, surely Thou seest and knowest how often we are brought to the verge of losing our faith and casting our confidence away. We are glad Thou art with us then, for it is Thy restraining hand and Thy pleading voice which draweth us back again from folly and turneth us again to true wisdom. Oh, let us never forget the wonderful recompense of reward which is ours because we have trust in Thee and Thy redeeming cross. Let us never forget that, if we cast away our confidence in Thee, there is nothing to hope for. It were a shame, dear Lord, if we could not be faithful for the brief span of this earthly life. We have Thy compassionate promise that Thou wilt not suffer any temptation to assail us which Thou dost not give us strength to resist. We know Thou wilt deepen our patience, so that we may never draw back from the lot which we have chosen with Thee. Yet, we will need a full abundance of Thy grace, lest we fail and fall in the great fight of afflictions which cometh against us. Master, make us more than conquerors. May we not alone stand firm ourselves, but may we rescue others who may be perishing. Use us somewhere, somehow, for the saving of those whom Thy blood hath redeemed. Grant us the happiness of helping them grow stronger in their trust. Should we find some despairing one who hath cast his confidence away, bless us so that we may restore him again. We ask it for Thine infinite love's sake. *Amen.*

NOVEMBER 24

Read Matthew 25: 14-30

VERSE 21 — *Well done, thou good and faithful servant, thou hast been faithful over a few things, I will make thee ruler over many things.*

O GOD, OUR FATHER, we feel the great responsibility of the life into which Thou hast called us. We had erred and gone astray, without purpose or goal in our lives. Thou hast come to us with the salvation of Jesus, and hast led us into the blessed life which we now have with Thee in Thy kingdom. What a treasure Thou hast committed to us by giving us this great salvation. What a trust Thou hast left with us by assigning us the great commission to make disciples of all nations. We look to Thee for guidance and succor in the many perplexities which we meet. Help us to be faithful in whatsoever Thou hast imposed upon us, so that we may please Thee and enable Thee to commit more and more into our keeping. Let it be our constant delight to look to Thee and heed Thy bidding. Let us repose our whole life-time into Thy keeping. Take us and make of us what Thou wilt. Not our wills, but Thine, be done. Bless us with visions of the things which are one day to be. We do not ask for reward. We know at our best we are only unprofitable servants. But Thou hast Thyself directed our eyes forward to the great day of the restoring of all things. We bide patiently here, O God, but our hearts are expectant of the marvelous glories which will one day be ours. Keep us humble in view of our coming glory. Keep us faithful in the least duties which Thou dost require of us. We ask it all in Jesus' wondrous name. *Amen.*

NOVEMBER 25

Read Esther 4:9-17

VERSE 14 — *Who knoweth whether thou art come to the kingdom for such a time as this?*

GREAT AND MIGHTY GOD, ruling by Thine omnipotent power all things in heaven and on earth, Thou with whom nothing is impossible: Thou dost choose to use us weak mortal men and women in the accomplishment of Thy wise purposes. It is not for us to ask why Thou dost, as it were, lean upon us in our weakness. It is for us to understand we must place ourselves at Thy disposal. Grant that we may always have the willingness and the courage to be made Thy humble instruments. Though Thy service may threaten to bring death upon us, help us to say, in sublime submission to Thee, "If I perish, I perish;" and grant us wisdom to believe it is better to die in Thy service than to live long in heedlessness of Thy will. What would our whole lives, what would our hopes be, if our Savior had not been faithful unto death? Knowing all our help and hope cometh through His obedience, may we not be found wanting when the hour cometh in which Thou dost expect great things of us. Through prayer and sobriety make us vigilant for opportunities. Let nothing in which we delight so occupy us that we may not hear the sound of Thy voice when Thou dost call us. Fill our hearts with concern for the welfare of others, so that we may be willing to serve them not only for love of Thee but likewise for love of them. As we accomplish service for Thee, make us thereby fitter for further service. We ask it in His name who was faithful unto death, our Lord and Savior. *Amen.*

NOVEMBER 26

Read Proverbs 15: 15-27

VERSE 17 — *Better is a dinner of herbs where love is, than a stalled ox, and hatred therewith.*

LORD JESUS CHRIST, may we not, as we view Thy sufferings and death, by which Thou didst redeem us from sin and death and the devil's power, forget that Thou didst lead the sinless life; and may we, when we look upon Thee as our Savior and Redeemer, without whom we have no hope whatever, likewise learn from Thy virtues how to walk unto all pleasing in the sight of God, unto whom Thou hast redeemed us. Thou wast loving and kind, righteous and pure. Thou wast zealous unto the giving of Thy whole self for the welfare of Thy fellow men. Although Thou wast the Man of Sorrows and acquainted with grief, yet Thou wast ever filled with peace and holy joy. It was meat and drink unto Thee to do the will of Thy heavenly Father. May we be like Thee. Make us contented with our lot in life. Grant us to have holy and sanctified dispositions, and kind and loving hearts. Let a sacred joy underlie all we say and do and suffer. Make us diligent to do our Father's will in all things and at all times. May we not spare ourselves. Drive pride and self-sufficiency from us. Make us a comfort to those who come to us with their griefs and losses. Build up within us so true a righteousness and so inflexible an honesty that nothing may be able to purchase us. Though we forfeit riches and position by our integrity, keep us without fault when temptation cometh against us. Make us the salt of the earth. We ask it all in Thy name and relying on the power of Thy blood. *Amen.*

NOVEMBER 27

Read Hebrews 11: 1-10

VERSE 1 — *Faith is the substance of things hoped for, the evidence of things not seen.*

O HOLY GHOST, who pourest sweet peace into our hearts, and who our souls restorest: Thy comfort ne'er depart. Let us, His name confessing whom we in faith have known, receive Thy constant blessing and be in death Thine own. Thou hast worked faith in our hearts, a faith which hath become so real and firm that it is our very life, the substance of things which we do not see but for which we have dared to hope, the sure evidence of the things which are not to be comprehended by our bodily senses. We know our God hath framed the worlds, although we did not behold Him as He worked; for the eye of our faith doth see plainly that it was He who made heaven and earth. We know our Savior hath redeemed us, although we did not stand beholding at His cross; for the hand of our faith is laid in His pierced hand, and the vision of our faith maketh Him real unto us. O Holy Ghost, make us always the objects of Thy watchful care and Thine unceasing labors, lest our faith droop and die, and we become as those who have no hope. Hold up before our gaze the example of the countless thousands who by faith have accomplished deeds of self-denial and exalted sacrifice. Show us that it is the heart's faith which maketh life noble and Godlike. Found our faith alone upon the story of Jesus' birth and life, His suffering and death, His resurrection. Let us in this faith triumph at last and see Him face to face. We pray this of Thee in His name. *Amen.*

NOVEMBER 28

Read Acts 24: 22-27

VERSE 25 — *As he reasoned of righteousness, temperance, and judgment to come, Felix trembled.*

LORD GOD, we thank Thee that Thou hast saved us from the terrors of sin and judgment. We rejoice in the liberty wherewith Christ hath made us free. We know we were carnal, sold under sin; but Thou hast sent us redemption and freedom, through Jesus Christ, who gave Himself a Ransom for us. Oh, let us never again become the slaves of sin and lust and appetite and greed. As we see the examples of sin's deadly sway about us, may we dread its awful power and its horrible destruction. May we so highly prize the liberty in which we stand that, though we may still through weakness of the flesh sometimes err, we may never again choose sin as our master. Lord Jesus, when we look upon the hideous work of sin in men's hearts, we understand how heavy was the load which rested upon Thine innocent shoulders. Do Thou, who didst die that we might live, pour into our hearts the zeal for dying men's souls which will send us forth to reason with them of righteousness and temperance and judgment to come, and to show men how Thou canst save them from the consequences of their wickedness. Sorely doth the world need Thee to-day, and sorely dost Thou need those who will testify for Thee in the midst of a wicked and adulterous generation. Strengthen us in our faith and in our courage to do Thy bidding and to accomplish the world's conversion, for Thy name's sake. *Amen.*

NOVEMBER 29

Read Proverbs 22: 1-16

VERSE 1 — *A good name is rather to be chosen than great riches.*

SAVIOR, Thou hast a name which is above every other name. Thou wast called Jesus before Thou wast born of Mary, because it was Thy Father's purpose that Thou shouldst save Thy people from their sins; and not only Thy people of Israel, but all the sons of men. No other name is given among us whereby we must be saved. We rejoice in the blessedness which Thy comforting name hath brought among us, and willingly and joyfully bear Thy name with Thee. Thou art our Christ, we are Thy followers. We glory in Thy name, and it is our desire that all men may know we are Thine. Grant that we may never do dishonor to Thy pure and righteous name, but may ever bear it as behooveth them whom Thou hast chosen. Grant also that we may, through the strength which we have from Thee, so live that our own names may be held in honor. A good name is rather to be chosen than great riches. Give us grace so that we may hold everything in abhorrence which might bring a stain upon our names or Thine. Help us to see that our fame will be secure if we but heed the promptings of the Spirit whom Thou dost bestow upon us. Let us willingly bear shame for Thee without fear of loss thereby, knowing Thou canst and wilt exalt all those who take Thy cross upon themselves. Make us distrust the promises which sin so readily giveth those who are willing to do evil deeds. Sinless Savior, draw us into Thine image, for Thy dear name's sake. *Amen.*

NOVEMBER 30

Read Nehemiah 2: 12-20

VERSE 17 — *Come, and let us build up the wall of Jerusalem, that we be no more a reproach.*

MERCIFUL HEAVENLY FATHER, Thou art pleased in Thy holy Word to call us Thy coworkers. Thou hast taken us into partnership with Thyself in the work of building the walls of Thy kingdom, the kingdom in which there is redemption through the blood of Jesus, the Savior of the world. Do Thou make the extension of Thy kingdom among men the chief delight in our lives. We have tasted and seen how good Thou art. We know all our blessedness cometh because Thou hast taken us into Thy kingdom. We know that other men can not find happiness unless they are brought into this kingdom. Thou hast made us debtors to all mankind by entrusting salvation to us. Endue us with zeal and joy in Thy service. Impress upon our hearts the misery of the heathen world. Commend to our sympathy the Israelite, still groping his way without the promised Messiah. Fill us with pity for the Black man in our own borders. Have us bear in mind that all the abandoned and sunken are laid at our very doors. Make us see that of such Thou canst, by the transforming power of Christ's blood, build up glorious walls of Thy gracious kingdom. Let us never tire in our labors, however often we may meet discouragement. Teach us to labor in harmony with others for the welfare of souls. Forbid that we should ever preach another gospel to others than the pure truth of the story of Jesus. To this end draw us ever nearer to Him in true and living trust. We ask it in His name. *Amen.*

DECEMBER 1

Read Nehemiah 13: 15-21

VERSE 17 — *What evil thing is this that ye do, and profane the Sabbath day?*

HEAVENLY FATHER, it was in great love Thou didst, before Thou hadst formed our race of men, so provide that we should have reminders of Thy goodness and opportunities to draw nearer to Thee, for whom our hearts thirst as the hart panteth for the water-brooks. Thou Thyself didst cease from the labors of Thy creation on the seventh day, and didst hallow the day, setting it apart for peculiar purposes. All through the centuries Thou hast so guided men that we still have the heritage of the day of the Lord. Nor hast Thou left this day poor and barren; for Thou hast given us Thy holy Word with its sacred truth, and Thy holy Church, with its sacred ordinances. Through Thy holy day Thou dost enable us, Thy children, the better to be the salt of the earth. We adore Thy wisdom and thank Thee for Thy fatherly divine goodness and mercy. Preserve in us the spirit of worship and faith and love. Preserve to us in its full purity and clearness the teaching of Thy Word. Enlighten us so that we will rejoice at the approach of Thy day; and make the service of Thy sanctuary so sweet and refreshing to us that we will welcome every day which may lead us to Thine altars. Grant that no unholy influence may rob us of the sacredness of our Lord's day. Remind us that it is the day of His rising from the dead, and may we ever use it for the strengthening of faith in Him and His redemption. We ask this of Thee for His name's sake. *Amen.*

DECEMBER 2

Read Matthew 3:1-10

VERSE 3 — *Prepare ye the way of the Lord, make His paths straight.*

O HOLY SPIRIT, work in our hearts and lives the things which please our Father in heaven, and which prove that we are in truth the followers of Him who came to deliver us from every evil work. Bring down every proud thought of our hearts into subjection to Jesus, our Savior. Do Thou rob our flesh of its power, and create in us the new man, who will live according to the pleasure of God. Leave us not, until Thou hast brought forth in us true repentance. Show us the wickedness, the rebelliousness, the misery of sin, and fill us with shame and contrition because we have transgressed the command of Him who loveth us. Remove from our minds the false and foolish confidence which we so often have in that which can never avail in the sight of Holy God. Terrify us, if need be, with the message of God's wrath against us on account of our iniquity. Choose our hearts as a way of the Lord, and prepare them for His coming. Impress upon us the truth that now is the accepted time, now is the day of salvation; that the kingdom is at hand; that, if we despise the day of our redemption, we may never again have opportunity to hear and heed. Preserve us from the hardness of heart which overcometh those who habitually enjoy the bounties of Thy grace but return to Thee only an outward obedience. Truly convert us, and constrain us by the love of Jesus. Let us count no cost too great for our discipleship. Grant this, for His name's sake. *Amen.*

Read Isaiah 54: 7-14

VERSE 10 — *The mountains shall depart and the hills be removed, but my kindness shall not depart from thee.*

ETERNAL GOD, who art from everlasting to everlasting, the thought of Thy Unchangeableness bringeth comfort to our hearts. All Thy creatures are as fleeting shadows. We see them as they come and go. Mountains depart, hills are removed, seas subside, rocks are rent, but Thou art the same forever. Great kingdoms and mighty empires have had their day and have gone down into dust; but Thy kingdom remaineth ever. The promises made to us by friends and lovers are often broken and forgotten; but Thou makest a covenant with us which endureth even to eternity. We bless Thee for this covenant, made with us through Him who came into our flesh to be our Friend and Brother, though He hath been our Lord and God from the beginning. We rejoice in this Thy covenant with us, which Thou dost make even though we are rebellious sinners against Thee. We trust in this Thy covenant, even though we have sometimes departed from it, yes, though we depart from it daily. We know Thou wilt never prove faithless to Thy promises. Sometimes Thou dost seem to forsake us and to forget Thy covenant; but it is only for a little while; and it is for our own good that Thou dost thus chasten us. We ask Thee now to make us more faithful. May every thought of Jesus and His coming create in us more fervent love for Thee, more faithful service of Thee. Enable us to walk as becometh the people of the holy covenant, sealed with the blood of Christ. We pray this in His name. *Amen.*

DECEMBER 4

Read Isaiah 4: 2-6

VERSE 2 — *In that day shall the Branch of the Lord be beautiful and glorious.*

O FAITHFUL GOD, how fully and truly Thou hast kept all Thy promises and brought to pass all Thy prophecies concerning the glorious Branch, which according to Thy Word was to grow up as a Root out of a dry ground. All Thy prophecies concerning Thy Son, our Lord Jesus Christ, have been Yea and Amen in Thee. Thou hast made the day glorious by the brightness of His coming. Thou hast filled the world with joy. Not a single soul need go its way disconsolate and suffering. Not a single heart need wander astray. Not a single one of us need suffer injury from storm or rain. Not one of us need feel the burning heat of noonday. In Christ Jesus Thou hast given us a Cloud of smoke by day and a shining of flaming Fire by night, to guide us on all our ways. In Him Thou hast built a Tabernacle for a shadow in the daytime. In Him Thou hast prepared a Covert for us from storm and tempest. Plenteous grace with Him is found, grace to cover all our sin. Let the healing streams abound, make and keep us pure within. Oh, bless us richly with all the mercies which He hath come to bestow on us. Let no evil inclination of our hearts make us come short of the fulness of His grace. Let Him grow beautiful and glorious in us. We know how unworthy and sinful we are, yet we cast ourselves upon Thy promises, and know Thou wilt not fail us. And Thou wilt not deny this our prayer, for we bring it before Thee only in His name. *Amen.*

DECEMBER 5

Read Isaiah 55: 1-11

VERSE 1 — *Ho, every one that thirsteth, come ye to the waters.*

LORD OF THE HEAVENS, to whom all things belong, to whom this earth and its fulness belongeth, and who dost bountifully refresh all Thy children with streams of life and love: what mercy on Thy part that Thou dost pardon all our transgressions, and dost call us to come to Thy fountains and drink of the waters of Thy goodness freely, without money and without price. We need not fear Thou dost not include us in Thy blessed invitation, for Thou hast called every one who thirsteth. Our need is guarantee that Thou hast bidden us to come to Thee. O, grant in Thy great goodness that we may not trifle with the days of our opportunity. Let us seek Thee while Thou mayest be found. Let us seek Thee early, in the days of our youth. Help us to forsake every wicked way on which our feet have walked, and grant us pardon so abundant that all of sin's load will fall from our shoulders and we may stand forth free of all its curse and power. Make Thy word effectual in us, to the working of true repentance and the building of true faith. Make Thy Church here on earth an exhaustless fountain of that living truth which alone can refresh poor dying souls, the truth of Jesus' coming into our flesh and our world, that we might have life, and that we might have it more abundantly. Hear this our prayer, which we have courage to plead only because He came to be our Mediator and Intercessor. *Amen.*

DECEMBER 6

Read Luke 1: 26-35

VERSE 33 — *Of His kingdom there shall be no end.*

JESUS, Thou art a King, Thou art our King, our only Sovereign and Lord, Thou who hast reigned with the Father and the Spirit, world without end. We rejoice because Thou hast called us into Thy marvelous kingdom, a kingdom of which there shall be no end. Ah, how gracious it is of Thee that Thou dost condescend to men of low estate. What a blessedness, that Thou dost commit to us, weak mortals, the glorious tasks of Thine endless kingdom. Thou hast not forgotten any of us in Thy boundless love. Though we may not all be so highly favored as have been some of the holy men and women of old, yet hast Thou a place for every one of us in the great work of Thy cause. Do Thou prepare our hearts for Thy service by making us Thy humble instruments, always ready to listen to Thy counsel, always willing to perform Thy good pleasure, always subjecting our own minds to Thy wisdom and guidance. To this end break down our sinful resistance to the influence of Thy Holy Spirit, and take away all self-will and self-love from our hearts. Show Thyself to us in all Thy beauty and greatness, in all Thy love and mercy. Make us happy in the consciousness that Thou dost accept us, and in the performance of the service which Thou dost require of us. Make us brave enough to bring any sacrifice which Thou mayest see fit to demand of us. Teach us not to fear the judgment of worldly-minded men. We ask it all, dear Savior, for Thy great mercy's sake. *Amen.*

DECEMBER 7

Read Acts 26: 12-23

VERSE 22 — *Having therefore obtained help of God, I continue unto this day witnessing.*

O GOD OF ALL GLORY, what wonderful manifestations of Thyself Thou dost vouchsafe to us. Even though the time of miracles may be past, our lives are filled with evidences that Thou art with us directing us on all our ways, protecting us from danger, and ever mindful of Thine own, especially of their souls' welfare. We do thank Thee for coming to us and abiding with us. We do thank Thee for attending us on our ways. We thank Thee most of all for coming to us in the birth of Jesus Christ, our only Lord and Savior. Through Him Thou hast made Thyself felt as a real presence in our lives. Oh, fill us with the spirit which He alone can impart to us. For His sake forgive our many sins of omission and commission. Assure us that we have Thy favor. Fill our souls with the happiness which cometh through faith in Him. Let us be living proofs of the saying that out of the abundance of the heart the mouth speaketh. Our hearts are truly filled with grace and glory by the mercy of our blessed Lord. Teach our lips and all our other members to sing His praise and to proclaim His power. Make us living messages to those who are yet separated from Jesus by the hardness of their hearts or the carelessness of their minds. Grant that nothing may be able to intimidate us in our confession of the unspeakable happiness which cometh into the world because Thou didst send forth Thy Son, made of a woman, and made under the law. We ask it in His name. *Amen.*

DECEMBER 8

Read Nehemiah 4: 7-18

VERSE 9 — *We made our prayer unto our God, and set a watch against them day and night.*

HOLY SPIRIT, Thou who dost come into our hearts and teach us to pray, who dost help our souls utter the desires which we of ourselves could not voice: continue in us Thy divine work and lead us deeper and deeper into the habit of prayerfulness. Do Thou fix our eyes on the greatness of our God's power and love. Help us believe, as surely as though we saw Him face to face, that He is with us on every day we live and on every way we go. We do not ask Thee to lead us upon paths where there is no danger. We do not ask Thee to spare us every trial. We know we have sinned and need the tribulations which come unto us. We know we daily transgress the law of our God and need the chastenings which are meted out to us. But we pray Thee to give our hearts assurance in the time of need and hope in the hour of trial. May nothing dismay us in our service of our Lord and God. Thou dost make us mighty in prayer, make us likewise mighty in deeds. Instruct us in the divine art of uniting our prayers and our labors. Preserve us from the weaknesses which come unto us by reason of unfaithfulness or of self-sufficiency. Grant us abounding hopefulness, no matter how dark the prospect. Remind us that our Savior, Jesus Christ, hath brought new hope among us by His birth as one of our human race. In Him make us equal to every task which may devolve upon us. We pray this in His all-prevailing name. *Amen.*

DECEMBER 9

Read Zechariah 9: 9-14

VERSE 12 — *Turn you to the strong hold, ye prisoners of hope.*

LORD JESUS CHRIST, our King, who comest unto us from perfect love to us and divine compassion for our souls, who hast salvation, who canst speak peace even to hearts which are tossed by the darkest tempests, Thou whose dominion extendeth from sea to sea, Thou whose arrows go forth as the lightning: what marvels Thou hast worked by coming into our flesh, a little Babe, born in the lowly stable at Bethlehem. We rejoice in Thy coming, and lift up our hearts in songs of praise and purest happiness. Without Thee we would be hopeless prisoners in the strong-holds of sin. Thou hast turned our despair into relief, and hast made us prisoners of hope, showing us the way to the strong-hold of righteousness, where we are secure from every enemy, even from the righteous wrath of Holy God. Blessed be Thy mighty name for the deliverance Thou hast worked for us. Blessed be Thy dear love, which hath moved Thee to come to us in the form of a servant, to bear the load of our wretchedness and guilt. Grant that we may never forget from what depths of wo Thou hast redeemed us. May the memory of our sinfulness keep us very humble before Thee. May the memory of our helplessness draw us very close to Thee. Let us prize Thy salvation above every other blessing which is given to us, and may we never stray from Thee and from the strong-hold which Thou hast built upon Thyself as a foundation. We ask this of Thee in Thy love and mercy. *Amen.*

DECEMBER 14

Read Acts 27: 13-26

VERSE 23 — *"There stood by me this night the angel of God, whose I am and whom I serve."*

DEAR HEAVENLY FATHER, Thou art a very present Help in trouble. Never dost Thou forsake those who put their trust in Thee. Never hast Thou forsaken us when we put our trust in Thee. If it seemed to us as though Thou hadst turned Thy face away from us, it was because we had forsaken Thee and lost our trust in Thy presence and help. We ask Thee again to strengthen our confidence in Thee and Thy wise and merciful providence. Didst Thou not send Thine only-begotten Son, who was with Thee from eternity, into our human family, making Him one of us in order that we might not be estranged from Thee? What more couldst Thou have done to draw us to Thee? Ah, it is our sinfulness which keepeth us from perfect trust. It is our wickedness which maketh us afraid when the storms come. It is our own waywardness which bringeth the shipwreck of our faith. Be merciful to us, and do Thou save us in spite of our own sinful selves. Send us messengers to assure us of Thy close presence. Make all things minister for the strengthening of our faith. Help us to see that we can by strengthening and cheering others exercise our own faith unto its deepening and strengthening. Let the joys of the coming festival work within us unto the refreshing of our souls and the cheering of our hearts. May our most blessed gift at this time be the bestowal of Thy Holy Spirit, who shall stand by us and give us assurance. We pray this in Jesus' name. *Amen.*

DECEMBER 15

Read Psalm 18: 25-36

VERSE 29 — *"By Thee I have run through a troop, and by my God have I leaped over a wall."*

GRACIOUS FATHER IN HEAVEN, what life and health and strength Thou hast brought into the world through the Babe of Bethlehem. We stand before the manger where His head is pillowed low and meek, and we draw from His advent into our race all the needed power to come back again to Thee, from whom sin had sundered us. In this little Child we behold the Lion of Judah, the Prince of Peace, the Lord of Life. It is He who saveth the afflicted. It is He who lighteth our candle in the darkness of sin and shame and sorrow. It is He who girdeth us with strength. It is He who supporteth us, so that our feet do not slip, no matter how treacherous the path and how feeble our steps. It is He who giveth us might, so that we run through every troop sent against us by the enemy. It is He who maketh us strong enough to escape from the imprisonment of walls and bars which sin and Satan have made firm round about us. Oh, do Thou humble us before the Child. O little Child of Bethlehem, descend to us, we pray; cast out our sin and enter in; be born in us to-day. All our hope is in Thee. We have no confidence in our own powers. We have nothing to bring Thee but our sin and distress. Send us forth from Thy presence, forgiven, blessed, enriched. Help us, whom Thou hast delivered, to bring deliverance and joy to the world. Make us Thy bearers to the souls of other sinners, and let them find pardon and peace in Thee. We ask this of Thy great mercy. *Amen.*

DECEMBER 16

Read John 1: 40-51

VERSE 51 — *Ye shall see heaven open.*

BLESSED LORD CHRIST, who didst come down to us from heaven, we thank Thee that, coming, Thou didst leave heaven's gate ajar, that we might have glimpses of the glory which through Thee shall one time be revealed in us. Heaven was opened wide when Thou didst come to be born a Babe of our own race. The light of heaven's glory streamed down upon our poor desolate earth; the angel of the Lord appeared to men; and there was with the angel suddenly a multitude of the heavenly host. Ever since that time we have dared to look upward to see that heaven's gate is still ajar, and that the way for us to God hath not been closed. We understand why Thou didst say to one of those who came to Thee that we should see heaven opened, and the angels ascending and descending upon Thee. Thou art in truth the Way to heaven, for Thou art the eternal Son of God, and Thou art the King of Israel, promised of old, the King, of whose kingdom there should be no end. Lord Jesus, preserve us from making the festival of Thy birth a time for earthly concerns and pleasures. Direct our minds always upward. Thou didst come to draw us of earth into the radiance of heaven above. Thou didst come to show us the surpassing worth of the unseen and eternal things. Save us from the blindness which sin hath brought upon us, and teach our eyes to see. Forgive us anew whenever we forget. Direct us daily to the Scriptures, which reveal Thee unto us. Do this of Thy great love. *Amen.*

DECEMBER 17

Read Isaiah 35: 1-10

VERSE 1 — *The desert shall rejoice and blossom as the rose.*

O HOLY SPIRIT, how wisely Thou didst prepare regeneration for this sin-stricken world when Thou didst overshadow the Virgin of Nazareth, so that the Holy Thing which was born of her was rightly called the Son of God. How surely Thou didst carry forward to their fulfilment the sayings of the prophets, when Thou didst anoint Jesus of Nazareth with Thyself and with the power of God. It is through Him the desert rejoiceth and blossometh as the rose. It is through Him the wilderness of our life hath been made a garden of delight. It is through Him the ravage of sin hath been healed, and all the ills of our mortal state have been changed into blessings. It is through Him that we, ransomed, return, with everlasting joy upon our heads. Our hearts are filled with exultation, and we are strangely moved as we consider His coming into our estate, only without sin. Do Thou grant that we may truly repent of all our sins, and bring forth fruits meet for repentance. Deliver us, O Spirit of God, from the deceitfulness and desperate wickedness of our old nature. Touch us effectually with the redemption which Jesus Christ hath worked for us. Have Thou Thy perfect way with us, and make us true children of the King. Uproot in us all the wilderness growth of the natural man, and plant in us the growth in which our Father delighteth. Water and enrich us with the dew of Thine indwelling. Fashion our lives into gardens of divine beauty and goodness, for Jesus' sake. *Amen.*

DECEMBER 18

Read Hebrews 12: 1-11

VERSE 1 — *Let us lay aside every weight.*

DEAR HEAVENLY FATHER, we know Thou lovest us. Our enemies, within us and without, tempt us to think we have lost Thy favor. But the coming of Thy dear Son into our flesh is proof sufficient that Thou lovest us with a boundless love and Thy mercy will never depart from us. Grant that, relying upon Thine unvarying grace, we may have patience to go the way of our lives, wheresoever it may lead us. Direct our vision always to Jesus, who is the Author and Finisher of our faith, and bestow upon us the virtues of patience, endurance, courage, and confidence. Hold before our eyes the life and sufferings and death of the Babe born in Bethlehem. Remind us that He, although He came into our flesh with the splendor of heaven shining down upon earth and the multitude of angels adoring Him, came nevertheless to go the way of sorrows which ended in the cross on Calvary. Make us partakers of His faithfulness. Help us to despise the shame of the cross, enduring its pain and resisting our enemy unto blood if need be, even as He did. Embolden us to deny our own flesh and its desires, laying aside every weight which may encumber us in our race. Chasten us, not in displeasure but in fatherly love. Do Thou choose our way for us. May we never forget that in the shame of Jesus' cross our own glory is found. In Him grant us full forgiveness of all our sins, and happiness and peace now and forever. We ask it for His name's sake. *Amen.*

DECEMBER 19

Read Isaiah 52: 7-15

VERSE 7 — *How beautiful upon the mountains are the feet of him that bringeth good tidings.*

GRACIOUS GOD, accept our thanks and praise this day because Thou hast not withheld from us the cheering message of our salvation by the coming of Jesus Christ. No other word which has ever been sounded into the ears of men is so beautiful as is the gospel of Thy love in Jesus. In His coming Thou hast made bare Thy mighty arm against the powers which despoil our souls. Though He was the Fairest among ten thousand, He did go forth into danger and death, His visage marred, His form dishonored, in order that with His sacrificial blood He might sprinkle all the nations and cleanse the souls of millions from the stain of sin. Through Him Thou hast sent comfort into this cheerless world, which sin had desolated. Truly, the story of His advent among men is the message of deliverance to the captive, the promise of sight to the blind, of healing to the wounded and sick, of hope to the prisoner, of life to the dying. Receive our endless praises and thanks for Thy wondrous mercy, and draw us ever closer to Him who is our only Redeemer. Give us foretastes of His glory as we follow Him in our lives. May the comfort of pardoned sin be ours every day. Keep us from the unclean things, and direct us to those things which are altogether lovely in Thy sight. Take us into partnership with Thee in the work of sprinkling the nations with His saving blood. May we serve Thee and Him unwearied, joyful, with increasing zeal. Hear us, for His sake. *Amen.*

DECEMBER 20

Read Isaiah 11: 1-10

VERSE 9.— *The earth shall be full of the knowledge of the Lord, as the waters cover the sea.*

LORD JESUS, blessed Savior, fill Thou the earth with Thy knowledge, as the waters cover the sea. Come to the hearts of men, and flood them with the blessed truth of Thy gospel. Teach them that Thou art the Rod of the stem of Jesse, the Seed of the woman, promised of old, and revealed when Thou wast born of Mary in Bethlehem's stable. Though a little Child, Thou didst come to be the Leader of men, to bear them by Thy strength forward into a reign of happiness and good will. Thy rule over us is one of pure righteousness and love, although Thou hast power to smite the earth with the rod of Thy mouth. Oh, make us duly thankful for the marvels of Thy glorious kingdom, in which we live, our sins forgiven, our peace made with God, our hearts transformed into His image. Cleanse us more and more, and help us forward to the time when they shall not hurt or destroy in all Thy holy mountain. Make us fountains of Thy mercy, bearers of Thy light, doers of Thy will among men. Let Thy blessing rest abundantly upon Thy Church, and upon every effort which is made to spread the knowledge of Thy redemption. Fill our hearts with good will toward all our fellow men, friends and enemies, near and far. Comfort us in our troubles, cheer us in our faintness, direct us in our perplexities, provide for us in every want of soul and body. Hear us, dear Lord, above that we are able to think and ask, for Thy mercy's sake. *Amen.*

DECEMBER 21

Read John 5: 20-25

VERSE 23 — *All men should honor the Son, even as they honor the Father.*

TRIUNE GOD, Father, Son and Holy Spirit, we look up to Thee, wondering at Thy greatness, unable to solve the mystery of Thy being, yet drawn to Thee by Thy love. O Holy Spirit, come into our hearts and empower us to worship God aright, even though we can not with our finite minds comprehend Him in His infinity. Thou hast revealed unto us that, even as we honor the Father, so are we to honor the Son who came into our flesh, born in weakness and poverty in Bethlehem. May our carnal reason be taken captive by Thy power; and may we render Jesus not only the love of hearts which can not deny Him their devotion, but likewise the worship of souls which acknowledge His true deity, and His equality with the Father and with Thee, O Spirit of God. Beautiful words, wonderful words, words of eternal life, have been brought unto us by Him who became Man for us. Receiving His Word, we escape the just condemnation which rested upon us. Through Him we have passed from death unto life. He hath power to give life, to quicken whom He will. O God, look upon us in mercy, and gather us unto those who are eternally saved by His merits. Seal our salvation to us at this happy season of the year, as we look forward to the festival of His incarnation. May His salvation work in us a new life, in which we give Thee the unrestrained love of our hearts, and render to our fellow men the service of unselfish kindness. We ask it all in His name. *Amen.*

DECEMBER 22

Read Isaiah 2:1-5

VERSE 5 — *Come ye, and let us walk in the light of the Lord.*

JESUS, with the day of the brightness of Thy rising approaching so near, we turn to Thee to thank Thee with deeply moved hearts for showing us that all the light of the world is but shadow, and that Thy light alone can bring us safety and happiness, health and growth, life here and hereafter. It is Thy kingdom which is established in the tops of the mountains, Thy kingdom, and Thine alone. Thy ways are the only ways which can lead us aright. We know full well Thy light was dimmed when Thou wast led into shame and death. But from the gloom and the deep darkness Thou didst shine forth again; and to-day, wherever men have found true light, it is because they have come to Thee. We rejoice in the power which Thou canst assume in the hearts of men. Thou canst move them to beat their swords into plow-shares and their spears into pruning-hooks. Lord, with Thee nothing is impossible. Yet Thou dost not desire to work in us by power, by storm, by earthquake, by fire: Thou dost desire to persuade us with the gentle voice of Thy love. Thou desirest us to walk in Thy light because we have learned to love Thee. Here, Lord, we bring Thee our hearts, our whole hearts. Cast out our sin and enter in. Be born in us to-day. Do Thou never leave us, but keep us in the light of Thy love, until we have accomplished what Thou hast sent us to do. Then receive us into everlasting light and life, for Thy love's sake. *Amen.*

DECEMBER 23

Read Luke 1: 46-55

VERSE 50 — *His mercy is upon them that fear Him from generation to generation.*

DEAR LORD, it is only by Thy pardoning grace we can stand before Thee. Hadst Thou not had compassion on us, hadst Thou not regarded us in our lost estate, we would long since have perished. Before our race fell into sin Thou didst plan our redemption. From generation to generation Thou didst behold us yet unborn, didst see the misery and wretchedness which would afflict us, and didst work out Thy mysterious plan for our salvation. When the fulness of the time had come, Thou didst send forth Thy Son, made of a woman, made under the law, to redeem us, who were under the law, that we might have the adoption of sons and daughters. It was because Thy tender mercy was upon us that Thou didst accomplish our salvation. Still this Thy mercy is upon us, regarding us, no matter how low our estate. With all Thy Church we are about to celebrate again the day of the coming of Thy Son into our flesh, His submission under the law, His mighty work to gain for us the adoption of sons and daughters in Thy household. Oh, keep our thoughts upon the high and holy things as we observe this glorious festival. Remove the worldly mind from us, and give us the heavenly mind. Glorify the Babe of Bethlehem in our eyes. Translate Him into our hearts. Cleanse us more fully. Bring us holy joy and divine peace. Move our hearts to thoughts and deeds of good will to all men. We ask it for His dear sake. *Amen.*

DECEMBER 24

Read Matthew 1: 17-25

VERSE 21 — *He shall save His people from their sins.*

O LORD GOD, Thou art the God of our salvation. On Thee do we wait all the day. Thou knowest the need of our souls, and Thou alone couldst provide for our wants. Only Thou, O Son of God, couldst become our Jesus, saving us from our sins; and Thou didst choose the only way, coming into our human family by birth of a virgin, conceived by the Holy Spirit. Thou art both God from all eternity and Man from the day of Thy birth at Bethlehem. Thou art true God, Thou art true Man. In Thy wondrous person Thou hast united God's nature with our own, and didst thus become Jesus. Thou hadst foretold Thy coming thus. Long before Thy birth of Mary Thou hadst chosen Thy name, Emmanuel, for Thou hadst planned that God should dwell with man, and man should be brought again to God. Our hearts are filled with precious joy at this holy season of Thy coming. Grant that we may have not a fear of anything which may come upon us because we confess faith in Thee. Help us to bear the slights which are cast upon us because we humbly confess our entire dependence on Thy salvation. Help us to remain firm in our faith even though hundreds who once stood with us have proved unfaithful. May their departure not discourage us. May it influence us to redouble our efforts to carry Thy salvation to others who have not yet tasted and seen how good Thou art. Hear us, dear Lord, and abundantly bless and prosper us, for Thy holy name's sake. *Amen.*

DECEMBER 25

Read Luke 2: 1-17

VERSE 14 — *Glory to God in the highest, and on earth peace, good will toward men.*

O JESUS, to Thee on this day of Thy birth be glory and honor through heaven and earth. True Son of the Father, Thou comest from the skies. To be born of a virgin Thou dost not despise. O holy Child of Bethlehem, descend on us, we pray. Cast out our sin and enter in. Be born in us to-day. We hear the Christmas angels the great glad tidings tell — oh, come to us, abide with us, our Lord, Immanuel. O holy Child, Thy manger gleams till earth and heaven glow with its beams, till midnight noon's bright light hath won, and Jacob's Star outshineth the sun. Our hearts tremble to-day with the wondrous joy Thou dost bring unto us. Our voices are vibrant with the happiness of Thy coming among us. Our minds are awe-struck by the miracle of Thine entrance into our flesh. Lord Jesus Christ, eternal praises be sung unto Thee; for Thou hast come to bring us freedom from the curse of sin, and everlasting rejoicing in our reconciliation with God. Hallelujah, hallelujah, hallelujah! Unspeakably great is our emotion at this manifestation of Thy love and the love of Thy Father, who hath again become our Father. Thanks be to Thee, likewise, O Holy Spirit, for the peace and rest and comfort Thou dost breathe into our souls by the gift of Jesus, our Savior. Now, do Thou make our Christmas truly blessed and happy. Give Thyself unto us without measure, and help us to give ourselves to Thee in complete surrender, and to our fellow men in unselfish devotion and charity. We ask it for Thy name's sake. *Amen.*

DECEMBER 26

Read Isaiah 9: 2-7

VERSE 6 — *His name shall be called Wonderful, Counsellor, The Mighty God, The Everlasting Father, The Prince of Peace.*

O HOLY CHILD OF BETHLEHEM, what wondrous names Thou dost bear; and how truly Thou art, in Thy person and in Thy work, everything these names express. Thou art wonderful, for there is no greater wonder known than Thy coming into our nature, for Thou art true God from all eternity, yet at the same time true Man, born of the Virgin Mary. Thou art a Counselor, the Counselor of all the minds of all the world; for Thou alone canst counsel our souls so that they will forsake the way of destruction and choose the way of life. Thou art the Mighty God, for with Thee nothing is impossible. Despite Thy deep humiliation, all power in heaven and on earth was Thine. Thou art the Everlasting, for Thou hast been from all eternity, and Thou wilt be to all eternity. Even though Thou didst become man, Thou art yet the Changeless One. Thou art the Prince of Peace; for Thou canst truly bring peace to everyone who cometh unto Thee. Look upon us and our restless hearts to-day, and grant us the mind and the will to embrace Thy peace. Have us remember that all our unrest cometh by reason of our sin, and that Thou art He who hast brought us our only deliverance from sin. Let us no longer walk in darkness. Lead us into the blessed light of fervent faith in Thee. Break the yoke of our burden, the rod of our oppressor. Let there be constant increase of Thy government both in our hearts and in this world. Do this, dear Christ, in love and everlasting mercy. *Amen.*

DECEMBER 27

Read Luke 2: 25-38

Verse 29 — *"Lord, now lettest Thou Thy servant depart in peace."*

FATHER IN HEAVEN, Thou carest for us from our cradles to our graves. In earliest infancy Thou dost take thought for us, on all our ways through life Thou dost attend us, in old age Thou dost not forget or forsake us. We would indeed be desolate as our time of life draweth to its close if we had not the comforting knowledge of Thy presence with us. The peace which Thou hast brought into our souls by the story of Jesus' birth and death for us is past understanding. The world can not comprehend it. But we feel its comfort and abide in its cheer, and no change of time or tide can alarm us. Thy Holy Spirit is upon us all, dwelling in us, making His presence felt in us, giving us assurance and unwavering trust. Through Him the Christ hath truly been born in us and hath made His abode with us, entering in and becoming our constant Companion and proving Himself to be our heavenly Lover and Friend. How could we fear, when Thou art so gracious to us? Keep us, Father, in Thy grace even unto the end of our earthly pilgrimage. When our eyes grow dim, give our faith clear vision to see Thee. When our limbs grow weary, renew the youthful strength of our trust in Thee. When our hands grow unsteady, let the hold of our hearts upon Thee be all the firmer. When the joys of this life pall, grant us a keener taste of the joys which lie beyond. When the end cometh, let Thy servants depart in peace according to Thy Word, for our eyes have seen Thy salvation. Hear us, for our Redeemer's sake. *Amen.*

DECEMBER 28

Read First Chronicles 16: 8-19

VERSE 12 — *Remember His marvelous works which He hath done.*

DEAR HEAVENLY FATHER, the year draweth to its close, yet Thou art still with us, and the holy covenant which Thou hast made with us is unbroken by Thee. The Church which Thou hast established among us, and into which Thou hast called us, still endureth, and trusteth in the promise of Thy Son, that the gates of hell shall not prevail against it. Through Thy holy Word Thou dost still bring unto us, in all its power and comfort, the gospel of our Lord Jesus Christ, who hath come among us to be our true Brother. We lift up our voices in happy thanksgiving to Thee, who hast kept us until this time. We speak of all Thy wondrous works, we glory in Thy holy name, our hearts rejoice in Thee, Thy judgments are upon our lips. Give us wisdom, that we may seek Thy face continually, that we may come to Thee for the strength which we need to go the way of life. Preserve us in our manifold temptations. May they not become snares of destruction for us, but do Thou make them the means of strengthening us in our trust in Thee. We know Thou hast pardoned all the sins which we have committed against Thy holy law. If Thou wouldst not pardon, we could not stand. But with Thee there is forgiveness, and boundless mercy. Draw us closer to Thyself as the years speed on their way, carrying us forward to the end of all earthly things. Bless all our crosses and trials unto the purifying of our hearts. Increase our confidence in Jesus, our only Lord and Helper. We pray this in His most blessed name. *Amen.*

DECEMBER 29

Read Second Timothy 4: 6-8

VERSE 7 — *I have fought a good fight, I have finished my course, I have kept the faith."*

SPIRIT OF GOD, who hast given us life and who hast thus far sustained our lives: we pray Thee still to attend us and to dwell in us with Thy comfort and Thy power. We have come through many a struggle unto this hour, and we know that many a field of battle yet lieth before us. It is by Thy grace we have thus far fought the good fight of faith. It is by Thy mercy we have kept our faith amid the many shipwrecks of men's faith round about us. It is only by Thy help we shall be able to finish our course in victory. Do Thou direct our eyes upon the glorious goal where there is laid up for us a crown of righteousness. Make us love the appearing of our Lord Jesus Christ, who hath promised one day to come again in the clouds of heaven, so that with our eyes we may behold Him. Preserve us against that great day, that we may be found watching for our Lord. Fill our hearts with daily thoughts of His goodness to us. Draw us who believe in Him nearer together, and make us like a mighty army, moving forward to certain triumph. Bless every effort of Thy Church to put down the power of Satan. Be with all who are in trials and afflictions, and grant them strength for their day. Assure us that we are God's elect, whenever our fears make us anxious. Let not one of us fail of gaining the incorruptible crown which Jesus hath purchased and won for us. We ask it in full reliance that Thou wilt hear and heed, inasmuch as He is our Lord and Savior to the uttermost. *Amen.*

DECEMBER 30

Read Revelation 22: 12-21

VERSE 13 — *I am Alpha and Omega, the Beginning and the End, the First and the Last.*

OUR GOD, our Help in ages past, our Hope for years to come, our Shelter from the stormy blast, and our eternal Home: under the shadow of Thy throne Thy saints have dwelt secure. Sufficient is Thine arm alone, and our defense is sure. Before the hills in order stood, or earth received her frame, from everlasting Thou art God, to endless years the Same. How good it is that we, as the fleeting years make us sadder and wiser, may rest assured in the knowledge that Thou art Alpha and Omega, the Beginning and the End, the First and the Last. We rejoice that Thou didst send us the bright Morning Star, Jesus, born for us. We rejoice that at the end of time He will come again, bringing His reward with Him. We know that in Him we are accepted in Thy sight, and that, as long as we desire Him as our Savior, no lapse of time can wear away the ties which bind us to Him. Watch over our hearts, O God, and let no deceitful imaginings ever turn our love away from Him. Keep us in His faith, so that we may have right to the tree of life and may enter in through the gates into the city of heaven. O Holy Spirit, do Thou breathe Thy gracious invitation day by day in our hearing, asking us to come and take of the water of life freely. Make all our days times of refreshing. Work daily repentance in our wayward hearts. Let none of us come short of the glory of our Savior. Send us forth to bring His salvation to others. Hear us in this our prayer, which we offer Thee in His name. *Amen*

DECEMBER 31

Read Isaiah 61: 1-9

VERSE 2 — *To proclaim the acceptable year of the Lord.*

O SPIRIT OF THE LORD, rest upon us as we close this year in Jesus' changeless name. Throughout this year Thou hast brought to us the good tidings of salvation by His precious blood. When our hearts were broken, Thou didst bind them up. When we were taken captives by the wiles of Satan, Thou didst deliver us and bring us forth again into the glorious liberty of the sons of God. Thou hast broken all the gates and bars which formed our prisonhouse. Thou didst make the year an acceptable year of the Lord. In all our mourning Thou didst bring us comfort. In our times of heaviness of heart Thou didst clothe us with the garments of praise. Our hearts are moved to sing the glory of our God, and to cry aloud, "Hitherto hath the Lord helped us." We believe, O God, Thou wilt not now leave us. Thou wilt be with us to the dying moment of this year, and wilt go with us into the coming year of grace. Thou, O Christ, wilt continue to apply to us the salvation which cometh by Thy blood. Assure us, ere this year closeth, that all the sins which we have committed as it ran its course are forgiven by Thy merits. Fit us for a better, truer life as Thy followers in the year which will soon be given to us. Help us throughout its course to bear Thee in mind, and to look to Thee as the only Source from which our help can come. So do Thou make of the new year a more acceptable year, and continue to bless us until all the years have passed and we are with Thee in eternity. Do this because Thou lovest us. *Amen.*

INDEX

Genesis

	PAGE
1: 1-16	5
1: 20-31	7
3: 1-13	148
3: 14-21	84
4: 3-15	9
18: 1-10	17
18: 20-32	21
19: 15-26	24
22: 1-12	89
28: 10-22	31
41: 38-49	41

Exodus

3: 1-10	64
4: 1-14	67
14: 5-14	128
14: 15-22	130
14: 23-31	202
15: 22-27	131
16: 14-26	132
17: 8-13	135
34: 1-7	140

Leviticus

10: 1-11	146
26: 3-13	254
26: 14-20	288

Numbers

13: 26-33	159
14: 1-10	160
14: 10-19	163
27: 12-22	176

Deuteronomy

	PAGE
6: 3-12	316
7: 1-6	345
8: 2-9	15
8: 10-18	44
9: 1-6	134
17: 14-20	47
20: 1-9	57
31: 1-8	180

Joshua

1: 1-9	183
4: 1-9	189
24: 14-22	199

Judges

6: 11-16	203

1 Samuel

2: 27-35	212
3: 2-13	215
7: 5-13	224
5: 13-23	228
17: 32-49	231

2 Samuel

1: 17-27	240

1 Kings

2: 1-12	261
17: 10-16	277
18: 30-39	281
19: 9-18	284
21: 15-24	287

INDEX

2 Kings

		PAGE
2:	9-18	299
6:	10-17	304
20:	1-7	313

1 Chronicles

16:	8-19	399
17:	1-12	257
22:	6-16	258

2 Chronicles

18:	6-17	290
20:	14-24	294
26:	14-21	309
29:	3-11	310
33:	11-16	325

Nehemiah

2:	12-20	371
4:	7-18	379
6:	1-13	383
13:	15-21	372

Esther

4:	9-17	366

Job

38:	1-12	260
41:	1-10	312

Psalms

1:	1-6	293
4:	1-8	298
5:	1-12	361
11:	1-7	72

		PAGE
14:	1-7	322
16:	1-11	350
18:	1-12	73
18:	13-24	87
18:	25-36	386
19:		20
23:		158
25:	1-11	127
25:	12-22	35
26:		65
27:	1-14	300
29:	1-11	69
32:	1-11	337
33:	6-18	137
34:	11-22	34
37:	16-25	171
42:	1-8	232
46:	1-11	222
48:	1-14	192
50:	1-15	208
61:	1-8	221
84:	1-12	235
90:	1-17	249
91:	1-16	315
103:	1-22	264
115:	1-15	296
139:	1-12	306
145:	8-21	326

Proverbs

1:	7-19	331
3:	11-24	336
11:	1-11	342
11:	24-31	353
15:	15-27	367
22:	1-16	370

INDEX

ECCLESIASTES

		PAGE
11:	1-6	333
12:	1-7	363

ISAIAH

1:	2-9	167
1:	10-20	266
2:	1-5	393
4:	2-6	375
8:	16-22	143
9:	2-7	397
10:	12-19	177
11:	1-10	391
26:	1-9	186
35:	1-10	383
37:	33-38	319
48:	12-19	268
52:	7-15	390
53:	2-9	78
54:	7-14	374
55:	1-11	376
58:	5-11	74
60:	1-11	12
61:	1-9	402
64:	1-9	280

JEREMIAH

6:	13-20	195
16:	5-11	216
22:	11-19	272

EZEKIEL

33:	7-16	348
18:	19-27	147
34:	11-22	274

DANIEL

		PAGE
1:	8-19	334
3:	13-27	354
5:	22-31	356
6:	13-23	357

HOSEA

6:	1-6	149
8:	1-8	211

JOEL

2:	23-32	154

NAHUM

1:	1-10	52

HABAKKUK

2:	12-20	58

ZEPHANIAH

1:	14-18	162

HAGGAI

2:	1-9	246

ZECHARIAH

9:	9-14	380

MATTHEW

1:	17-25	395
2:	1-12	10
3:	1-10	373
3:	11-17	8
5:	13-20	11
5:	38-48	23
6:	2-13	43

MATTHEW — Cont'd

Reference	Page
6: 19-25	60
6: 26-34	70
7: 12-20	142
7: 21-29	156
8: 5-15	19
8: 18-27	25
9: 27-38	27
10: 28-39	168
11: 1-10	33
11: 25-30	175
13: 3-10	194
13: 31-35	204
14: 22-33	40
15: 21-28	45
15: 29-39	49
16: 13-20	56
16: 21-27	61
17: 1-13	63
18: 23-35	219
20: 1-16	245
21: 18-22	259
22: 2-14	286
22: 35-46	301
23: 24-33	75
25: 1-13	355
25: 14-30	365
26: 14-25	97
26: 26-35	98
26: 36-46	99
26: 47-58	100
19: 23-30	233
26: 59-68	103
27: 11-23	106
27: 24-31	107
27: 35-44	109
27: 45-49	112
27: 50-56	116
27: 57-66	119
28: 1-15	120

MARK

Reference	Page
1: 21-31	68
1: 35-45	71
3: 20-35	133
5: 24-34	144
5: 35-43	139
7: 31-37	150
9: 14-29	153
9: 30-40	53
9: 41-50	136
10: 1-12	230
10: 42-52	157
11: 1-11	113
13: 28-37	329
14: 66-72	104
16: 1-14	121

LUKE

Reference	Page
1: 26-35	377
1: 46-55	394
2: 1-17	396
2: 25-38	398
2: 41-52	238
5: 1-11	250
5: 17-26	255
6: 17-26	14
7: 11-17	265
9: 51-62	269
10: 25-37	39
10: 38-42	275
11: 5-13	129

INDEX

LUKE — *Continued*

	PAGE
12: 13-21	278
12: 29-40	181
12: 49-57	214
15: 1-10	241
15: 11-24	253
16: 1-9	285
16: 19-31	297
17: 11-19	292
18: 9-14	324
22: 39-51	101
23: 1-12	105
23: 26-37	108
23: 39-43	110
23: 44-49	115
24: 13-24	124
24: 25-36	125

JOHN

	PAGE
1: 1-14	344
1: 19-28	381
1: 29-39	384
1: 40-51	387
2: 1-11	317
3: 1-12	321
3: 13-21	358
3: 25-36	327
4: 31-38	332
5: 20-25	392
5: 26-35	18
5: 36-47	48
6: 26-35	152
6: 37-44	165
6: 60-71	338
7: 40-53	340
8: 23-32	201
10: 11-18	263
10: 22-33	346
11: 1-11	349
11: 17-29	351
11: 33-44	352
12: 1-11	90
12: 20-30	76
12: 31-37	91
13: 1-17	92
14: 1-11	93
14: 15-24	94
16: 1-15	95
17: 1-17	96
18: 1-9	102
19: 1-27	111
19: 28-30	114
19: 31-37	118
20: 1-10	122
20: 9-29	126
20: 11-18	123

ACTS

	PAGE
1: 1-11	166
2: 1-13	172
2: 37-47	178
3: 1-11	182
4: 1-12	191
4: 13-20	196
5: 24-33	205
8: 26-37	217
9: 1-12	220
9: 13-22	225
10: 34-44	234
16: 4-15	303
16: 23-35	305
17: 22-32	311

ACTS — *Continued*

	PAGE
24: 22-27	369
26: 12-23	378
26: 24-32	382
27: 13-26	385

ROMANS

1: 8-17	6
3: 20-28	13
4: 20-25	169
5: 3-11	77
6: 3-12	83
6: 13-23	173
7: 14-25	252
8: 1-10	256
8: 11-18	81
8: 24-31	328
8: 32-39	330
10: 9-18	51
11: 33-36	161
12: 9-21	170
13: 8-14	29
15: 1-7	237

1 CORINTHIANS

1: 1-13	16
1: 18-29	22
2: 1-9	26
2: 9-16	174
3: 1-11	179
3: 16-23	184
9: 24-27	267
10: 1-12	335

	PAGE
11: 23-32	117
13: 1-13	291

2 CORINTHIANS

1: 3-12	28
4: 1-10	30
4: 11-18	188
5: 7-17	193
5: 17-21	85
6: 14-18	270
9: 6-15	339

GALATIANS

2: 11-21	36
3: 6-14	86
3: 21-29	197
4: 1-11	200
6: 1-10	343

EPHESIANS

2: 1-10	38
3: 13-21	262
4: 11-20	273
4: 22-32	276
5: 11-21	347
6: 10-18	320

PHILIPPIANS

1: 19-30	42
2: 1-11	206
4: 4-13	279

INDEX

COLOSSIANS
	PAGE
1: 12-20	88
2: 6-15	46
3: 1-11	209
3: 12-21	282

1 THESSALONIANS
4: 1-7	50
4: 13-18	187
5: 12-24	283

2 THESSALONIANS
2: 13-17	54
3: 6-16	210

1 TIMOTHY
1: 12-20	59
2: 1-10	213
6: 6-16	359

2 TIMOTHY
2: 1-10	218
2: 11-19	289
3: 12-17	362
4: 6-8	400

TITUS
2: 9-15	223
3: 3-11	295

HEBREWS
4: 11-16	226
6: 10-20	227
7: 19-28	229
9: 6-15	82
10: 19-29	302
10: 30-39	364
11: 1-10	368
11: 29-40	341
12: 1-11	389
13: 1-9	37
13: 11-21	66

JAMES
1: 2-12	138
1: 16-25	141
2: 10-17	236
3: 3-12	307

1 PETER
1: 3-9	145
1: 13-25	79
2: 1-10	239
2: 11-25	242
3: 8-18	308
5: 1-10	198

2 PETER
1: 1-11	151
1: 12-21	244
2: 1-9	314
3: 3-15	248

1 JOHN
1: 1-10	155
2: 1-11	80
2: 15-23	247
3: 1-12	251
3: 13-18	318
4: 9-21	323

INDEX

Jude
	PAGE
1-7	164

Revelation
		PAGE
1:	1-8	32
2:	1-11	55
3:	1-12	62
3:	14-22	185
4:	8-14	190
7:	9-17	207
19:	1-9	243
21:	1-8	271
22:	1-7	360
22:	12-21	401